Sean K

Sean Kingsley is a London-based archaeologist with several years experience running excavations and surveys from Montenegro to Israel. He specialises in the Holy Land, where he discovered and researched the largest cluster of ancient shipwrecks in the eastern Mediterranean. He is Managing Editor of *Minerva*, the International Review of Ancient Art and Archaeology, and Visiting Fellow at the Research Centre for Late Antique and Byzantine Studies at the Reading University. He writes for various popular magazines. This is his sixth book.

God's Gold

*The Quest for the Lost Temple Treasure
of Jerusalem*

SEAN KINGSLEY

JOHN MURRAY

© Sean Kingsley 2006

First published in Great Britain in 2006 by John Murray
A division of Hodder Headline

Paperback edition 2007

The right of Sean Kingsley to be identified as the Author of the Work has been asserted by him in accordance with the Copyright, Designs and Patents Act 1988.

1

A CIP catalogue record for this title is available from the British Library

ISBN 978-0-7195-6804-6

Typeset in Monotype Bembo by Servis Filmsetting Ltd, Manchester

Printed and bound by Clays Ltd, St Ives plc

Hodder Headline's policy is to use papers that are natural, renewable and recyclable products and made from wood grown in sustainable forests. The logging and manufacturing processes are expected to conform to the environmental regulations of the country of origin.

John Murray (Publishers)
338 Euston Road
London NW1 3BH

To my family past and present,
lost in the concentration camps of Nazi Europe,
reborn on the streets of London

Contents

CONTENTS

Revolution

Imperial Rome

Vandal Carthage

Constantinople – New Rome

The Holy Land

Illustrations

Photographic credits: 1 and 14, photographed by Sean Kingsley courtesy of the Museum of Roman Civilisation, Rome; 2, 12 and 13, Classical Numismatic Group, Inc; 3–6, 9–10, 15–21, 23, 25, 27–33, photographed by Sean Kingsley; 7 and 11, Z. Radovan, www.BibleLandPictures.com; 8, Ussishkin 1982, fig. 83; 22, E-Spaces and Unesco; 24, *Revue Africaine* (1934), pl. 2; 26, Onofrio Panvinio

Preface

O N THE SUMMIT of the Sacred Way in the Forum of Rome, an infamous monument conceals damned memories and an enduring secret. Passage through the Arch of Titus is today blocked by request of the government of Israel and by order of the Italian prime minister. The last dignitaries said to have walked formally through the Arch were Benito Mussolini and Adolf Hitler. Tour guides give visiting Jews permission to spit on its walls.

A relief on the southern wall of the Arch immortalises one of the pivotal moments in history. Fifteen men can be seen parading through the streets of Rome in a Triumph celebrated in AD 71 by the emperor Vespasian and his son, Titus, who, a year before, had crushed Israel and the First Jewish Revolt. On their shoulders Roman soldiers carry the broken dreams of the Jewish nation, the gold menorah (candelabrum), a pair of silver trumpets and the gold and gem-studded Table of the Divine Presence ransacked from the Temple of Jerusalem – intimate instruments of communication between God and man.

Priceless, and steeped in religious and political power, what happened to these defining symbols of the God of the Old Testament? While the Arch of Titus today is a well-known monument, the fate of the Temple treasure of Jerusalem has slipped through the net of modern exploration. Western consciousness hungers for ancient treasure. Hundreds of books, television documentaries and Hollywood movies have trawled lands and seas for the Ark of the Covenant, the Holy Grail, Noah's Ark and Atlantis.

Yet the Temple treasure remains the most valuable and accessible of all these iconic objects and themes, most of which are, in reality, no more than the stuff of myth and legend. The Ark is a different matter, but most scholars accept that it was destroyed by or in 586 BC, when

King Nebuchadnezzar of Babylon torched the First Temple of Jerusalem. It no longer exists to be discovered.

If the real Temple treasure has, until now, remained elusive, Hollywood has recently glossed over the fact. In 2004, Nicolas Cage played a guardian of Jerusalem's vanished secrets, Ben Gates, in Walt Disney Pictures' *National Treasure*. This adrenalin-fuelled romp crosses the globe in search of ten billion dollars' worth of artistic treasures originating in Solomon's temple and spirited away by the Knights Templar. Finally, using crypts, codes and maps, Gates uncovers the greatest fortune known to man deep beneath Trinity Church on the corner of Wall Street and Broadway in New York. All extremely exciting and entertaining, but only make-believe: you'd be hard pushed to explain how statues of Egyptian pharaohs, mummy coffins and papyrus scrolls from the great library at Alexandria ended up in a Jewish temple.

When most people think of treasure, their eyes mist over and they succumb to what Freud called the 'oceanic' feeling. Certainly the three central objects shown on the Arch of Titus are artistic masterpieces worth billions at auction. Money, however, is not what makes the Temple treasure so intriguing to me. On this occasion I am happy to borrow the closing lines of Ben Gates in *National Treasure*, who promises to donate his discoveries to the Smithsonian, the Louvre and Cairo Museum because 'There's thousands of years of world history down there and it belongs to the world and everyone in it.' For me, archaeology has always been about knowledge rather than possession.

This book, an account of the first methodical quest for the Temple treasures of Jerusalem immortalised on the Arch of Titus, seeks to restore to the world the history of these awesome icons. So little is known about their antiquity, artistry, symbolism and, most crucially, their fate down the centuries. Did the Romans melt them down to swell the imperial coffers? Did the swirling winds of change – as Rome was succeeded by Barbarians, Vandals, Byzantines, Persians and Arabs – destroy them or could they have survived into the modern era? To address these questions I have circled the Mediterranean twice since 1991 and time-travelled across 600 years of history.

Along the way I confronted a host of ancient ghosts, from famous emperors and politicians to theologians and general troublemakers. Although the quest incorporates rich textual and archaeological remains, the testimony of two brilliant minds have contributed enormously to the cause. The first is Flavius Josephus, a Jewish priest of royal descent born in Jerusalem in AD 37. Josephus started the First Jewish Revolt as commander of the Jewish forces in the Galilee, but ended it as special adviser to the Roman emperor. For swapping sides and turning imperial 'supergrass', he remains vilified in many religious and political circles. Yet in many ways, he was simply an opportunist who realised the game was up for his fellow revolutionaries. The iron fist of Rome could not be resisted.

After Vespasian's victory, Josephus did not abandon himself to a life of luxury under his Roman masters, but set about memorialising the complete history of biblical Israel in *The Antiquities of the Jews* and the *Jewish War* (cited in this book as *AJ* and *JW*). Both are rich mines of knowledge tapping stories – often fascinating and harrowing – about the social, military and religious history of Palestine from the days of Exodus to the AD 70s.

My second major source wove his literary magic centuries later. Born in the late fifth century AD, Procopius of Caesarea in Palestine lived until around AD 562. His was a world of profound change, and he witnessed first-hand the end of classical antiquity and rise of the Byzantine 'orientalist' era. As the court historian of the emperor Justinian (ruled AD 527–65), Procopius in his *History of the Wars* wrote lively accounts of the empire's battles with Goths, Vandals and Persians, and in *Buildings* chronicled Justinian's colossal building programme across the Mediterranean. Despite his formal position at court, however, the historian secretly seethed with disgust at the emperor's immoral behaviour and anarchic style of rule, and in the dark hours penned a clandestine poison book. *The Secret History* lifts the lid on numerous courtly scandals and, miraculously, still exists.

We don't know what Josephus or Procopius looked like. No portraits survive; we have only their writings. And both historians are less well known than the fifth-century BC word-spinners Herodotus and Thucydides, though they deserve equal billing as important historical voices. I hope the reader will appreciate their fine attention to fact, as well as their love of a good yarn.

God's Gold is a quest for truth. I have no political or religious axe to grind, no preconceived ideology to promote. I write this as an

Acknowledgements

L IKE MANY OF the most exhilarating moments in my life, the seeds of this book go back to my work as a marine archaeologist along the shores of the ancient harbour of Dor in Israel. For falling asleep in our archaeological lab one stormy day in 1991, shrouded in the *Jerusalem Post*, and for unwittingly revealing a letter on its pages about the Temple treasure of Jerusalem, I am grateful to Kurt Raveh for initiating this quest.

Numerous scholars have generously given academic advice during my quest: Géza Alföldy, Rupert Chapman, Amanda Claridge, Frank Clover, Shimon Dar, Ken Dark, Jerome Eisenberg, Stefania Fogagnolo, Shimon Gibson, Richard Hodges, Dalu Jones, Paolo Liverani, Jodi Magness, Eilat Mazar and David Stacey. For other information, thanks to Shuli Davidovich at the Israel Embassy, London, Philippe Van Nedervelde of E-Spaces, and to Gershon Salomon in Jerusalem. The template of the map used in this book was provided by Vince Gaffney and Henry Buglass from the Institute of Archaeology and Antiquity, the University of Birmingham.

Eric McFadden and Italo Vecchi of the Classical Numismatic Group Inc. patiently answered endless questions about Roman coins and modern value equivalents. From Jerusalem, Ibrahim Raï (Abou George) carefully drove me into the West Bank and experienced a shared fright for the cause.

Due to its politically and religiously controversial subject matter, this book was written under a veil of secrecy. For the necessary smoke screens, I offer apologies to all of the above.

At John Murray I am especially indebted to Roland Philipps for his guidance and faith in the book, to Rowan Yapp for her efficiency and patience, and to Howard Davies for his hawk-eyed excellence.

Vivienne Schuster at Curtis Brown has been a constant beacon of support, enthusiasm and advice; it is a privilege to work with her. Special thanks are also due to Josie Lloyd and Emlyn Rees for their ambassadorial generosity, and to Mark Merrony for reading and commenting on the text and for his friendship and encouragement.

As ever, the highs and lows of writing are shouldered by family, and for their understanding, interest and belief, endless thanks to Andrew and Sally. However, the star of this production is Madeleine Kingsley, a veritable Old Testament matriarch with unrivalled energy and passion, who read and advised on the manuscript with boundless enthusiasm despite huge pressures on her time. She is a source of constant inspiration. This book is for her and the family and roots she lost during the brutality of the Second World War.

———◆———

Permissions to reproduce ancient sources have been kindly granted by: Elizabeth Jeffreys (*The Chronicle of John Malalas*); Cyril Mango (*The Chronicle of Theophanes Confessor*); John Moorhead (*Victor of Vita*); and the Loeb Classical Library of Harvard University Press (*Ammianus Marcellinus III*, tr. J. C. Rolfe; *Cicero X*, tr. C. Macdonald; *Pliny. Natural History IV*, tr. H. Rackham; *Pliny. Natural History X*, tr. D. E. Eichholz; *Procopius of Caesarea. Buildings*, tr. H. B. Dewing). Very special thanks to Sebastian Brock for permission to read and reproduce from his unpublished translation of *The Khuzistan Chronicle*. Full reference to these titles is provided in the Select Bibliography. Every effort has been made to obtain reproduction permission for all titles in copyright cited in this book. The author and publisher will include any omission in subsequent reprints.

Abbreviations

AJ: Josephus, *Antiquities of the Jews*
HVP: Victor of Vita, *History of the Vandal Persecution*
JW: Josephus, *Jewish War*
Legends of the Jews: L. Ginzberg, *The Legends of the Jews, I–IV*
Secret History: R. Atwater, *The Secret History of Procopius*
Wars: Procopius, *History of the Wars*

I

River of Gold

Yet there was no small quantity of the riches that had been in that city [Jerusalem] still found among its ruins, a great deal of which the Romans dug up . . . the gold and the silver, and the rest of that most precious furniture which the Jews had, and which the owners had treasured up underground, against the uncertain fortunes of war . . . as for the leaders of the captives, Simon and John, with the other 700 men, whom he [Titus] had selected as being eminently tall and handsome of body, he gave order that they should be soon carried to Italy, as resolving to produce them in his triumph.

Josephus, *Jewish War*, 7.114–18

JERUSALEM WAS LOST, its ashes returned to the soils that gave birth to the holiest city on earth a thousand years before. The end of the world was nigh – just as the omens of impending doom had foretold. For months, waves of portents had petrified Jerusalem's High Priests. A sword-shaped star hung over the great Jewish Temple; across Israel, chariots cavorted past the setting sun and armed battalions hurtled through the clouds. During the festival of Passover a sacrificial cow inexplicably gave birth to a lamb in the Temple court, surely the work of the devil. And finally the eastern gate of the Temple's inner court, crafted of brass and so monumental that twenty men could hardly move it, opened of its own accord in the middle of the night. Terrified High Priests swore they heard the voice of God proclaim, 'We are departing hence.' The day was 26 September, AD 70, and Rome had just crushed the last drop of life out of the First Jewish Revolt of Israel.

Battleground Jerusalem was hell on earth, an inferno of blood, smoke and tears. With typical Roman efficiency imperial troops razed the city to the ground. Fire consumed the Temple, the holiest place on earth, where Abraham had prepared to sacrifice his son, Isaac, to the Lord. The graceful architecture of the 150-metre-long precinct – the largest religious forum of classical antiquity – was one immense fireball. The eye of the devil was rising from the house of God.

Satanic flames danced across stores of holy oil used in animal sacrifice, shooting columns of fire and thick plumes of smoke high into the night sky. Along with the natural smells of this religious bonfire, the autumnal air was choked with the abominable stench of burning flesh. The Jewish zealots of Jerusalem had been put to flight, every man for himself. The bodies of Jewish revolutionaries lay piled across the altar steps of the Temple's Holy of Holies where they had died in combat, its once pure stream of spirituality now profaned by a river of blood. As the corpses roasted, the cedarwood roof crumbled. The gold-plated ceiling crashed with almighty force on to the elegant marble paving below, entombing the holy warriors.

Across the upper city, once home to the rich and famous of Jerusalem – High Priests and wealthy landlords – fortunes were going up in smoke. Villas as opulent as any gracing the Bay of Naples, playground of Rome's aristocrats, fell to Titus' ruthless storm-troopers. Judaea's rulers, provincial puppets appointed by Rome to secure the empire, had proved inept. No subject power had ever dared lock horns with its masters so brazenly. Death and destruction would be the reward.

Amidst a landscape of Armageddon, the groans of hundreds of crucified Jews rent the air daily. Wooden crosses lined the streets as far as the eye could see. Roman soldiers maliciously taunted dying Jews with wine and beer; others downed food in front of famished prisoners who had not touched a morsel for weeks. The noose of the siege had strangled the city and starvation alone would take 11,000 lives inside beleaguered Jerusalem. Jews over seventeen years old were chained together in readiness for the long march south to Egypt's desert, where forced labour awaited them in the imperial gold and marble mines; Jews under that age were simply sold into slavery, converted into loose change for Rome.

And yet these were the fortunate minority: 1.1 million Jews were allegedly killed across Israel during the First Revolt. A further 97,000 prisoners became fodder for gladiatorial games in the Roman provinces, butchered by sword or wild beast in the name of entertainment. Perhaps these 'performers' would have preferred the roll of the dice that led to crucifixion rather than death in a distant land amongst a crowd of foreigners baying for blood in tongues they could not fathom. All across the Temple Mount Roman troops methodically flushed out the revolutionaries hiding amid dunghills and the rat-infested underground passages honeycombing the Temple complex.

As the curtain fell on one of the bloodiest and most savage battles of history, Rome was getting high on the spoils of war. Rumour had gathered during the siege of Jerusalem that the Temple was stuffed with a wealth of fabulous treasures. Jews trying to desert the front line and escape Jerusalem had taken to swallowing gold coins in a desperate attempt to conceal their surviving valuables from the grasp of the enemy. But following a tip-off, Romans soldiers, and their Arabian and Syrian mercenaries, had revelled in slicing open and disembowelling Jewish deserters. Even though Titus expressly forbade this barbarism, 2,000 Jews were dissected in one night alone. The taste for booty was contagious.

But such spoils were minor compensation compared to the vision of the Temple, plated throughout with gold, that had inspired the Roman soldiers during ferocious battles. They assumed, rightly, that its secret subterranean storerooms overflowed with wealth, and were entranced to find vast money chests, piles of garments and other valuables within the treasury chambers. Since the Temple was a sanctuary both holy and fortified, many Jewish High Priests and aristocrats had transferred their own personal wealth to this supposedly secure repository over the months. Now as fire danced across the dry cedar timbers, the precious wall plating melted into a river of gold at the soldiers' feet.

While low-ranking Roman soldiers dreamt of a little plunder to soften the blows of a weary battle campaign and to impress their wives and families back home, their generals were privately negotiating a delicate deal to secure the greatest sacred treasure known to man. Inside the Jewish sanctuary lay items of immeasurable wealth and religious value, the very symbols of state passed down from generation to generation and locked away in the Temple's secret places.

The High Priests knew they were cornered like rats in a sinking ship – nowhere to go but into Roman chains or through the gates of heaven. So it did not take long for Titus to cut a deal with the priest Jesus, son of Thebuthi, who, in return for a royal pardon, handed over the wall of the sanctuary two candelabrums, along with tables, bowls and platters, all crafted of solid gold. Next Jesus gave up the exquisitely woven veils that divided the Holy of Holies from the impure outer world, together with the High Priests' religious paraphernalia, precious stones and many other articles used in public worship. Once taken prisoner the Temple treasurer, Phineas, also squealed at the sharp tip of Roman steel, disclosing a plethora of purple and scarlet tunics and girdles worn by the priests, a mass of cinnamon, cassia and other spices, as well as a mountain of treasures and sacred ornaments. Suddenly Titus and his father, the emperor Vespasian, were rich beyond their wildest dreams.

While Titus and his troops mopped up Jerusalem and jostled and joked about marching south to relax amidst the luxuries of the great port city of Alexandria – with its baths, brothels and fine wines from the shores of Lake Mareotis – the harbour of Sebastos at Caesarea witnessed an altogether different scene. A crack unit of 200 army officers sped to Israel's chief port under a veil of secrecy. In the dead of night they slipped into the city by the back gate near the southern amphitheatre and followed the shadows down to the shore. Only eighty years before, King Herod's harbour had been built between 22 and 10 BC to honour the emperor Augustus and as a port of call for Egyptian grain destined for Rome. With its temple-lined streets, vaulted warehouses, fountains, latrines and inns, Sebastos was a bastion of *romanitas* – Rome away from home.

The port was designed as the first purely artificial harbour of antiquity, a state-of-the-art facility on which no expense had been spared. Ingenious engineers had conjured up islands in the sea along a completely unsheltered coastline. On to the seabed were sunk lines of wooden caissons filled with *pozzuolana* – a hydraulic concrete that solidifies in contact with water – imported from the Bay of Naples. Over the submerged foundations master architects created a bustling mercantile quarter. Gleaming white marble adorned the foreshore and a colossal bronze statue of Drusus, stepson of the emperor Augustus, bestrode the entrance mouth of this 20-hectare basin. Two protective breakwaters sheltered the harbour, the southern arm protruding 500 metres into the sea like the pincer of a giant crab, greedily pulling in the commercial fruits of the empire.

At the far tip of the southern breakwater, twenty warships and five of Rome's most robust, 35-metre-long merchant vessels with double-planked wooden hulls were moored menacingly by the inner harbour. Rapidly and without ceremony, rugged officers lugged heavy straw baskets deep into the ships' holds, as the remainder of the troops sealed off the area. After half an hour of toil, the operation ceased as abruptly as it had started. The air was calm and windless; waves caressed the shore. Suddenly, a procession of three priests swinging gold censers, accompanied by six generals, descended from the darkness of the Temple of Augustus and Rome fronting the port along the quay and carefully stepped up the gangway of the largest warship. 'Lift anchor,' barked a heavily bearded general clad in bronze breastplates embossed with the personification of a smiling Nike, the goddess of Victory.

The ship's captain acknowledged the order by shining a bronze oil-lamp overboard. For a split second the pitch-black night was pierced, silhouetting a white-robed figure with a long priestly beard, clutching close to his chest a seven-pronged golden candelabrum. The spoils from the Temple of Jerusalem, razed to the ground not a week before, were on their way to Rome.

2

Awakenings

THE MOTHER OF all storms ripped along the coast of Israel as I stood on the beach at the ancient port of Dor in May 1991. Just 13 kilometres to the south, the ghostly outline and blinking lights of the power station at Caesarea loomed through the sea mist, close to the spot where King Herod's colossal lighthouse once welcomed sea-battered sailors home to port. The howling wind and swirling sand threatened to sweep me off my feet. Café owners rushed to secure their shutters and villagers of the Carmel took to the roofs to escape rising rainwater. Even hardy Arab fishermen, who had spent all their lives on the moody Mediterranean Sea, dragged their boats high on to beaches and battened down their hatches. As they savoured thick, muddy coffee from within a ruined Ottoman house they nodded wisely. This was one of the periodic great storms that ravage this quiet backwater of the eastern Mediterranean once or twice a generation.

Poseidon's wrath was bad news for me. At the end of the First Gulf War following Saddam Hussein's invasion of oil-rich Kuwait, I had packed my snorkel, wetsuit and underwater camera to work as a marine archaeologist in Israel. Along with a colleague I had founded the Dor Maritime Archaeology Project to explore ancient shipwrecks in the waters of Dor, a city of Canaanite origin perched on a rocky promontory midway between Caesarea and Haifa. This ancient port city is a well-kept secret hidden in a breathtaking landscape. Its tantalising waters conceal myriad unanswered secrets about the ancient maritime world. The concoction of rich history, archaeology and out-standing natural beauty is magical; in a place like this you awake each morning tingling with excitement at the endless promise of a new day.

For several weeks, with my project co-director and diving buddy, Kurt Raveh, I had dived the ancient sea-lanes, spending more time underwater than on land, scouring a seabed choked with ton upon ton of sand blankets that it would take lifetimes to remove by hand or even with the help of powerful air-lifts – underwater vacuum cleaners. The underwater visibility was astonishingly clear but only revealed a desert of sand and shell. Frustrated, I yearned to know what lay beneath. Day after day we lived in hope of finding the preserved timbers of a Phoenician or Roman ship peering out of the sediment.

With growing impatience we watched the storm set about its mischief and I killed time in our laboratory drawing the few fragments of Roman terracotta wine jars discovered so far. This was a long way to come for a bag of broken crockery, a very small return for a huge gamble at a time when my peers were climbing corporate ladders and enjoying the high life. Fidgeting over lost time, I pulled the back page off the *Jerusalem Post* that Kurt had been reading before he fell into deep slumber on the office sofa.

Whilst chilling spring winds made me shiver and dream of English fish and chips drenched in salt and vinegar, a small headline tucked away on the back page caught my attention. Israel's Minister of Culture had dispatched a formal letter to the Vatican demanding the return of the Temple treasure looted from Jerusalem in AD 70. The Eternal City stood accused of deliberately imprisoning the prime symbols of Israel's national birthright (central to hopes of resurrecting a new synagogue on the Temple Mount) deep in its centuries-old, dusty storerooms.

To my scientific mind, any idea that this treasure might have survived 2,000 years sounded ludicrous – at least at first. After all, war and greed have robbed mankind of many of the artistic wonders of the classical past. The original Greek bronze statues fashioned by the master craftsmen, Myron, Pheidias and Polykleitos, were largely melted down in antiquity. Where are the 120,000 talents of gold and silver, the enormous chests stuffed with jewels and gold that Alexander the Great looted from Persepolis in Iran in 330 BC? What happened to these spoils after they were carried away on 10,000 mules and 5,000 camels, according to the ancient writers Diodorus Siculus and Plutarch? The Greek treasuries, *thesauroi*, uncovered at the Oracles of Delphi, Olympia and Gela are impressive forms of architecture in their own right, but their once fabulously wealthy interiors lie barren today. Why should Jerusalem's loot be any different?

Initially, Israel's historical thunderbolt seemed preposterous – fantasy born of fanaticism. Yet as storm waves pounded the shore and lightning illuminated pewter grey skies, I recalled a historical reference to this very treasure being publicly paraded by the emperor Vespasian in a Roman Triumph following the bloody subjugation of Palestine. Pen in mouth, I pulled a dog-eared copy of Flavius Josephus' *Jewish War* from the dusty lab shelf.

Much of the detail that Josephus describes, particularly figures rather than facts, has to be taken with a plentiful pinch of salt. But as Kurt slept and fishermen played cards in ruined shacks along the shore, I read how in AD 71, following Titus' victorious return from Israel, Jerusalem's looted silver, gold and ivory were borne by soldiers along the streets of Rome like a river of wealth. Pageants on floats up to four storeys high re-enacted the bloody siege of Jerusalem, with the Temple on fire and ships clashing in sea battles. Meanwhile, humiliated Jewish military leaders were dragged in chains in front of the triumphant emperor and his son.

According to Josephus, the most impressive moment in the parade was the passage of the Temple spoils: a heavy golden table and a seven-branched golden candelabrum, the *menorah*. As the Triumph reached its conclusion at the Temple of Jupiter Capitolinus, a silence gripped the crowd as Simon, son of Giora and general of the Jewish revolt, was executed in the Forum.

Once the excitement of the Triumph had died down, so Josephus explicitly tells us:

> Vespasian decided to erect a temple of Peace. This was very speedily completed and in a style surpassing all human conception. For, besides having prodigious resources of wealth on which to draw he also embellished it with ancient masterpieces of painting and sculpture; indeed, into that shrine were accumulated and stored all objects for the sight of which men had once wandered over the whole world, eager to see them individually while they lay in various countries. Here, too, he laid up the vessels of gold from the temple of the Jews, on which he prided himself. (*JW* 7.158–61)

This revelation made my senses tingle and a wave of adrenalin shot through my body. Could this report be historically accurate or was it the kind of hyperbole of which Josephus is so often guilty? Did the holy treasures of Herod's Temple find a home in the Eternal City? If so, were they eventually melted down for liquid capital? If not, what was their fate during the fifth-century Gothic and Vandal invasions? Could they even still survive today?

The very idea was exhilarating. If true, the implications for humanity were enormous. Not only would this treasure be worth a king's ransom of hundreds of millions of pounds but, as the symbolic insignia of a people lost and found – Judaism and the modern state of Israel – the political implications were highly sensitive, even dangerous.

My fascination with this enigma was not to be satisfied in 1991. The following day the skies cleared and the sea ceased to swirl. Diving eagerly, we realised that Poseidon had generously bestowed his blessings on us. Three-metre-deep sand blankets smothering the seabed had been blasted away by the force of a thousand sea horses in a single storm, exposing parts of Dor's ancient harbour floor never before seen by the human eye.

Throughout those heady spring and summer days we found twelve shipwrecks along an 80-metre-long stretch of seabed – the richest concentration in the eastern Mediterranean – recovering a fifth-century BC Greek war helmet, Roman bronze bowls and, gratifyingly, the noble timbers of those elusive Late Roman wooden hulls. I got my hands on more ancient pottery than I could ever have wished for. To my corporate friends this may have looked like old rubbish, but to me it was living history, a vast jigsaw that had important stories to tell. In those days I wouldn't have swapped my museum of broken pots for a case of Bollinger. As I lived through the most invigorating time of my life, recording the archaeology, participating in television documentaries and writing articles, the riddle of Titus, Josephus and the case of the missing Jewish treasure was relegated for ten long years to a back drawer of my mind – stored away germinating, but never erased from memory.

3

Ghosts of Israel Past

STRANGE HOW A blast from the past resurfaces when you least expect. By 2001 I had swapped my facemask and wetsuit for reading glasses and a smart suit to edit *Minerva*, the International Review of Ancient Art and Archaeology. Fighting crowds on my way to work in London's West End was a far cry from those heady days of shipwreck exploration in Israel.

Each morning I would ritually savour my first cup of life-sustaining coffee while scanning the latest newspaper cuttings for ancient ruins making the news. As a familiar time-traveller into the vortex of antiquity, I usually only found old news re-spun for fund-raising campaigns or chanced upon by an over-excited journalist unwittingly sold the emperor's new clothes rather than a hot new discovery. However, I was always alert for some exception to the rule.

One memorable day in August 2001 I spluttered into my coffee as my eyes feasted on a story publicising the opening of the *Blood and Sand* exhibition in the Colosseum at Rome. The Amphitheatrum Flavium, as it was originally called, was one of the engineering wonders of classical antiquity, a four-storey entertainment facility built by the emperor Vespasian from AD 72 and finished by his son, the emperor Titus, in AD 80. When complete, the Colosseum boasted 80 entrances, was 189 metres long, 48 metres high, seated 50,000 people, and was by far the largest amphitheatre of the Roman Empire. The noise and atmosphere generated by this stone theatre of death must have been terrifying, unlike any of today's comparatively tame entertainment facilities, even Madison Square Garden on a world championship boxing night.

To the side of the Colosseum's main entrance is a massive marble architrave that once spanned a major passageway. Until very recently it lay idly on the ground at its original place of discovery, neglected by the three million visitors passing by each year. Ancient relics like these are scattered throughout Rome. However, this turned out to be no ordinary stone. Since 1813 historians have been familiar with a Latin inscription running across the front surface of the architrave referring to a restoration of the Colosseum sponsored by Rufius Caecina Felix Lampadius in AD 443/4. Very interesting and useful in its own right for working out the complex surgery which this monument has been subjected to over the decades.

Far more compelling, though, are a series of sixty-seven small holes studded across the architrave's surface, a couple of centimetres deep, that originally pegged in position bronze letters from a far earlier inscription. Once Lampadius decided to reuse this piece of architecture, the original bronze letters were melted down. So today all that remains are the empty holes from this earlier 'phantom' inscription.

On that stifling summer's day in August 2001, in an office down Old Bond Street, I was intrigued to read how Professor Géza Alföldy from the University of Heidelberg, an expert in so-called ghost epigraphy, had reconstructed three lost lines of Latin beneath the fifth-century inscription:

IMP(ERATOR) T(ITUS) CAES(AR) VESPASIANVS AVG(VSTVS)
AMPHITHEATRVM NOVVM
EX MANVBIS FIERI IVSSIT

The importance of this inscription, dating to AD 79, far transcends the massive weight of the architrave, and can be translated as:

The Emperor Titus Caesar Vespasian Augustus ordered the new amphitheatre to be made from the [proceeds of sale of the] spoils.

Titus never served as a general before going to war in Judaea where he earned his spurs, so the *manubiae* (spoils) concerned were without doubt those plundered from the Temple of Jerusalem in AD 70.

The looting of Jerusalem must have had a huge impact on Rome's economy. The holy Temple had been a massive gold mine. This architrave, a living piece of history that has outlasted the centuries, was tangible confirmation that Josephus had been reporting fact all along. Jerusalem's treasures were indeed brought to Rome, impacting powerfully on the everyday landscape not only of the pagan city of antiquity but also the contemporary skyline.

The success of Vespasian and Titus in suppressing the First Jewish Revolt (AD 66–70) had brought the empire spoils beyond its wildest dreams, exceeding the exploits of all of Rome's celebrated rulers. Josephus leaves us in no doubt of the enormity of the windfall: 'So glutted with plunder were the troops, one and all, that throughout Syria the standard of gold was depreciated to half its former value' (*JW* 6.317).

The cities and towns of the Near East were saturated with Temple gold and, as the Colosseum's phantom inscription verifies, Vespasian's slice of the bounty was easily sufficient to sponsor the grandest place of entertainment the ancient world ever boasted. Recent estimates put the cost of the Colosseum's foundations alone at £28.5 million (excluding labour, drainage and any superstructure). The end product must have been closer to £100 million. The enormity of the Temple treasure was also sufficient to bankroll the entire Flavian dynasty (AD 69–96) from the emperor Vespasian to Domitian. The economic windfall of the looting of the Jewish Temple is estimated to have brought the treasury of Rome an immense 50 tons of gold and silver. Just how much of Flavian Rome was built from Jewish blood money?

Grappling with this exciting revelation, I recalled the shores of Dor and the great storm of May 1991. Now intrigue had been replaced by scientific curiosity. When I contacted Professor Alföldy to congratulate him on his discovery and confirm a few details, his reply was modest but telling: 'Now we know what happened with this immense booty.'

By the end of the same week I had completed a short article for *Minerva* entitled 'The Roman Siege of Jerusalem and Fate of the Spoils of War'. Once again I was consumed by intense speculation; not so much amazement and awe at the scale of the treasures as a resolute curiosity to determine what precisely happened to the great gold candelabrum, the Table of the Divine Presence and silver trumpets looted from Jerusalem – one of the most important lost treasures of history. My mind was in turmoil, I couldn't sleep. I would have liked to close the offices of *Minerva* there and then to head straight to

Jerusalem and Rome in search of answers. But reality bit and magazine deadlines pressed.

Intrigue had turned into obsession. Already I found myself processing the lost Temple treasure story through a series of critical scientific filters. Why, I wondered, did Rome destroy King Herod's Temple in Jerusalem in AD 70? Was it deliberate or just an unavoidable by-product of war? If the Jewish loot really made it to Rome, did it survive the decline and fall of the Roman Empire in the fifth century? When did the great gold candelabrum – symbol of a displaced civilisation – finally disappear from the pages of history?

With so many unanswered questions, I determined to unravel the truth about one of the most important, yet neglected, stories of history. During the next four years I would circle the Mediterranean twice on this quest, visiting four of the greatest cities of antiquity – Jerusalem, Rome, Carthage and Constantinople – clarifying some questions, burying others as red herrings and uncovering a web of facts more startling than any work of fiction. The journey drew me to dangerous places and people that reminded me of the age-old proverb: treasure is trouble.

4

Exodus and Exile

INSPIRED IN 2001 by the revelations of the Colosseum's phantom inscription, I itched to jump on a plane and head for the Eternal City. Just as all roads led to Rome 2,000 years ago, so the threads of the Temple treasure now seemed to converge there. Preliminary research flagged Rome as the crucial link in the disappearance of the Jewish spoils – the Temple of Peace was the last place where they were spotted in public. Or so I thought at the time.

But for now the lure of Rome had to wait. First I needed to separate fact from fiction in the epic story of the Roman Empire's destruction of Israel in AD 70. At the moment the quest felt abstract: I was hunting a monumental treasure without having clearly unravelled why Rome had attacked Israel in AD 66 and how the war unfolded.

If I was going to track down the Temple treasure of Jerusalem successfully, I needed to evaluate its physical, spiritual and monetary value to the Roman Empire and the Jews of ancient Israel. Without an accompanying historical, political and psychological profile, the spoils would lack context. Imagine investigating a murder scene without dusting for fingerprints or taking samples for DNA analysis. You would have no forensic evidence. My attitude towards the Temple treasure was exactly the same.

I needed to turn the clock back to the moment when the Temple fell, to reconstruct the final weeks of the siege and assess Titus' rationale for razing Jerusalem. Had he plotted with his father, the emperor Vespasian, to burn down the Temple deliberately so they could fill the imperial coffers with Jewish blood money? If so, perhaps they liquidated all of the treasure. After the great fire of Rome in AD 64, the Eternal City was certainly an eyesore that badly needed a face-lift. Did the Temple treasure pay for this plastic surgery?

In art and literature the image of the Temple treasure of Jerusalem has assumed legendary status. Steven Spielberg and George Lucas, in *Raiders of the Lost Ark*, famously presented the Ark of the Covenant as an omnipotent force of divine power, capable of wiping out Nazi units at the lift of a lid. In this portrayal the movie moguls were deeply inspired by the Ark's biblical prowess against enemies of the Israelites. More recently, *National Treasure* saw Nicolas Cage successfully hunt down Solomon's treasure beneath the sewers of New York.

A few books have flirted with the theme of Jerusalem's Temple treasure but, astonishingly, without defining its character. The nature of the supposed Temple treasure that ended up in the French village of Rennes-le-Château, uncovered by the Abbé Bérenger Saunière around 1885, has never been specified, although the effects of its deadly power allegedly filtered down the generations for two millennia. Elsewhere, the eccentric spiritual leader of the Parker Expedition to Jerusalem in 1909–11, Valter H. Juvelius, anticipated discovering riches beyond his wildest dreams beneath the Temple Mount: a $200 million treasure hidden away when King Nebuchadnezzar conquered Jerusalem in 586 BC. Following nocturnal probings of the Dome of the Rock, local rumour ran wild with speculations that the Crown and Ring of Solomon, the Ark of the Covenant and the Sword of Mohammed had all been plundered. But what artistic wonders did the Temple really conceal in AD 70?

Truth is a rare commodity in the zealous world of treasure hunting, where the fertility of the human mind finds the perfect playground. This is a field where clairvoyants are known to swing rings over maps to locate shipwrecked treasure and where virtually any method will be employed in the pursuit of gain. By no means restricted to modern Western greed, treasure hunting was well-established in nineteenth-century Palestine. Writing in *Pictured Palestine* in 1891, James Neal colourfully described a common tendency to hide wealth in the ground in an Ottoman world where banks and security of property were unavailable. Accordingly,

> all that is not turned into jewellery and worn by the women on their persons is hidden in the ground . . . The owner of such buried treasure, until at his last gasp, will seldom if ever reveal the secret hiding-place even to his wife, and therefore when he dies suddenly or amongst

strangers, his secret dies with him. Hence the country, through thousands of years, has come to be honeycombed with hidden treasures. In consequence of this, there has arisen a class of men who, like gamblers, abandoning their proper calling, and often neglecting their families, spend almost their whole life in wandering about to seek out buried property . . . One class of treasure-hunters are called *Sahiri*, or 'Necromancers'. Their method of procedure is to seek out certain nervous and highly sensitive individuals, who are credited with the faculty of perceiving objects concealed under ground, or in any other place of hiding.

In *Domestic Life in Palestine* (1862), Mary Eliza Rogers explained how the medium was coerced to pronounce:

the faculty is only active when raised by the influence of necromantic ceremonies, which are understood by the professional treasure-seeker. He properly prepares the medium, and calls into full activity the visionary power; then, in obedience to his command, the hiding-places of treasures are said to be minutely described. On being restored to the normal state, the medium does not remember any of the revelations which may have been made. The practice of this art is considered *haram*, that is, 'unlawful', and is carried on secretly . . . Those people of whom I made enquiries on the subject spoke with fear and trembling, and mysteriously whispered their explanations.

Just what oddities these speculators teased out of the soils of Palestine will never be known. In reality, however, the various methods initiated to track down the Temple treasure of Jerusalem have, to date, turned up nothing more than old horseshoes. To seek the Temple spoils, or write about their effects on later history, without determining what these treasures actually consisted of, is to construct a house of straw.

———◆———

Unravelling the mystery of the Temple treasure of Jerusalem hinges on two points in time, historical periods that could not be more culturally different. The first is the biblical Exodus, when proto-Israelite groups allegedly wandered in the wilderness of Sinai around the end of the thirteenth century BC before establishing a Jewish homeland in Israel. The second fixed point dates to AD 81, when the Arch of Titus was built on the summit of the Sacred Way in the Forum at Rome. The Arch is famous for its remarkable wall relief showing a scene from the Triumph of Vespasian and Titus celebrated along the streets of the Eternal City ten years earlier. This epic masterpiece depicts various Romans and the most important spoils plundered from the Second Temple of Jerusalem in AD 70. The scene is the equivalent of a detailed photograph of its age. Some form of table is carried at shoulder height on wooden poles; two cylindrical trumpets with flaring mouths are tied to its frontal plane. Behind, a seven-branched candelabrum is marched conspicuously through an archway. But what connects these two moments in time, the first from the dawn of organised religion, the second associated with the peak of pagan worship and the zenith of Roman civilisation?

The answer is God's detailed instructions to Moses about the formation and doctrine of Judaism in the Book of Exodus. Here the first record of the dominant symbols of the Jewish faith are plucked out of thin air to become constant beacons of faith for the next 3,500 years. If you want to fathom the composition of the Temple treasure of Jerusalem in AD 70, you have to focus on the Arch of Titus. But to set the spoils depicted in an accurate context, you must start with Exodus. Only in this way is it possible to determine whether the Arch of Titus menorah, Table and trumpets were original heirlooms passed down the centuries or products of the Roman era.

In Exodus the central tenets of First and Second Temple Judaism (tenth century BC to late first century AD) – sacrificial worship based around a single 'temple', commandments and objects of worship – emerge in fully developed form. The language used is precise, leaving no room for error. For instance, two one-year-old lambs must be sacrificed daily, one in the morning and one in the evening offered with one-tenth of choice flour mixed with one-fourth beaten oil and one-fourth of wine (Exodus 29.38–46). During his lengthy dialogue with God on Mount Sinai, Moses was bombarded with information – the prophet must have possessed a fine memory.

Exodus 25.1–9 records his instructions:

> The Lord said to Moses . . . Tell the Israelites to take for me an offering; from all whose hearts prompt them to give you shall receive the offering

for me . . . And have them make me a sanctuary, so that I may dwell among them. In accordance with all that I show you concerning the pattern of the tabernacle and all its furniture, so you shall make it.

Even though the Tabernacle was only a glorified reed tent inspired by Egyptian Late Bronze Age architecture – essentially little more than the tents of Bedouin encampments today – from the very beginning it was furnished with fine art and precious metals. The Ark of the Covenant, for instance, was decorated with two gold cherubim with spread wings (Exodus 25.18–20) and the Court of the Tabernacle contained twenty pillars and twenty bases of bronze to the south, covered with silver bands and beads (Exodus 27.10–11). The sanctuary also featured a bronze basin and washstand to maintain the cleanliness of Aaron and his priestly sons. A central feature of early Judaism, ritual purity is embedded within the religion from the very beginning: 'They shall wash their hands and their feet, so that they may not die: it shall be a perpetual ordinance for them, for him and his descendants throughout their generations' (Exodus 30.21). The dazzling array of *mikvehs* – ritual cleansing pools – surrounding the ancient site of Qumran on the shore of the western Dead Sea attests to the longevity of this religious observance.

Equally remarkable were the instructions regarding priestly clothing passed down to Moses, which offer a startling insight into the wealth associated with the central Jewish sanctuary throughout the ages. These garments were lavishly decorated, making the High Priests visibly shine in the presence of God:

> You shall make a breastplate of judgement, in skilled work . . . of gold, of blue and purple and crimson yarns, and of fine twisted linen . . . You shall set in it four rows of stones. A row of carnelian, chrysolite, and emerald shall be the first row; and the second row a torquoise, a sapphire, and a moonstone; and the third row a jacinth, an agate, and an amethyst; and the fourth row a beryl, an onyx, and a jasper; they shall be set in gold filigree. There shall be twelve stones with names corresponding to the names of the sons of Israel . . . You shall make for the breastplate chains of pure gold, twisted like cords . . . So Aaron shall bear the names of the sons of Israel in the breastplate of judgement on his heart when he goes into the holy place, for a continual remembrance before the Lord. (Exodus 28.15–29)

From its elaborate exposition in Exodus, the word of God offered vast opportunities for architectural and artistic embellishment over time. If you accept the Bible verbatim, the tenth century BC witnessed a watershed in building and an economic boom for the fledgling nation of Israel. At this time, 'Judah and Israel were as numerous as the sand by the sea; they ate and drank and were happy. Solomon was sovereign over all the kingdoms from the Euphrates to the land of the Philistines, even to the border of Egypt' (1 Kings 4.20–21). With his mighty 40,000 stalls of horses for his chariots and 12,000 horsemen, this wisest of rulers was lord of all he surveyed.

The First Temple built by King Solomon was one of the wonders of the age. Enormous financial resources were invested in the new sanctuary and political alliances exploited to turn a dream into reality. King Hiram of Tyre arranged for Lebanese cedars to be floated down the Mediterranean coast to Israel in return for annual tribute of 20,000 kors of wheat and 20 kors of fine oil (1 Kings 5.10–11). Solomon sent teams of 10,000 people into Lebanon each month to speed up the construction business, and dispatched 70,000 labourers and 80,000 stonecutters into the hill country of Judaea.

The Bible describes Solomon's Temple as 60 cubits long and 20 wide (30 x 10 metres), with a timber inner sanctuary overlaid with pure gold. Much of the cedar wood was sculpted with cherubim, palm trees, gourds and open flowers, while the floor of the inner and outer rooms was again overlaid with gold. The entrance door to the inner sanctuary repeated the same decorative scheme, but this time the artwork was overlaid with gold (1 Kings 6.2–20; 29–32). The Temple must have been a major drain on regional gold resources, then mined in the legendary land of Ophir – probably either Ethiopia or the Yemen:

> Solomon overlaid the inside of the house with pure gold, then he drew chains of gold across, in front of the inner sanctuary, and overlaid it with gold. Next he overlaid the whole house with gold, in order that the whole house might be perfect. (1 Kings 6.21–2)

Mirroring the Tabernacle sanctuary of the wilderness, the king also housed two monumental gilt-veneered olive wood cherubim within the inner sanctuary, each 5 metres wide (1 Kings 6.23–8). The bronzes adorning the Temple were equally staggering. Hiram of Tyre was commissioned to cast two bronze pillars in the Temple vestibule known as Jachin and Boaz. Each measured 9 metres high and 6 metres in diameter. Two vast bronze capitals surmounted each pillar, each 2.5 metres high and decorated with 200 bronze pomegranates (1 Kings 7.15–22). Next Hiram crafted the 'cast sea', essentially a 5-metre-wide cauldron that could hold the equivalent of 2,000 baths, with a brim shaped like the flower of a lily standing on twelve cast oxen (1 Kings 7.23–6). This was accompanied by ten bronze basins, each capable of holding the equivalent of forty baths (1 Kings 7.38). Finally, the master craftsman modelled ten bronze stands decorated with lions, oxen and cherubim, each standing on four bronze wheels (1 Kings 7.27–37). To these artistic masterpieces were added the treasures of King David.

King Solomon was one of the most celebrated characters of history, a powerful ruler of proverbial wisdom and a master builder. For these reasons he has become a victim of his own success, with popular perception immediately linking images of the Temple treasure to this man. Such a view, however, has to surmount two major pitfalls. First, extensive archaeological exploration conducted throughout Jerusalem and the surrounding hills has failed to produce one iota of evidence for a ruler called Solomon or, more damagingly, for monumental tenth-century BC building operations. If Jerusalem was really inhabited at this time, then the very meagre pottery unearthed proves it can only have been a small, rural village and hardly the epicentre of a magnificent United Israel. This image is completely at loggerheads with the Bible's elaborate description of major urban development.

Second, and equally conclusive, the Bible paints a vivid canvas of severe political and cultural disruption in sixth-century BC Jerusalem, when Israel was dismantled. As Israel was ransacked by the generals of King Nebuchadnezzar of Babylon, the superpower of the day, the religious symbols of Judaism were deliberately destroyed – at least according to one biblical tradition. Thus, 2 Kings 24.13–14 emphatically narrates how Nebuchadnezzar

carried off all the treasures of the house of the Lord, and the treasures of the king's house; he cut in pieces all the vessels of gold in the temple of the Lord, which King Solomon of Israel had made . . . He carried away all Jerusalem, all the officials, all the warriors, 10,000 captives, all the artisans and the smiths; no one remained except the poorest people of the land.

The plunder of the wealth of Jerusalem's Temple, it is safe to say, was comprehensive.

As emphatic as the reports relating to the timing and effects of these events seem to be, later testimony clouds the subject. For some reason the Bible contradicts itself over the fate of the Temple treasure. Rather than being completely destroyed and melted down for reuse in Babylon, Ezra (1.7–11) records them as suffering a completely different fate when, in 538 BC, King Cyrus of Persia handed the exiled Jews their freedom and returned the Temple treasures:

King Cyrus himself brought out the vessels of the house of the Lord that Nebuchadnezzar had carried away from Jerusalem and placed them in the house of his gods. King Cyrus of Persia had them released into the charge of Mithredath the treasurer, who counted them out to Sheshbazzar the prince of Judah. And this was the inventory: gold basins, 30; silver basins, 1,000; knives, 29; gold bowls, 30; other silver bowls, 410; other vessels, 1,000; the total of the gold and silver vessels was 5,400. All these Sheshbazzar brought up, when the exiles were brought up from Babylonia to Jerusalem.

Over time even this version of repatriation was replaced by over-imaginative Late Roman and medieval legends that attempted to reinforce the survival myth of Solomon's treasure. One source supposes that the vessels were entrusted to the prophet Jeremiah, under whose protection the Ark of the Covenant, the altar of incense and the 'holy tent' were carried by an angel to Mount Sinai. There, Jeremiah concealed the vessels in a spacious cave. Another medieval tradition places Solomon's Temple treasure under a stone next to the grave of Daniel (of lions' den fame) at Shushar in Persia. Legend states that anyone trying to remove the stone fell dead; people digging near the spot were crushed by a storm.

The tale of the concealment and preservation of the Temple vessels during the exile in Babylon became increasingly embellished down the centuries. One intriguing legend preserved amongst a wealth of medieval folklore demonstrates the fantastic dimensions to which the story had swollen. As a unique document of messianic hope and projection, it deserves quoting at length:

> Even the temple vessels not concealed by Jeremiah were prevented from falling into the hands of the enemy; the gates of the Temple sank into the earth, and other parts and utensils were hidden in a tower at Baghdad by the Levite Shimur and his friends. Among these utensils was the seven-branched candlestick of pure gold, every branch set with 26 pearls . . . and 200 stones of inestimable worth. Furthermore, the tower at Baghdad was the hiding-place for 77 golden tables, and for the gold with which the walls of the Temple had been clothed within and without. The tables had been taken from Paradise by Solomon, and in brilliance they outshone the sun and the moon, while the gold from the walls excelled in amount and worth all the gold that had existed from the creation of the world until the destruction of the Temple.
>
> The jewels, pearls, gold, and silver, and precious gems, which David and Solomon had intended for the Temple, were discovered by the scribe Hilkiah, and he delivered them to the angel Shamshiel, who in turn deposited the treasure in Borsippa. The sacred musical instruments [trumpets] were taken charge of and hidden by Baruch and Zedekiah until the advent of the Messiah, who will reveal all treasures. In his time a stream will break forth from under the place of the Holy of Holies, and flow through the lands of the Euphrates, and, as it flows, it will uncover all the treasures buried in the earth. (*Legends of the Jews* IV.321)

Here, in fully romanticised form, the description of the gold candelabrum departs from the concise biblical version to stud the artefact with all manner of precious stones. The original narrative is now overlain with glorious fantasy to evoke a dream-like myth of hope for the communities of the Diaspora, tenuously peering back through the mists of time for a bridge to Temple days that might offer comfort amid the religious persecutions of contemporary medieval life.

Such rich folklore is fascinating in its own right, important documentation revealing the psychological condition of medieval Jewry. Yet, as fantasy, it has no historical bearing on the true movements of Solomon's Temple treasure. At no point does the Old

Testament pretend that the major vessels of faith – the menorah, Table of the Divine Presence and trumpets – were returned to Jerusalem in the reign of King Cyrus of Persia. On balance, every shred of evidence suggests that if they ever really existed, the treasures of the First Temple went up in a puff of smoke during the destruction of Jerusalem in the sixth century BC. So when and in what context did the treasures of Herod's Temple emerge?

5

Herod's Treasure Chest

To DEFINE THE unique character of the Temple treasure plundered by Rome in AD 70, and crassly paraded along its streets a year later, we must leave behind the murky world of Iron Age Palestine. Sieving through the texts, one specific event emerges as a defining moment that dictated the treasure's composition. In the second century BC the borders of Palestine were creaking under the pressures of a regional power struggle. Palestine was a crucial geographical land and sea bridge linking Egypt and the Middle East with the northern Mediterranean. Control Palestine and you controlled the entire eastern Mediterranean basin and the world beyond: lucrative caravan routes meandering into Arabia and over the horizon to the Indies. Not without reason, in 1799 Napoleon Bonaparte's Chief of Staff still dubbed Palestine 'the key to the East'.

Just before the mid-second century BC, Egypt and Syria were at loggerheads over Israel, and the ruling elite of Judaea exploited the frosty political circumstances to try and bring about internal regime change. At the same time as the Syrian Seleucid king Antiochus IV Epiphanes was quarrelling with Ptolemy VI of Egypt over control of greater Syria, in Jerusalem the High Priest Onias III cast the sons of Tobias from the city gates. Aware of the territorial squabble between Egypt and Syria, the sons of Tobias fled to Antiochus and petitioned the king to appoint them his client rulers, a policy that suited his intention of Hellenising all of Syria.

Antiochus was spoiling for a fight and eagerly exploited this opportunity to attack Jerusalem with a mighty force, which triggered a bloodbath against Ptolemy's supporters in 169 BC. Writing some two hundred years after the event, Josephus confirmed that the king 'also spoiled the temple, and put a stop to the constant practice of offering a daily sacrifice of expiation for three years and six months' (*JW* 1.34).

The sons of Tobias proved to be naive political pawns rather than experienced political rulers and had no clue that they were being exploited as dispensable puppets in a brutal realpolitik. In the event, the schemers' dreams backfired. Rather than support his Jewish 'allies', in 167 BC Antiochus forced the Jews to dissolve their laws, defiled the Temple by ordering sacrifices to pigs, and forbade circumcision. The seditious sons of Tobias thus paid dearly for presuming that the wider world cared a fig about religious sensitivities.

In *Antiquities of the Jews*, Josephus explained Antiochus' megalomania as inspired by pure greed, and described the looting in detail. The king turned against the sons of Tobias,

> on account of the riches that lay in the temple; but, led by his covetous inclination (for he saw that there was in it a great deal of gold, and many ornaments that had been dedicated to it of very great value), and in order to plunder its wealth, he ventured to break the league he had made. So he left the temple bare, and took away the golden candlesticks, and the golden altar [of incense], and table [of showbread], and the altar [of burnt offering]; and did not abstain from even the veils, which were made of fine linen and scarlet. He also emptied it of its secret treasures, and left nothing at all remaining; and by this means cast the Jews into great lamentation. (*AJ* 12.249–50)

Not for the first time in history the Jews proved convenient scapegoats, on this occasion taking the backlash for Antiochus' impotence in failing to outmanoeuvre Ptolemy VI of Egypt. The Syrian king proceeded to burn the Lower City of Jerusalem, torch the sacred books of Jewish law, and strangle circumcised children. The bodies of murdered sons were hung around the necks of crucified fathers and 10,000 men were enslaved. Here was Jerusalem's Kristallnacht, 2,100 years before the Nazis ethnically cleansed the streets of Germany of its Jewish minority.

The bloody actions of Antiochus guaranteed that no Temple treasures survived the year 167 BC. The Bible reinforces the historical accuracy of this event, providing complementary written evidence that the gold candelabrum, Showbread Table and all other treasures were seized and taken into Syria (1 Maccabees 1.21–4; 2 Maccabees 5.16).

Following three years of abomination and the suspension of Jewish ritual, Jerusalem was recaptured by the Maccabean dynasty, a family of priestly descent from Modi'in in the outskirts of the Holy City. After Matthias defeated Antiochus and expelled the Syrians, his son, Judas Maccabeus, returned Israel to Temple worship:

> He then got the temple under his power, and cleansed the whole place, and walled it round about, and made new vessels for sacred ministrations, and brought them into the temple, because the former vessels had been profaned. He also built another altar, and began to offer the sacrifices. (*JW* 1.39)

The Bible confirms the creation of 'new Holy vessels' and dates the rededication to 25 Kislev, 165 BC. Soon after, Judas rebuilt the Temple sanctuary and consecrated the courts (1 Maccabees 4.48–9). In memory of this famous victory, the Maccabees 'decorated the front of the temple with golden crowns and small shields' (1 Maccabees 4.57). Yet in an ironic twist of fate, Josephus hints that Judas' success was supported through an alliance with a new political power whose voice was starting to rumble across the Mediterranean Sea: the Romans. At the very moment when Israel was refounded and the Temple rededicated, the seeds of its eventual demise were sown.

The ferocity of Antiochus IV Epiphanes ensured that any Temple spoils plundered by Titus from the Temple in AD 70 must post-date 165 BC. Between these two chronological stepping stones, the Temple of Jerusalem experienced a golden age. As the central religious institution of Judaism, it received a level of patronage unparalleled in preceding centuries. We will never know exactly what Titus and his generals found sparkling within the treasure chests of the Temple Mount. No inventory survives and I doubt that anyone outside the inner circle of High Priests really knew exactly what wealth the Temple had amassed.

Over the centuries, kings, generals and the ordinary farmer alike offered donations varying from the magnificent to the humble. And as history ebbed and flowed, passing despots and greedy rulers seized parts of the national wealth of the Jews. From time to time ancient writers illuminated this complex tapestry, enabling us to appraise a portion of the immense riches lying within the sanctuary in the first century AD.

The central vessels of worship were certainly safe and sound in 63 BC, when Pompey the Great and his entourage invaded Jerusalem on the pretence of resolving the civil war between two brothers of the ruling Jewish Hasmonaean dynasty. There, they 'went into the temple itself, whither it was not lawful for any to enter but the high priest, and saw what was reposited therein, the candlestick with its lamps, and the table, and the pouring vessels, and the censers, all made entirely of gold, as also a great quantity of spices heaped together, with 2,000 talents of sacred money' (*JW* 1.152).

Back in Rome, Pompey undoubtedly boasted about how he had demonstrated Rome's greatness over the god of the Jews by violating the Holy of Holies. So when Crassus was later appointed governor of Judaea, he took the opportunity in 51 BC to remove the Temple gold and 2,000 talents untouched by Pompey to cover the costs of a military expedition against the Parthians.

Only in the final century of its existence did the Temple of Jerusalem become one of the greatest wonders of antiquity, with the reign of King Herod, a former general and son of the pro-Roman Antipater of Idumaea. Eager to cement a reputation as one of the supreme leaders of the Mediterranean world, King Herod (ruled 37–4 BC) was obsessed with ambitious building projects. With his network of royal palaces at Caesarea, Herodium, Jericho and Machaerus (in modern Jordan), the king established a reputation as a man of immense wealth and style. By building the world's first deepwater artificial port, and naming it Sebastos, the Greek for Augustus, the king proved the depth of his allegiance to his Roman masters. Herod was the perfect client king for safeguarding the economic and political interests of the empire. And to appease the local population, around 20 BC he initiated the most ambitious building plan in the entire Near East – the redesign and rebuilding of the great Temple of Jerusalem.

The Temple would be Herod's crowning glory, a perpetual memorial of his omnipotence. Even though it is this Temple, generally referred to as the Second Temple (although more accurately a third sanctuary after those of Solomon and Zerubbabel), that went on to inspire generations of world religions, politicians, artists and poets, not one contemporary artistic representation of the site survives. From the air, at least, the scale of the Temple Mount on which the sanctuary stood can still be marvelled at. Measuring 485 x 315 metres, the area of five football pitches, it was twice the size of the emperor Trajan's Forum in Rome. Today, however, the ground plan of Herod's Temple – both standing architecture and foundations – is wholly annihilated by later structures.

Fortunately, various ancient writers recorded the basic form of the sanctuary in detail, to which archaeology has added a few physical features. Herod essentially started from scratch, removing the foundations of the former Temple and superimposing a new edifice measuring 50 metres in height. Single blocks of masonry weighed up to 5 tons, and an exceptional stone built into the western wall of the Temple Mount measures a staggering 12.1 metres in length and weighs about 300 tons.

Just as no expense was spared on the architecture of the Temple, so its lavish decoration stretched the boundaries of extravagance and taste. While most of the complex was built of white limestone and marble, the exuberant display of precious metal increased with proximity to the central Holy of Holies. The nine gates of the Lower Court, for example – donated by Alexander, the father of Tiberius Julius Alexander (governor of Judaea AD 46–8, and later a Roman commander in the First Jewish Revolt, though himself a Jew) – were covered with gold and silver sheet, as were their doorjambs and lintels. Josephus explicitly states that the outer face of the Temple 'wanted nothing that was likely to surprise either men's minds or their eyes', being covered all over with heavy gold plate. At sunrise, the Temple reflected the fiery splendour of the sun, blinding onlookers. From a distance the golden façade was said to resemble a snow-capped mountain. To cap this spectacle, King Herod bolted an enormous golden eagle above the entrance gate.

According to the Mishnah (the earliest post-biblical codification of Jewish oral law, written c. AD 200), the entire Holy of Holies, the most sacred part of the Temple, was overlaid with gold except for the rear side of the doors, and its inner door was crafted of Corinthian brass. Above the twelve steps leading up to its entrance was suspended from lintels the famous sculpture of the golden vine, replete with clusters of grapes as tall as men. Over the decades individuals donated additional golden leaves, berries or even clusters. Eventually it became so heavy that 300 priests were needed to lift it. Another artistic masterpiece displayed here was a silver and gold copy of a crown worn by the High Priest Joshua son of Jehozadak after the return from Babylonian exile. The original crown symbolised his divine appointment as architect of a new Temple and to serve as God's mouth-piece on earth (Zechariah 6.11–13).

The wealth of the Temple that fell into Rome's hands in AD 70, as summarised by Josephus, included an extraordinary array of precious materials and objects. Alongside entire golden walls and doors were High Priests' clothing, including golden bells signifying thunder and pomegranates worn on garment fringes symbolising lightning. The High Priests' breast girdles were embroidered with five rows of gold, purple, scarlet and blue thread, on to which were sewn gold buttons enclosing large sardonyx gems (sardius, topaz, emerald, carbuncle, jasper, sapphire, agate, amethyst, ligure, onyx, beryl, chrysolite), each engraved with a name of the twelve tribes of Israel. The High Priest also sported a golden crown engraved with the name of God, which was worn once a year when he entered the most sacred part of the Temple. The Mishnah also refers to chambers beneath the Court of the Israelites at the entrance to the inner Temple complex, where the Levite temple servants stored their harps, lyres, cymbals, and other musical instruments.

The daily administration of the Temple was a labyrinthine business, whose inner workings largely remain a mystery. This was not simply a house of worship but, in many ways, a world of its own with unique quirks of operation, not dissimilar to the Vatican City today. Independent offices existed for rinsing the hides and innards of sacrificial victims and for their salting. A small army of priestly bureaucrats ran this holy 'city'. Yohanan ben Pinhas was in charge of seals, and Petahiah supervised bird offerings. (Petahiah was renowned for his knowledge of seventy languages, which presumably allowed him to converse with Jewish pilgrims from the four corners of the world.) The House of Garmu looked after the baking of the Showbread while Ben Ahiah was charged with supervising bowel sickness, a very serious threat to Temple purity if not controlled.

Temple economics was an imprecise science rotating around two streams of revenue. Every Jew in Israel and the Diaspora annually contributed half a shekel taxation. Donations comprised a second major source of income. The daily contributions were processed in underground chambers descending to depths of 20 metres. The Mishnah refers to 'shofar' chests kept in the sanctuary and inscribed in Aramaic 'New shekels' (for current year Temple tax) and 'Old shekels' (for people who had failed to pay in the former year). Other chests were incised for the relevant donations: 'bird offerings', 'frankincense', 'gold for the Mercy seat' and 'for freewill offerings'. This cash was collected three times a year, half a month before the festivals of Passover, Pentecost and Sukkoth.

Beyond the annual imposition of the Temple tax, it is impossible to estimate the value of further arbitrary offerings. People harbouring secrets and private fears, for instance, offered personal gifts, whose proceeds went to the poor. Equally enigmatic in AD 70 would have been the contents of the Chamber of Utensils, donations assessed every thirty days and either used in Temple upkeep or sold with the revenue going to the sanctuary. None of this patronage was constant. Other than registering the general prosperity of the period, which would have made the Temple essentially a national bank of Jewish wealth, it would be grossly misleading to attempt any calculation of that wealth.

Alongside donations made by the local Jewish citizens of Judaea, rulers contributed artworks to the Temple as political tribute. King Herod had spoils captured in Israel's wars with 'the barbarous nations' mounted all around the Temple complex. Sossius, the Roman governor of Syria who in 37 BC helped Herod capture Jerusalem from Antigonos, the last ruler of the Hasmonaean dynasty, also donated gold to the Temple, including a crown (*JW* 1.357). There is every reason to expect that this pattern of political patronage was mirrored by vast unknown riches, such as the precious cauldrons, dishes, tables and pouring vessels donated by the Roman emperor Augustus and his wife (*JW* 5.562).

Herod Agrippa, grandson of Herod the Great, spent much of his youth in Rome, where he paid the price for supporting Caligula's imperial power struggle. Although the emperor Tiberius imprisoned Agrippa for his duplicity, when head of the empire Caligula subsequently appointed him puppet king of Israel (AD 37–44). At this time Agrippa also contributed to the splendours of the Temple:

> And for the golden chain which had been given him by Caius [the emperor Caligula], of equal weight with that iron chain wherewith his royal hands had been bound [in prison], he hung it up within the limits of the temple, over the treasury, that it might be a memorial of the severe fate he had lain under . . . that it might be a demonstration how the greatest prosperity may have a fall, and that God sometimes raises what is fallen down; for this chain thus dedicated, afforded a document, to all men, that king Agrippa had been once bound in a chain for a small cause, but recovered his former dignity again. (*AJ* 19.294–5)

The issue of what Rome encountered in the Temple in AD 70 is complicated even further by increased instances of deliberate plunder in the first century AD, as Rome's political tentacles closed more tightly around Israel's neck. In 4 BC Sabinus seized the Temple treasury by force (*JW* 2.50) and, as the fifth procurator of Judaea (AD 26–36), Pontius Pilate later diverted sacred monies to build aqueducts (*JW* 2.175), no doubt including those arches still standing today to the north of Caesarea. Gessius Florus, Roman procurator of Judaea and described as 'eager to obtain the treasures of God', extracted 17 talents in the name of the emperor in AD 66 (*JW* 2.293), allegedly to make up for arrears of tribute, but really to stoke up war with the Jewish state.

Such 'withdrawals' generated a slow simmering hatred across Israel for Roman institutions. By dipping into the Temple funds, however, Rome was merely replicating its behaviour elsewhere in the provinces. But in treating Jerusalem's Temple simply as a place of worship, Roman policy would backfire disastrously. To Judaism, the Temple was the spiritual core of Israel's state religion.

But it wasn't just the Romans who plundered the Temple in the first centuries BC and AD. Once Jew took up sword against Jew inside Jerusalem during the First Revolt of AD 66–70, the various splinter factions deemed the Temple treasury acceptable prey because it contained wealth donated by groups whose authority they refused to recognise. After looting most of the richest houses of Jerusalem around AD 69, John of Gischala 'betook himself to sacrilege, and melted down many of the sacred utensils, which had been given to

the temple, including the vessels donated by the Emperor Augustus'
(*JW* 5.562). By ignoring the greater Roman threat, and immersing
themselves in constant internal bickering and battling, the Jews were
courting catastrophe and bringing the destruction of the Temple and
its treasures closer by the day.

Israel – Land of God

6

Dark Secrets in the Vatican

IN AD 70 the Temple of Jerusalem was a veritable gold mine for Vespasian's invading Roman army. Now, having compiled a solid image of the physicality and history of the treasures stored in the Jewish sanctuary, it was high time for me to explore the Holy City itself. Jerusalem is the scene of the crime from where a trail of historical and archaeological clues was disseminated across the Mediterranean basin. Before hotly pursuing this ancient evidence, I wanted to unravel what Judaism believed befell this biblical legacy and what the Temple and its holy treasures mean religiously, politically and symbolically to modern Israeli society.

Rather than a story solely relevant to ancient Israel, the fate of the Temple treasure resonates fiercely across modern politics. Since the mid-1990s a heated political wrangle has been simmering between the Vatican and Israel, who has accused the papacy of imprisoning the treasure looted by Titus in AD 70. Israel is adamant that the spoils have remained in Rome uninterrupted for two thousand years and, not surprisingly, covets the repatriation of its birthright to rectify an ancient wrong.

Certain Jewish politicians and factions remain committed to recovering the lost sacred vessels and, not least, to benefiting from association with their divine powers. This war of words boiled over in 1996, when Israel's Minister of Religion, Shimon Shetreet, presented the Vatican with historical research, allegedly compiled at the University of Florence, which is said to leave no shred of doubt that the gold candelabrum and other treasures still languished in Rome. Shetreet claimed to possess statements from former popes confirming that the Catholic Church holds these objects. An official enquiry leading to the return of the sacred vessels was demanded.

37

Then, in 1999, Moshe Katzav, President of Israel, formally asked Cardinal Angelo Sudano, Prime Minister of the Vatican, to prepare a list of all the Temple treasures and Judaica in his possession. Israel's Chief Rabbis, Yehuda Metzger and Shlomo Amar, joined the battle lines in January 2004 by requesting permission from Pope John Paul II to search the Vatican storerooms for artefacts. Reports in the Israeli newspaper *Maariv* claimed the rabbis planned to buy back the gold candelabrum.

The case for the repatriation of the Temple treasure from the Vatican is also vehemently championed by the Temple Mount and Land of Israel Faithful Movement. The ultimate goal of this extremist Zionist organisation is the establishment of a Third Temple in Jerusalem over the ground space of the historical Solomonic and Herodian edifices, the Temple Mount – today occupied by the Muslim Haram al-Sharif (Noble Sanctuary) and, at its centre, the Dome of the Rock. The Movement boldly asserts that Israel has 'very clear evidence' that the Vatican continues to imprison the 2,000-year-old Temple treasure, 'making this an undeniable fact'. A newsletter released by the movement summarises the argument thus:

> The information regarding the taking of the Menorah and the holy vessels to Rome and later, when the Roman Empire became Christian, being placed in the basement of the Vatican, has been passed down from generation to generation of the Jewish people. During the exile the holy Menorah and vessels remained at the focus of the memory of the Jewish people. Their dream was that one day soon they would recover them from the Vatican and return them to Jerusalem. This would be a sign of the beginning of the rebuilding of the Temple in Jerusalem and the redemption of the people of the land of Israel.
>
> The fact that the Vatican holds these holy Temple vessels has been very well known since 70 CE. Many Jews travelled to the Vatican when they could do so to look for them and to see them. Some of the travelers testified that they had personally seen the golden Menorah and the vessels in the basements of the Vatican. Some priests have even confirmed this fact . . .
>
> Israel is now living in the prophetic endtimes of redemption, that the Temple of the God of Israel is soon to be rebuilt in Jerusalem, and that the golden Menorah from the Second Temple and the other vessels will soon be returned to Jerusalem to be used in the Third, endtime Temple . . . This should move the heart of everyone in the world.

Further expectation and curiosity has been aroused by Steven Fine, Professor of Judaic Studies at the University of Cincinnati. Although he found the University of Florence confused by its supposed association with research pinpointing the Temple treasure in the Vatican, he contributed further tantalising ammunition. An unpublished inscription on a mosaic in a chapel of St John Lateran, Rome, and dated to 1291 reads: 'Titus and Vespasian had this ark and the candelabrum and . . . the four columns here present taken from the Jews in Jerusalem and brought to Rome.' Pope Pius XII (1939–58) was even alleged to have shown the gold menorah to Isaac Herzog, Chief Rabbi of Israel, but refused to return it.

My own research corroborated the existence of a rich vein of tradition placing the Temple treasure in Rome uninterrupted from the Late Roman period onwards. As late as the nineteenth century, the Eternal City's Jewish colony believed that early Christian soldiers threw the seven-branched candelabrum into the River Tiber, whose bed miraculously turned bronze from Rome to Ostia. The Jewish community even petitioned the pope for permission to excavate the Tiber and recover the menorah, a request denied. Hence, diverse threads woven at disparate times have created a climate of zealous hope and anticipation.

Without personally reading the 'undeniable facts' underlying Israel's accusations against the Vatican, I intended to exercise extreme caution in dealing with this war of words and to accept nothing as the gospel truth. In my own scientific work I had confronted many brilliant biblical scholars with elaborate theories born of passion and emotion, but these were often straw houses lacking secure foundations. My own interest in the Temple treasure of Jerusalem had no religious or political agenda. As a humanist and 'man of science', I was committed simply to historical integrity, to exposing the truth in whatever shape it might take.

The Vatican and its museums are renowned for their hollow legs, endless winding storerooms that contain myriad shelves of ancient masterpieces. Like Earth's oceans, nobody really knows exactly what's down there and, of course, Dan Brown's *The Da Vinci Code* has recently added great weight to conspiracy theories surrounding the papal residency. Could the Temple treasure really be languishing in those vaults? Simply discounting the idea out of hand wouldn't make the intrigue disappear: a Catholic priest even claims he once saw several Temple relics in a vault buried four storeys under the West Wing.

If anything of the great treasure of Jerusalem lies within these holy precincts, then word of its presence ought to be inked into the Secret Archive. But excavating this evidence would be a Herculean task. Although this collection currently meanders along seven and a half miles of bookshelves in the Tower of the Winds, a Baroque astronomical observatory built by Pope Paul V Borghese in the early seventeenth century, the archive's contents today owe much to chance survival and random removal and relocation.

There is no doubt that great wonders and mysteries lurk under lock and key. Even the Tower of the Winds' staff has no knowledge of some documents residing behind a heavy door at the end of a corridor on the lower floor. Always closed, its key never leaves the side of the Chief Prefect. Behind it are stored the Vatican's most sensitive and precious documents: Greek letters exchanged between the popes and emperors of Byzantium – for instance, discussing the protection of the Crusaders in 1146; the last letter sent to the pope by Mary Queen of Scots a few days before she fell under the axe of Queen Elizabeth I in 1587.

If word of the Temple treasure of Jerusalem truly lies amidst these tantalising documents, we have to assume that it – or a facsimile – has survived undisturbed for at least 1,700 years. Are such ancient scrolls capable of long-term survival in the humid microclimate of Rome? Probably not: papyrus scrolls tend to be preserved only in highly arid desert climates. To make matters worse, in the Hall of Parchments alone, thousands of medieval documents have been turned purple by a violet-coloured fungus that scientists have failed to contain.

The tumultuous history of the Secret Archive makes survival extremely unlikely, especially of documents covering the first two hundred years of the Temple treasure's presence in Rome. In AD 303 Eusebius Pamphilus, Bishop of Caesarea in Palestine and the father of Church history, recorded how in the reign of Diocletian: 'I saw with my own eyes the places of [Christian] worship thrown down from top to bottom, to the very foundations, and the inspired holy scriptures committed to the flames in the middle of the public square' (*History of the Church* 8.2.1). Rome's early Christian archive went up in smoke. Nothing survived for monks to make copies from. The crucial documentation covering the five and a half centuries after the reign of Constantine the Great are also irretrievably gone, and the earliest surviving entry, register Number 1, dates to the papacy of John VIII in AD 872–82. And even these early depositions are random and highly disparate.

At this time, and in a bizarre quirk of fate, the papal archive was stored in the Patriarchum on the Palatine Hill, alongside a castle-fortress that abutted the Arch of Titus. Because this Roman arch depicted some of the holy treasures of Jerusalem looted by Titus, including the mighty gold candelabrum, the ninth-century building was known as the Turris Cartularia, the Tower of the Seven Lamps. The safety of the archive was entrusted to the Frangipani family, who were also in charge of the public granaries. However, in the course of endemic fighting between Rome's noble families, the archive vanished. So, in its current form the bulk of the archive dates from 1612, when it was re-established by Pope Paul V Borghese. Preservation of word of the Temple treasure within the Secret Archive, confirming its current existence within the Vatican, is beyond a million-to-one chance.

What about the treasure itself, though, which various high-powered Israeli politicians argue passionately to be within the Vatican City? In England I spent six tortuous weeks politely harassing the Israel Embassy to reveal its sources. Although they contacted universities, the Israel Antiquities Authority and various political offices, no one could locate the original documentation or 'undeniable facts'. In the face of my frustration, the embassy's Press Secretary did finally provide me with a hollow answer: 'If anyone knows the Vatican does!' For this I had been kept waiting six weeks?

No doubt the embassy had tried its best on my behalf, but no one was going to go on the record about this sensitive issue. The official line claimed that the historical documentation had gone missing when Prime Minister Ariel Sharon dissolved the corrupt Ministry of Religion for financial irregularities in 2004. Its duties had been carved up between various other ministries, such as the Department of Culture and Ministry of Education, with some interests 'falling between the cracks', or so I was informed. It sounded to me as if someone was plastering over those cracks. A whitewash was in progress, but why?

The only logical response was to pass the buck. So next, I pursued the Vatican, although I suspected that a portcullis of silence would swiftly fall. If they did have the Temple treasure they surely wouldn't come clean; if they didn't, why waste time answering disrespectful questions? In the end, part of my communication with Dr Paolo Liverani, Curator of Classical Antiquities in the Vatican Museums, made the Vatican's formal position succinctly clear: 'In later times there is not the smallest evidence that any part of the treasure of the Temple arrived in Rome and I do not think that the Vatican has any interest to hide the Menorah or any other part of the booty of Titus.'

With various doors slammed in my face, but with Israel's 'undeniable facts' still beyond my grasp, I had one card left to play. Uncomfortable as I was talking to a group that wanted to eject Islam from the Temple Mount and replace it with a third Jewish Temple, I was optimistic that the director of the Temple Mount and Land of Israel Faithful Movement, Gershon Salomon, would be forthcoming with facts. If there was any validity to Israel's allegations against the Vatican, the truth would out.

7

Temple Prophecies

THROUGHOUT ITS HISTORY Israel has always been a time bomb with a short fuse. Middle Eastern politics are extreme. Bomb threats, street skirmishes and murder are daily occurrences that can arise at the drop of a Hassidic Jew's fedora. Israeli politics is wild and spontaneous; people suck the marrow out of every hour of the day as if it might be their last. You certainly know you're alive when you visit the Holy Land.

The morning I flew out to Israel in April 2005 to meet the director of the Temple Mount Faithful, the Middle East was once again in uproar. Three fourteen-year-old Palestinians had been caught red-handed smuggling weapons in Gaza and were shot dead by the Israel Defence Force. Gazan militia responded in the usual biblical fashion – an eye for an eye, tooth for a tooth – by pumping eighty mortars and Qasam rockets into the Jewish settlement of Gush Katif. The same day, extreme right-wing Jews from the Revava movement marched on the Temple Mount to demonstrate against its 'occupation' by Arabs. For three days some 8,000 police were drafted in to patrol the entrances to the site, preventing the extremists from breaking into the holy places. At the same time, thousands of Palestinians, including the leader of the West Bank's Hamas cell, Hassan Yousef, flooded the Mount to create a human shield.

Meanwhile, dozens of right-wingers, opponents of the Gaza disengagement plan, burned tyres along Tel Aviv's Ayalon highway, chained the gates of seventeen Tel Aviv schools, and hung signs on their railings reading 'Jews do not expel Jews'. Should the Israeli withdrawal go ahead, they threatened to paralyse the country with civil disorder. Jew fighting Jew is a familiar theme stretching back to the First Jewish Revolt of AD 66–70, an historical event that effectively destroyed the House of Israel and lost the Temple treasure to Rome. The cliché that history repeats itself is a deadly truth in the embattled Middle East. Lessons are not learned.

Elsewhere, a bored Jordanian workman repairing the bulging eastern wall of the Temple Mount of Jerusalem was accused of defacing this UNESCO World Heritage Site by incising the word 'Allah' into the masonry. At the Hawara checkpoint outside Nablus, a fifteen-year-old Palestinian suicide bomber was arrested as he tried to take out as many Israeli soldiers as possible. His long woollen over-coat concealing five home-made pipe bombs, worn in a temperature of 30 degrees Centigrade, gave his deadly plot away. To travel from the UK to Israel is a complete metamorphosis, a culture shock that sees inertia replaced by thunderous passion.

Jerusalem's Temple Mount is a place of extremes. With its tranquil landscaped gardens, breathtaking blue-tiled Dome of the Rock mosque, and endless fountains and soothing water features, it is extremely beautiful. When you escape the winding alleys of the Arab souk surrounding the Mount, and emerge from the oriental bustle into the open spaces where the Jewish temples of Solomon and Herod once stood, the air somehow seems cleaner, suffused with an atmos-phere of spirituality. The accumulation of history on the Temple Mount enhances the sense of other-worldliness.

However, the holiest place on earth is also one of the deadliest, a seething volcano of hatred that emits tremors that erupt down the centuries. Over the past 4,000 years, 118 conflicts have been fought in Jerusalem. It only takes a minor provocation for all hell to break loose. Witness the Tunnel Riots of September 1996, when the government of Benjamin Netanyahu opened an ancient tunnel complex leading beneath the Western Wall. Fierce fighting ensued with the deaths of seventy Palestinians and seventeen Israeli soldiers. In 2000 Ariel Sharon's politically insensitive visit to the Temple Mount triggered the Second Palestinian Intifada. With good reason Meron Benvenisti, the former deputy mayor of Jerusalem, calls the rival Jewish and Muslim claims to the Temple Mount 'a time bomb . . . of apocalyptic dimensions'.

In recent years this bomb has started to tick increasingly loudly. One of the fundamental reasons why extremist right-wing Jewish organisations like the Temple Mount Faithful have pressurised the Vatican for release of the Temple treasures looted by Titus in AD 70 is to prepare for the pending liberation of the Mount from Arab occupation and for the rebuilding of a Third Temple. According to Rabbi Yisrael Ariel, a paratrooper who helped free Jerusalem during the Six Day War of 1967, and founder of the Temple Institute, 'The State of Israel can only be one thing – a State with a Temple at its centre . . . All of today's troubles originate in the sin of abandoning the Temple Mount and the site of the Holy Temple.'

Such right-wing Jews are convinced that we are living in 'endtimes' that will witness a new Jewish Temple emerge on the Temple Mount. Signs of long-held biblical prophecies shine all around us, exemplified by the bizarre case of the red heifer. During the exodus from Egypt and the First and Second Temple periods, anybody entering the Tabernacle or Temple had to be ritually clean. Purity was ensured through immersion in ritual water baths called *mikvehs*, still visible to this day clustered around the southern entrance to the Temple. However, people who had come into contact with dead bodies were more seriously contaminated, especially priests taking funerals. In such instances, cleansing revolved around the ashes of an unblemished red heifer, typically sacrificed on the Mount of Olives.

The Bible describes how God commanded Moses and Aaron to manage such ritual:

> Tell the Israelites to bring you a red heifer without defect, in which there is no blemish and on which no yoke has been laid. You shall give it to the priest Eleazar, and it shall be taken ouside the camp and slaughtered in his presence. The priest Eleazar shall take some of its blood with his finger and sprinkle it seven times towards the front of the tent of meeting. Then the heifer shall be burnt in his sight; its skin, its flesh, and its blood, with its dung, shall be burned. The priest shall take cedar wood, hyssop, and crimson material, and throw them into the fire in which the heifer is burning. (Numbers 19.2–6)

From the time of the establishment of the earliest proto-Temple, the Tabernacle, in the wilderness of Sinai, through to Herod's construction of a Second Temple in the late first century BC, nine red heifers were allegedly born. The tenth, so tradition promises, will appear during the end-times heralding the Third Temple. Yet following the destruction of the Second Temple, no such beasts were born for 2,000 years. By stark contrast, since 1997 a rash of appropriately pure animals have been born at Kfar Menachem in northern Israel (a heifer called Melody), in the religious youth village of Kfar Hasidim near Haifa, and on the Texas ranch of a member of the Temple Mount and Land of Israel Faithful Movement. Whereas extremist right-wing Jews have welcomed these signs with unbridled excitement, secular Israel is highly concerned. Various sources have recommended that Melody be shot. To the liberal *Haaretz* newspaper, 'The potential harm from this heifer is far greater than the destructive properties of a terrorist bomb.'

Further minor miracles continue to herald the fast approach of the prophetic end-times in Jerusalem. Thus, on 18 July 2002 the Western 'Wailing' Wall of Herod's Temple inexplicably started to weep. A section of masonry 15 metres high became wet. As foreseen in the Book of Joel, water flowing from the hill of the house of God will signal the redemption of the people of Israel:

> And it shall come to pass on that day, that the mountains shall drop sweet wine, and the hills shall flow with milk, and all the streams of Judah shall flow with waters, and a fountain shall issue from the house of the Lord, and shall water the valley of Shittim. Egypt shall be a desolation, and Edom shall be a desolate wilderness, for the violence done against the people of Judah, because they have shed innocent blood in their land. But Judah shall remain for ever, and Jerusalem from generation to generation. (Joel 3.18–20)

The attitude of the Temple Mount Faithful cannot simply be dismissed as the ramblings of a lunatic minority. In the sensitive world of Temple Mount politics, it takes very little to shatter the fragile peace. Nevertheless, plans continue apace to prepare for the end-times. Since 1998 the Temple Mount Faithful have been preparing to lay the cornerstone for the Third Temple. These stones were cut by the Allafy family, immigrants to Israel from Iraq (the ancient Babylon of Jewish exile after the destruction of the First Temple by Nebuchadnezzar in 586 BC), and, coincidentally, one of the largest workers of stone in modern Israel. The Allafys believe they are descendants of the original Temple builders, thus fated to build the Third Temple. For them, an historical circle is closing today.

Three cornerstones of the Third Temple have already been marched to the Temple Mount. Fortunately, Israeli authorities barred their movement beyond the gates, so these objects of certain death now sit in Jerusalem's City of David district. Meanwhile, in 2004 the Passover animal sacrifice was resumed on the Mount of Olives in sight of the Holy of Holies. Since Israel reopened the Temple Mount to the non-Muslim world in August 2003, 5,000 Israelis have visited the site every month, evidence of a fast-moving Third Temple culture, according to Israel's right-wingers.

In the political climate of these apocalyptic end-times, the resurfacing of the Temple treasure would create an unparalleled frenzy leading to appalling conflict, as Jew and Muslim fought over the sacred spaces of the Holy City. Monetary and historical value aside, this is the core reason why the quest for the Temple treasure of Jerusalem is so central and dangerous to contemporary Middle Eastern politics.

8

Volcano of Hate

Spiritual and historic heart of the world, Jerusalem is also an unstable city of extremes. Ever thrilling, the Western Wall and Temple Mount are a stressful environment. The high-level security, distasteful political baggage and fanatical emotions stoking this religious volcano leave you feeling edgy and disoriented. But in April 2005, before heading into the centre of modern Jerusalem to discuss Jewish treasure in the Vatican with the Temple Mount Faithful, I had no alternative but to face the most 'peaceful battleground' on earth. Once again, the Temple Mount had been dragged into the Arab-Israeli peace process, only this time the argument felt personal: the archaeology of the Temple Mount itself was on trial.

Between October 1999 and January 2000 the Islamic trust charged with overseeing the site, the Waqf, dug a massive hole measuring 50 metres long, 25 metres wide and 12 metres deep into the south-eastern corner near 'Solomon's Stables'. Although the architecture above ground is the work of the Crusaders and Knights Templar, its subterranean hall of thirteen vaults and eighty-eight piers is ancient, an original design of King Herod to create an inclining entrance leading on to the Temple Mount from the southern triple Hulda Gate complex. The term Solomon's Stables is wishful thinking based on the reference in 1 Kings 4.26 to the wise ruler's 40,000 stalls of horses for his chariots and 12,000 horsemen. Over the centuries the legend stuck.

The latest wounds inflicted on the Mount annexed both Solomon's Stables and the eastern Hulda Gate into a new mosque extending over one and a half acres, with a 10,000-person capacity, making the structure the largest mosque in Israel. In all, an estimated 6,000 square metres of the ancient Temple Mount's surface has been ripped up and paved over.

To the neutral observer, there can be no doubt how provocative these developments have been. In 1967 Moshe Dayan infamously handed back the Temple Mount's keys to Jordan at the end of the Six Day War to prevent military escalation and even greater bloodshed with the Arab world. So today the site is legally controlled by the Islamic Waqf. Traditionally, however, the Waqf has respected the Mount's sacred status to both Judaism and Christianity, as well as Islam. The large-scale building operations have now shattered this spirit of accommodation.

Virtually nothing is known about the archaeology of the Temple Mount, so any building work carried out without recording ancient deposits is a major opportunity lost to contribute to global cultural knowledge. That ancient remains were destroyed is undeniable – but exactly what was lost is disputed. Israeli police claim that an arched water channel dating to the time of King Herod was wilfully destroyed (although other sources claiming a medieval date are more realistic). Yet according to an Arab Waqf worker, stones with decorations and inscriptions were deliberately recut to destroy religious marks, including ancient Hebrew text.

Israeli intelligence believes the Waqf has cleaned out ten giant subterranean cisterns on the Mount with the intention of filling them with water from Mecca's holy Zamzam Spring. Zamzam is a major pilgrimage station in the Hajj, holy to Muslims as the traditional site of the ancient well where Hagar and Ishmael rested after being banished from the home of Abraham and Sarah (Genesis 21.8–20). This action would thus elevate Jerusalem's sanctity within Islam, making al-Aqsa as important as the Great Mosque in Mecca. The entire project is seen as an Arab political ploy to deny Israeli claims to a Jewish Temple Mount.

Far more archaeologically destructive, however, was the hushed-up dumping across Jerusalem of 1,500 tons of soil extracted from the Mount – most prominently in the Kidron Valley just east of the city walls, but also in the municipal city dump of El Azariah. The Waqf claims it has nothing to hide: the disturbed soil was mere fill lacking archaeological value. Conversely, elements of Israeli society accuse the Islamic clerics of de-Judaising the Temple Mount and deliberately Islamicising it.

Clearly passions surrounding these extremist positions run very high. I wanted to examine both sides of the argument and to flush out any signs of major destruction to the ancient cultural heritage on my mission to the Temple Mount. I also planned to speak to Dr Eilat Mazar of the Hebrew University, an outspoken opponent of the development works and a high-profile member of Israel's Committee for the Prevention of Destruction of Antiquities on the Temple Mount.

As I walked through the Jewish Quarter of Jerusalem, I was struck by the city's extremes. Birds chirped merrily amidst landscaped trees, while Hassidic Jews traded Kabbalistic blessings in the guise of red wool bracelets for hard cash. The ancient Jewish quarter of 2,000 years ago is today the centre of global Jewish identity. The Pinchas Sapir Jewish Heritage Center and Women's Torah Institute straddle the ruined homes of Roman Jerusalem's High Priests, rejuvenated as museums, and stores peddling Judaica, trinkets, cups and T-shirts announcing 'Don't Worry Be Jewish' and 'Jerusalem, Just Do It'. A fresh desert breeze rolled in from the southern Judaean Desert.

The Western Wall looks dry today; no signs of weeping. There is, however, a cherry-picker crane parked on the sacred ground with its operator examining the wall and cheekily peering over its summit at what his Muslim brethren are up to. Bar Mitzvah boys are proudly carried aloft on fathers' shoulders. A grandfather tells his wide-eyed grandson, 'This is the centre of the world.' Past and present converge. The western outer wall of King Herod's magnificent Jewish Temple dwarfs the plastic chairs and a diverse Israeli society. A crooked old man in traditional black religious garb retreats backwards from the wall, bending down as he moves to touch the sacred ground and run his fingers down his chest in blessing. Another elderly man exits walking sideways for some esoteric reason. A Russian girl dolled up in a pink leather belt and matching lipstick wafts by. Jewish soup kitchens ring the Western Wall.

As in antiquity women are barred from approaching and profaning the Western Wall. Instead, they peer over a wooden screen and emit shrill screams, a celebratory cacophony that seems more appropriate to the tribal boiling of a Westerner in a remote African jungle. They throw silver glitter into the air, which twinkles like fairy dust in the midday sun — messages from God. White doves glide along the summit of the Temple Mount, offering peace to Jew and Muslim alike.

At the checkpoint leading up to the Temple Mount, the police have a pressing security issue to tackle: confiscating Bibles. A white-haired English gentleman with a well-polished middle-class accent is quizzed about his brown book. 'Is this a Bible?' he is asked. An emphatic no is the response. Much police huddling and discussion ensues. 'Are you sure this isn't a Bible?' reiterates the main security guard. The confused Englishman nods an affirmative. More huddling and finally the chief guard is summoned to referee the stalemate. 'If this isn't a Bible, what is it then?' he challenges. 'Well, if you must know,' replies the inno-cent abroad, 'it's a history book about cannibalism at sea.' The black humour of this ludicrous scenario is lost on the guards. All they know is that they must temporarily confiscate Bibles to prevent Christians praying publicly on the Temple Mount and potentially inciting reli-gious conflict.

I entered the Morocco Gate where, according to Muslim tradition, Mohammed harnessed al-Barak, his trusty horse, when he flew into Jerusalem. To my left, well-manicured gardens conceal the 70,000 Muslim *shahid* (dead holy warriors) of the twelfth-century Crusades. The Mount today is seemingly devoid of Roman architecture. The smell of strong Turkish coffee wafts through the air from the Old City, home to 15,000 Arabs and 5,000 Jews.

If you didn't know the dark history of the Temple Mount, you could be forgiven for judging this place an oasis of peace. In reality, the site has been a production line of death and destruction over the millennia. On cue, I picked up a spent bullet from the 1967 Six Day War. Yet tranquillity reigns today. The northern quarter, where Titus finally broke through the mighty Antonia Tower fortress to set alight the cloisters of the Second Jewish Temple, is now a garden of olive and cypress trees and exotic fountains. A teacher shrieks at her pupils along the eastern wall, where hundreds of Arab kids sit within the vaulted classes of the 'Al Aqsa Sec. Religious School – 1901 Est', as a sign suggests. This could be any classroom in the world.

But I was not on the Temple Mount for tourism. Instead, I was searching for traces of destruction that would confirm or refute Israel's claims of an ongoing cultural intifada on the site. Was Israel presenting a balanced case or was Sheik Ikrima Sabri, chief Muslim administrator of the Mount, correct when he stated recently that 'The Temple Mount was never there . . . There is not one bit of proof to establish that. We do not recognise that the Jews have any right to the wall or to one inch of the sanctuary . . . Jews are greedy to control our mosque . . . If they even try to, it will be the end of Israel.' If the defence of basic building work can excite such a tongue lashing, what would be the repercussions of the reappearance of the Temple treasure?

The signs did not look good for Sheikh Sabri. A bulldozer was parked immediately outside the entrance to the Dome of the Rock mosque. Something fishy was clearly afoot. Traces of massive earth-moving activities quickly became obvious. Olive tree gardens had been filled with freshly relocated earth and, on closer examination, revealed a high density of Roman, Islamic and Crusader pottery, including unequivocal proof of a first-century BC to first-century AD presence on the Temple Mount.

No pottery has ever been published from the Temple Mount, yet here was tons of the stuff beneath my feet – an archaeologist's dream. Sheikh Sabri had been speaking nonsense. With such a collection of potsherds archaeologists can spin wonders and tease fresh and important historical data from silent soils.

Nearby, what can only be described as a breaker's yard had been shoddily assembled. On one side stood piles of ancient stone masonry, and on the other newly cut blocks of stone 'repackaged' for reuse in modern structures on the Mount. While I had no problem with the Waqf developing the site to accommodate growing numbers of Muslim worshippers and wasn't partisan about the politics involved, the level of destruction coupled with a lack of documentation of this vital site's ancient remains was seriously disturbing.

Imagine if developers cut chunks out of Rome's imperial Forum and threw out the cultural debris without sieving the soils or recording what lay in the exposed trenches. The Eternal City would be in uproar, no doubt the Pope would protest, and the collective archaeo-logical community would denounce these sacrilegious activities. In scientific terms, the Temple Mount is without doubt more important than Rome's Forum. But this is Jerusalem, where passions run high and politics pervade. Few outsiders are willing to stick their neck out and be seen as anti-Islamic. To me, however, this is not a political matter but an ethical debate about protecting the past.

If the Waqf had nothing to hide, I couldn't help wondering why it had offloaded 300 truckloads of soil and debris under cover of night. Why had important ceramic remains been concealed under olive groves and, most grievously, how could it explain and justify the recutting of ancient masonry without specialist archaeological super-vision? Ancient inscriptions may well have been erased.

———◆———

Great destruction had without doubt already been perpetrated on the Temple Mount. To discuss the scale of the problem, and the political fallout, I had arranged to meet Dr Eilat Mazar of the Hebrew University, an outspoken critic of the Waqf's activities. On the way to the site of the biblical City of David, where she was cur-rently excavating Iron Age remains, I emerged from the Temple Mount by the northern Katemin Gate, desperate for a refreshing drink. But all I could find along the long, shadowy market alleyway approaching the Mount was a bewildering array of children's toys. Not dolls and action men, as you might naively expect – appropri-ate for kids of all faiths – but a vast armoury of plastic guns and weapons: imitations of 'Swat Police', 'Power', 'Space' and 'Tommy' pistols; curved scimitars and straight-edged Crusader plastic swords; even sets of guns, face masks and moustaches. In this way new gen-erations of religious hatred are born a hair's breadth away from the holiest place on earth.

The religious volcano seethed, and as swarms of Muslims pushed on to the Mount a lone Hassidic Jew approached the entrance to the ancient Temple and started to pray, genuflecting sharply at the waist. Had the world gone crazy? Were both Muslims and Jews bent on fomenting further bloodshed and hatred? An Arab boy looked at me, pointed and smirked. I asked him whether the Hassids do this a lot. 'Yeah,' he replied, 'they're head-cases.'

Clambering down the Ophel hillside, I found Dr Mazar sorting ancient pottery in her laboratory on the edge of the City of David. The vast pit of her excavation was hidden from prying eyes by a tall screen, security guards and a fearsome Alsatian dog. Only back in London would I discover why such secrecy shrouded her dig: Dr Mazar claimed to have discovered part of the biblical palace of King David, no less.

Eilat Mazar has both a professional and an emotional interest in the problems of the Temple Mount. Her grandfather, Professor Benjamin Mazar, excavated at the southern foot of the site for ten years, and from him she inherited a love of antiquity and also the more serious responsibility of his extensive publication backlog. To her credit, both scientific and popular articles and books have now started to flow. When complete, her work will comprise the most important body of scientific information about the history and archaeology of the Mount throughout history.

Though critical of the Islamic Waqf's clearance operations and the Israel Antiquities Authority's weakness over the scandal, she is nevertheless a balanced archaeologist. Rather than ignoring all cultural evidence other than Jewish remains attributable to the periods of King Solomon and Herod, books such as her *Complete Guide to the Temple Mount Excavations* cover all aspects of antiquity from the tenth century BC to the end of Ottoman rule in 1917 with equal justice and without historical bias.

As the Muslim call to prayer wailed from a nearby minaret, Dr Mazar emphasised that the Waqf's development work breaks the law because the Haram al-Sharif is subject to Israel's legal system. She considers the physical damage perpetrated to be extreme. Although it would be far too politically insensitive for her as a Jew to monitor the archaeological destruction personally, the Committee for the Prevention of Destruction of Antiquities on the Temple Mount has used an eye in the sky – aerial photography – to observe and record the changes over the past five years. The camera reveals trenches cut up to 13 metres deep into the ancient Mount.

'Ancient structures have been greatly damaged,' she confirmed. 'We calculate that 20,000 tons of ancient fill have been dumped outside, of which we are trying to save about 5 per cent. The majority is lost for ever amongst the modern rubbish of the Azariah garbage dumps.' Literally hundreds of trucks unloaded their ancient cargoes into these abandoned places and no one knows what precious finds have been lost. For Mazar, the Temple Mount is an archaeologically sealed box preserving many of antiquity's original deposits. 'The percentage of probability for finding treasures is very high,' she argues. 'There is no reason why inscriptions shouldn't be preserved deep amongst the ruins.'

Surely both sides have learnt from these mistakes now that the scale of the destruction is widely known. But no, 'The Waqf couldn't care less,' bemoaned Dr Mazar. 'It doesn't even care about its own Islamic heritage. The goal is religious fundamentalism, and archaeology is absolutely not going to stop them on their way. The Arabs believe they can twist and rewrite history and that a mosque has existed here since the time of Adam and Eve. Their actions are deliberately provocative, an extreme fundamentalist Islamic approach. Similarly, the Israel Antiquities Authority has to fulfil Israeli law, but it doesn't due to political pressure from the Prime Minister.' It was an issue which Dr Mazar was sure would come back to haunt Israel.

The ever-swirling politics make objectivity difficult. Even though I found Eilat Mazar's tone harsh, I sympathised with her frustration born of a deep love for the archaeology of the Temple Mount area. Her words continued to ring in my ears while I plodded back up the hillside of the City of David: the Temple Mount is the most amazing site in the world, yet many scholars won't debate its cultural fate because politics monstrously overshadows all else. Why is UNESCO impotent in this matter, I wondered, as I set off to confront a worldview that made the archaeological battle for the Mount sound like child's play. Gershon Salomon, director of the Temple Mount and Land of Israel Faithful Movement, awaited me in central Jerusalem.

9

Keeping the Faith?

JERUSALEM IS AN ultra-modern city in an ancient, battered and bruised skin. Propped up economically and culturally by its big brother, America, impressionable Israel swiftly embraced the consumer revolution in the late 1980s. Away from the winding medieval alleys of the Old City bazaar, many of Jerusalem's bars are as hip as any in Soho. Its pampered youth are more conscious of changing fashions than down-dressing London and, in terms of quality and value for money, from breads and salads to seafood, its restaurants put the UK to shame. Israelis love complaining, and skimping on portions or stale servings will buy you an earful of abuse.

The Temple Mount Faithful occupy offices tucked away behind Jerusalem's busiest commercial district. Almost all the trade around Yafo Street is local these days, and has been since tourists stopped visiting once the Second Intifada kicked off in 1999 and suicide bombers targeted pizza and falafel restaurants. Consequently, local Israelis go out infrequently. As a friend explained, every time you put on a coat, hat and lipstick, you prepare for a game of Russian roulette: who will bite the bullet today?

Gershon Salomon's office occupies an old British Mandate period townhouse, not unlike a Roman villa with a main corridor and two side wings flanking an open courtyard. Overgrown vegetation droops down the sides of a run-down building which has seen better days. There is no nameplate, no hint of end-time plans hatched behind a closed portal. I knocked on a ground floor door to be greeted by a bemused student who had never heard of the Temple Mount Faithful and was quite sure they didn't operate from his building.

This meeting had taken enormous patience to set up. An endless stream of messages on answerphones, flying faxes and e-mails looked like being all for nothing. Crestfallen, I left the building's grounds and was about to give up the chase when a dark blue Cadillac parked under the shadows of an alley flashed its lights at me. I was being watched. Inside sat the director of the Temple Mount Faithful, Gershon Salomon, cautiously vetting me from a vantage point of quick escape should the need arise. Clearly I passed the test and wasn't considered an immediate threat. Within five minutes I found myself seated in the sanctuary of a rather scruffy office.

Back home in England I had steeled myself to dislike Mr Salomon. I had no sympathy with a political mindset obsessed with ridding the Haram al-Sharif (Judaism's Temple Mount) of Islam and seeing God establish a Third Temple on the Mount. I couldn't see how it could work peacefully and firmly believed that this was a political problem, not to be resolved through direct religious channels. The way the Faithful went about their business also disturbed me. Publicly dragging cornerstones for a new Temple to the edge of the Old City, and searching out unblemished red heifers in order to revive Temple ritual based on sacrifice, isn't a very subtle way of negotiating your business. However, having been firmly shown the door by the Vatican and Israel's politicians, I was relying on Gershon Salomon to give up the golden key to those 'undeniable facts' proving the Temple treasure of Jerusalem to be imprisoned in Rome's Vatican City. To uncover these facts I was prepared to sup with the devil.

To my surprise, I ended up rather liking Mr Salomon. Contrary to the image I had envisaged – of someone loud, self-opinionated and arrogant – he neither dressed nor spoke like a fanatic. Perhaps it was the way he hobbled with a cane after surviving a life-threatening military skirmish as a youngster, or the glimpse of a broken man, weary from a lifetime battling for a cause he believed in heart and soul, that caused me to change my view. Gershon spoke eloquent words with passion and without ego. His eyes shone like an evangelical prophet as he outlined dreams of the Promised Land he hoped to create.

Gershon Salomon established the Temple Mount Faithful Movement immediately after the Six Day War of 1967 with the object of returning Israel to a biblical nation, a kingdom of priests. He was born of old Zionist stock, his family having emigrated to Jerusalem from Vilnius in Lithuania in the late eighteenth century. The new-comers dreamt of forging a messianic revolution, and his forefathers believed that the messiah would arrive in 1840. So the dream of a biblical nation has been in Gershon's heart since childhood; he drank this idealism with his mother's milk.

Just before the Six Day War, he experienced a revelation that would transform his life. At the age of nineteen he was serving as a commander in northern Israel, defending kibbutzes and villages from Syrian attack. A mere three days before he was due to finish his tour of duty, his unit was caught in a terrible ambush and attacked by thousands of Syrians during an eight-hour battle.

'God saved my life,' Gershon maintains. 'A tank drove over my body and I lay in the corner of the field of battle, more dead than alive. At night the Syrians surrounded me, but as they prepared to shoot, they suddenly turned and ran back to the mountains. Illuminated by a shining light from the God of Israel, lying there I felt the presence of the spirit of God around me in my heart, as if he were telling me "you still haven't finished your work, you still have something great to accomplish in your life".' Salomon was taken to hospital in a coma.

After a few weeks he re-awoke to the world and tried to make sense of his surreal experience. Eventually, United Nations officers fed back to him a first-hand report from the Arab officer who had commanded the battle against his unit.

'Why didn't they shoot me?' enquired the bemused Israeli soldier.

Apparently they had harboured every intention of finishing him off, but simply couldn't. At the exact moment when they were ready to inflict the *coup de grâce*, thousands of angels allegedly appeared out of thin air and surrounded his body. The Syrians fled in horror back to the Golan Heights.

Gershon Salomon spent a year in hospital contemplating what God planned for him. Despite his severe injuries, he returned to his unit and participated in the liberation of the Temple Mount in 1967. He told me how he stood with his troops inside the Dome of the Rock weeping, and heard God tell him, 'For this moment I brought you here. Build my House, build Israel as a kingdom of God, a biblical Kingdom.' A historical circle had closed for Gershon Salomon.

At that date, when the world's spotlight was firmly on Israel and the entire Arab world was up in arms, the commander of Jerusalem's liberation, Moshe Dayan, chose to return the administration of the Temple Mount to the Jordanians. Although many Israelis still denounce him as a senseless traitor for this single act, Dayan knew that even with the aid of America, Israel would never know peace if it retained the Mount. The image of 1.5 billion Muslims descending on Israel from surrounding countries was enough to make him gamble on returning the keys to the House of God.

Salomon remains intensely bitter at this action. Thousands of Jews may recognise the Western 'Wailing' Wall as the holiest site to Judaism, but for the leader of the Temple Mount Faithful it symbolises exile and destruction: 'As long as the Temple Mount is not liberated and does not become a Jewish site with a Temple, as long as our mentality will not change to become a free biblical nation, never will there be peace in this land. What they call peace is a false peace. Actually the country will be cut up, piece after piece.'

The sun set over the Old City and against the backdrop of an Israeli flag unfurled across Gershon's office wall we discussed the dreams and fears of the Temple Mount Faithful. Salomon is convinced that we are living in an exciting end-time and that a Third Temple will be built within his lifetime. He calls this event 'the biggest in the history of mankind and Israel. This event is irreversible. God wants a different kind of life, not based on materialism or chasing after physical achievements.'

As it turns out, the prophetic promise of the red heifer story was somewhat premature. For the animal to be certified for sacrificial purity rites, it has to remain red for the first three years of its life. Those reported in 1992 failed this test by turning white and brown after a few months. However, in recent years at least three red heifers raised on a Texas ranch owned by a fundamentalist Christian pastor have passed the litmus test to be deemed completely 'kosher'.

So why isn't Salomon re-establishing biblical sacrifice? For obvious reasons, it turns out. The Israeli government has blocked delivery of the red heifers to Israel for sacrifice on the Mount of Olives because this act is considered excessively provocative. The Faithful's tenets also run contrary to Orthodox Judaism's belief that a spiritual messiah, not a secular human, will redeem Israel. Opponents of a Third Temple call the red heifer story a nuclear bomb that could have apocalyptic repercussions.

After hearing Gershon Salomon's side of the story, I dropped the million dollar question about the whereabouts of the Temple treasure of Jerusalem. Certainly there is no shadow of doubt in Gershon's mind that the menorah and other Jewish symbols of faith looted by Titus in AD 70 languish deep in the Vatican. He finds the lack of a formal denial from the Vatican deeply suspicious.

But what about the primary evidence to back up these claims? He reeled off the names of medieval travellers who documented Jewish customs across the Mediterranean basin and who personally claimed to have seen the Temple treasure in Rome. Now we were getting somewhere, although it was becoming clear that Gershon was good on the big picture but poor on detail. To be fair, however, why should he be? He is neither an academic nor an historian. The main sources, it turned out, were Benjamin of Tudela, Benjamin II and David Hareuveni, who all travelled to the Vatican, saw the sacred vessels and recorded their experiences in travelogues. Regrettably, Gershon Salomon didn't have the evidence to hand, but relied on the expert advice of an enigmatic Jewish bookseller in Canada, who possesses the relevant papers and historical books. I was informed that the President of Israel also holds a personal copy of the incriminating evidence.

So my meeting with the leader of the Temple Mount Faithful passed off successfully. I had new leads from unfamiliar sources and a frightening first-hand impression of a biblical future that hoped to turn the world on its axis. The objectives of the Faithful are explosive, incapable of implementation without immense suffering and bloodshed. Yet the individuals leading the Movement's battle are far less dangerous than the waves of fanatical Islamic suicide bombers who have plagued Israel in recent years. The main weapon of the Temple Mount Faithful is the spoken and written word.

Despite their extreme beliefs, Gershon Salomon's warriors exert significant influence. The Faithful receive donations from India, at least two Arab countries, Australia, the Philippines, Japan, and almost every country in Africa. Gershon has been invited to lecture from Norway to the Congo and claims that a revolution is spreading across the world. I pushed for statistics about what percentage of Israeli society the Temple Mount Faithful speak for and raised my eyebrows at the response. Apparently a Gallup poll taken eight years ago had shown that more than 60 per cent of Jews supported the Movement's ideas. Its leader claims that it has grown increasingly since then to represent 80 per cent of Israeli Jews.

'We are the only surviving idealistic movement left in Israel,' Gershon Salomon concluded as I prepared to leave. 'Israel is in a very deep spiritual and idealistic crisis and we give the nation hope. Emptiness looks for something to fill it.'

I left the shadowy back streets of central Jerusalem promising to read Isaiah 2.1–5 and Zechariah 8, from which the Movement draws its inspiration. My head spun with thoughts and ideas. New names now preoccupied my quest: what exactly did Benjamin of Tudela, Benjamin II and David Hareuveni see in Rome, and could their testimony be trusted? Would the President of Israel release his documentation to me?

Walking back to the nineteenth-century quarter of the German Colony where I was staying, I passed restaurants and shops all defiantly open to the world but from behind iron barriers patrolled by eagle-eyed security guards determined to thwart suicide bombers. This is the real face of the Arab-Israeli conflict, this hypersensitive volcano that blows its stack at the smallest provocation. I was just a visitor to Jerusalem and so could escape back to my own comparatively cosy world. And as I travelled home, Gershon Salomon's final words echoed in my mind: 'I believe that when the Vatican basement is opened, all the world will be shocked by what we find there.'

10

Benjamin of Tudela

Driving south out of Jerusalem down the Judaean Hills to the Dead Sea, the lowest place on earth, my ears popped. The lush, manicured parks of the Holy City gave way to an alien world of huge open spaces, uncultivated and barren. Even under pleasant April skies the hills were largely bare. Sporadic wiry green bushes rooted desperately for water amid arid sandy brown soils. From afar, the undulating terrain looked like the skin of a badly plucked chicken.

Unchanged since antiquity, this wilderness remains hostile to all forms of life – the perfect place to retreat from society and meditate about the meaning of life, like various biblical prophets, but home to no man: wilting 40 degree Centigrade temperatures for nine months of the year, few fresh water sources, and infertile saline soils. Here and there Bedouin lazily attended their herds of goats, and the occasional camel sneered from the roadside (bizarrely clad in fancy leg reflectors to stop speeding desert drivers crashing into these well-camouflaged, moody beasts).

Haze danced off the looping road winding down to the northern tip of the Dead Sea. Already in springtime it was baking hot. A particularly vile smell of rotting eggs drifted off the distant lake, a noxious concoction of naturally formed dry salt and sulphur. The road plateaus out at sea level and I swept past the military checkpoint and the turn-off north to Tiberias and Beth Shean in the Galilee through the West Bank.

I was steering south on a deserted sea road meandering towards the oasis of Ein Gedi, Beer Sheva, and eventually Eilat and the Red Sea. Not a single person could be seen, not one welcoming blade of grass. The landscape is stunningly alien. The Dead Sea refuses to sustain marine life; the flat foreshore is thick with reeds, and sulphurous spits of sand form narrow bays far too shallow for use as natural harbours.

What on earth did the Romans make of this place when they were dispatched here in AD 68 to decapitate the few Jewish revolutionaries making trouble on the edge of the civilised world? Were they proud of the sheer magnitude of the expanding empire or, after sweating pounds marching south, did they start to question the wisdom of war? The Tiber's cool, caressing winds must have seemed a world away.

Back in England I had tackled Gershon Salomon's leads in the Bodleian Library in Oxford. The director of the Temple Mount Faithful had introduced me to three travellers who had allegedly viewed first-hand the Temple treasure of Jerusalem imprisoned in the Vatican: Benjamin of Tudela, Benjamin II and David Hareuveni. Very swiftly I had discounted the last two figures. Benjamin II was a nineteenth-century traveller who was born in Moldavia in 1818 and recorded his wanderings across the Near East, Asia and Africa from 1846 to 1851 in search of the Ten Tribes of Israel in *Cinq Années en Orient*, published in France in 1856. Actually born Israel Joseph Benjamin, he assumed the name Benjamin II in imitation of Benjamin of Tudela. However, I. J. Benjamin was living in times when travel was far easier and much of his testimony had already been comprehensively covered in earlier travelogues. There was nothing about Rome he could add to his namesake's far earlier testimony.

Although David Hareuveni was a relatively early and thus revealing source, his highly subjective religious agenda makes him positively unreliable. In the 1520s David declared himself the messiah and his brother king of lost ancient Jewish tribes living in Africa. So soon after the Spanish Inquisition trials and the forced conversion of Jews to Catholicism of 1486–92, Europe's literary and religious circles were intrigued by Reuven's originality and boldness. Although he did engineer a meeting with the pope to propose a military alliance between the tribes of Reuben and the pope's army against Islam, David Hareuveni was an extremist whose testimony is inadmissible.

Of all three characters, Rabbi Benjamin Ben Jonah of Tudela is by far the most important historical source. A Jewish merchant from what is today modern Navarre in Spain, he spent significant time in Rome after the election of Pope Alexander III in 1159 and again in the years 1165–7. Rabbi Benjamin was a true pioneer, whose mission was to record the presence and lifestyle of Sephardi Jews across Europe and

Everything written and resolutely placing the Temple treasure of Jerusalem in Rome today comes down to this single sentence written almost 850 years ago. To say the least, I was sorely disappointed: no validation of why or how the spoils had ended up there, or how they had been retained. In fact, reading between the lines it was patently obvious that Rabbi Benjamin made no claims of his own at all: he was just passing on a piece of folklore, undoubtedly based on a kernel of truth rooted in Josephus' *Jewish War* and on historical memories of Vespasian's Temple of Peace. Exactly the same folklore undoubtedly also underlies the mosaic inscription of 1291 later built into the same church complex.

Nowhere does the rabbi explicitly state that he saw the treasure in the Lateran or elsewhere with his own eyes. While pondering this text I casually skimmed the rest of his *Itinerary* and soon realised that as a pioneer Benjamin was also very much an innocent abroad. In an age preceding the widespread translation of ancient writers and scholarly commentators, knowledge of antiquity was largely based on word of mouth, which always leaves ample scope for misinterpretation. One particular passage convinced me that while Rabbi Benjamin should be much respected, his testimony is unreliable as true history. Around Sorrento in Italy, he described how 'From this place a man can travel 15 miles along a road under the mountains, a work executed by King Romulus who built the city of Rome. He was prompted to this by fear of King David and Joab his general.'

Not only is Romulus a mythical figure for whom no concrete proof exists, but the relocation of the biblical King David to Iron Age Italy is historically irrational. With dedication I had chased the Israeli government, the Vatican and Gershon Salomon all down to their major source, which had shown itself wanting. Frustratingly, I had been on one very time-consuming wild goose chase. But I did have my answer. The 'undeniable facts' locating the Second Temple Jewish treasure in Rome and the Vatican was fable, an elaborate castle in the air.

My experiences with the Temple Mount Faithful had brought home just how time and faded memory have distorted the truth about the Temple treasure and replaced it with alternative pseudo-histories from the logical to the absurd. Historically, each generation rewrites the past to dovetail with its own particular ideologies. But which, if any, might be accurate? Four very different legends vie for the trophy of historical truth, and I had come to the lowest place on earth, the Dead Sea, to ponder the most complicated and persuasive case.

My destination was Qumran, a tiny oasis in this desert wilderness, whose occupants are credited as the authors of the 2,000-year-old Dead Sea Scrolls. Craggy mountains composed of loose pockets of sandstone and rock – giant dollops of geological apple crumble – dominate Qumran. With the lapse of centuries, earthquakes and landslides have concealed a labyrinth of caves overlooking the ancient settlement. But between 1949 and 1962 illegal looting by roaming Bedouin, and subsequent research by Jordanian, Israeli and American archaeologists, uncovered one of the most sensational finds of the twentieth century: religious books and social commentaries written on 850 leather and papyrus scrolls.

One document, however, turned out to be unique: scroll 3Q15 was the only example written on copper and has nothing to do with divine issues. When first translated by John Marco Allegro in Manchester, England, in October 1955, the Copper Scroll (as it is more conveniently called today) proved a sensation by purportedly revealing the hiding places of 31 tons or more of gold and silver worth a vast $3 billion. Many specialists maintain to this day that the scroll lists the hiding places of Jerusalem's Temple treasure, spirited away around AD 70 to prevent it falling into Rome's greedy hands. Back in England I had ploughed through endless research about Qumran and the Dead Sea Scrolls, and was highly suspicious of this theory. To test my own view of events, however, I needed to look the beast in the eye. Reading about these subjects is one thing, but gauging the truth is quite another.

I I

The Philosopher's Folly

THE EARLIEST PHYSICAL quest to uncover the great legacy of the Temple treasure was ill-advised wishful thinking based on very shaky grounds. In 1908, the eccentric Swedish biblical scholar and philosopher, Valter H. Juvelius, unravelled a coded passage in the Book of Ezekiel in a library in Constantinople describing the precise location of Solomon's treasure – or so he claimed. Juvelius believed that a fabulous $200 million windfall awaited him beneath the Temple, where it was hidden when King Nebuchadnezzar conquered Jerusalem in 586 BC.

After much hunting for a suitable project leader, Juvelius was fortunate to come across a former soldier, bored and itching for adventure. Thirty-year-old Englishman, Montague Brownslow Parker, the son of the Earl of Morley, had served with distinction in the Boer War, rising young to the rank of captain in the Grenadier Guards. An eager Parker was easily persuaded by Juvelius's mouth-watering scheme. After raising $125,000 from various wealthy donors, the Parker Expedition left for the Holy Land and two years of excitement, toil and trouble.

In August 1909 the team anchored off Jaffa, the port of call for Jerusalem. In Constantinople, Parker had already eased the passage of the expedition by promising the commissioners of the Ottoman government 50 per cent of any treasure uncovered. Meanwhile, Juvelius had secured the services of a Danish clairvoyant to 'guide' the search, and had bought up land around the slopes of the hill of Ophel, where his new employee and partner had advised him to dig.

The instructions of the Danish clairvoyant were followed to the letter, and a shaft first dug by Charles Warren of the Palestine Exploration Fund in 1867, leading down to the so-called Virgin's

Well, was reopened. The expedition believed this would expose a secondary tunnel veering straight to the Temple and its underlying treasure. Here Parker made his first bad move. The unwanted curiosity and attention of the local inhabitants was immediately aroused by the stationing of bodyguards and soldiers around the excavation. Jerusalem's cosmopolitan archaeologists, resident in the city's European and American archaeological schools, were suspicious of the cloak and dagger secrecy of the project and its failure to record the ancient remains scientifically.

Complaints were formally submitted to Jerusalem's Turkish Governor. Parker responded shrewdly by inviting Père Louis Hughes Vincent of the Dominican Fathers in Jerusalem to join the team as archaeological adviser. As the director of the French Ecole Biblique et Archéologique de Saint-Etienne, and one of the most respected authorities on ancient Jerusalem, Vincent was a perfect front to dampen down protest. And for Père Vincent this was a heaven-sent opportunity to study more of the biblical past. Everyone seemed content with this marriage, even though Parker conveniently kept the French priest in the dark about the true objectives of the mission.

By early 1910 heavy winter rains had forced the team to retreat home to England empty-handed. The poor weather was compounded by further bad news: back in Jerusalem the local Jews had accused Parker of violating King David's and King Solomon's tombs, a profound offence with extremely disturbing implications. By August, however, he was back in the Holy City, reinforced with the more efficient skills of British engineers who had worked on the recently opened London Underground. By now the honeymoon period extended to the expedition by the Ottoman government was over. The Turkish patrons were bored by the absence of treasure, and had given up hope of any discoveries.

To make matters worse, the excavators now had serious competition in the form of Baron Edmond de Rothschild, who backed the Jews' claims of ancestral disturbance and bought up land around Parker's excavation to safeguard their heritage. Faced with this political containment and isolation, Parker now had to contend with the Turks announcing the project's closure at the end of summer 1911. The team only had eleven months to find the legendary treasure.

Even though the engineers did manage to clear out the entire length of Hezekiah's Tunnel, recording some curious Bronze Age burial caves along the way, the secret passage to the Temple never materialised. Time was running out fast. At this stage Parker played his last card, taking a huge gamble by offering the Ottoman governor of Jerusalem, Azmey Bey, a bribe of $25,000 to let him excavate on the Temple Mount itself, whose holy ground was closed to Westerners. The image of Parker and a select team disguised in Arab costume sneaking over the walls of this religious compound is straight out of *Indiana Jones*. Yet for a week they did excavate the south-east corner of the Temple Mount under the shadow of night. This time, the Danish clairvoyant assured the expedition that the riches were close by, awaiting them beneath 'Solomon's Stables'.

Despite the geographical relocation, the team was still getting nowhere. Desperation spread, and as the sands of time ran out, Parker made one final mad decision. On the night of 17 April 1911, the engineers entered the sanctuary of the Dome of the Rock itself – epicentre of the religious world – to explore a natural cavern beneath the sacred rock where, according to legend, Abraham offered Isaac as a sacrifice to God and where Mohammed ascended to heaven. Hardly surprisingly, the ungodly sound of pick and shovel awoke a mosque attendant, who shrieked in horror at the scene of sacrilege he discovered, and ran into the city like a banshee to expose the violation.

Rumours spread rapidly that the English had dug up and stolen the Crown and Ring of Solomon, the Ark of the Covenant and the Sword of Mohammed. Jerusalem was in uproar, and several days of violent rioting broke out. Governor Azmey Bey was mobbed, spat at and called a pig for his complicity, and the Parker Expedition sped off to their yacht at Jaffa in fear for their lives. Even though their personal baggage was impounded by customs officers, the team managed to escape by sea, only to come home to a seven-column headline in the *London Illustrated News* enquiring, 'Have Englishmen Discovered the Ark of the Covenant?'

The answer to the question was a resounding no. Public ridicule put Parker in an impossible situation with his sponsors. Although he managed to arrange for Père Vincent to publish the 'scientific' results in the book *Underground Jerusalem* in an act of damage limitation, the scaffolding around the project was collapsing. Even Vincent couldn't help but remark in his book that 'Subterranean tunnels have always been a favourite element in oriental romance, and their popularity in contemporary folklore has certainly shown no signs of diminution.' Meanwhile, in Jerusalem a Turkish Commission of Inquiry appointed a new sheikh as guardian of the Dome of the Rock, and Azmey Bey was dismissed as governor. In Constantinople, the Turkish Commissioners who had brokered a deal with Parker were censured and the entire event hushed up.

From the critical distance of the modern day it is easy to discount the Parker Expedition and its search for the Temple treasure of Jerusalem as a fatally flawed caper. After all, clairvoyants, government bribery, illegal excavations and wild Arabs brandishing swords are the stuff of popular fiction, not of science. Obviously the background and methodology of this project were flawed from the outset. The team hadn't even bothered to assess the true character and history of the treasure they sought. So how could it really know what to look for?

But how different was their dream from modern quests that hunt for Noah's Ark on remote Turkish hilltops and Atlantis off the coast of Crete? Renowned institutions that ought to know better still dig deep into their pockets to sponsor such 'scientific' ventures. I cannot help but admire the political manipulation, logistical know-how and energy that went into the Parker project. And when it comes to this particular Temple, we must bear in mind one overriding factor: passions here always run very high, strangling logic and common sense.

The Parker Expedition is a potent reminder that we should be extremely wary of quests that first concoct an idea, nail it to a wall and then set about proving it. Putting the donkey in front of the cart in the world of treasure hunting has absolutely no chance of success.

Even more disturbing and ill founded are theories obsessed with the intrinsic power of ancient treasure to influence political history, even hundreds of years later. In a world enchanted by works of fiction, where codes and crypts unlock the secrets of untold wealth, the foundations of Guy Patton and Robin Mackness' *Sacred Treasure, Secret Power. The True Story of the Web of Gold* set the alarm bells ringing. The authors proposed that the spoils of Jerusalem were seized by the Visigoth leader, Alaric, during the sack of Rome in AD 410 and then carried off into the French Pyrenees around AD 415 by his successor, Ataulphus. When threatened by the Franks and the rise of early Islam, the Visigoths allegedly retreated to their last stronghold at Rennes-le-Château in the Languedoc region of southern France, where the treasure was hidden underground.

Patton and Mackness weave a fantastic conspiracy theory, which strings together a web of coincidences linking the Temple treasure to numerous infamous historical organisations from the Knights Templar to the Nazis. In the shadows lurks the veiled institution of the secretive Priory of Sion, supposedly a medieval Order that succeeded the Templars and remains dedicated to this day to protecting the bloodline of the Merovingian kings. With its shadowy Grand Master, alleged to have included Leonardo da Vinci and Sir Isaac Newton, the Priory is also considered by some to be the guardian of the secret of the Temple treasure of Jerusalem.

For all their meandering argument, and its far-reaching and long-term implications, Patton and Mackness neglect to characterise the nature of the very 'treasure' that apparently influenced many major acts of history – exactly like Valter Juvelius and Montague Parker ninety years earlier. Again, I was mystified how the transferable powers of a treasure or the scale of its wealth can be understood without its composition being clear.

The Rennes-le-Château enigma has long been a favourite stamping ground for treasure hunters and conspiracy theorists. Over the decades its association with the Knights Templar and the Priory of Sion has spawned a minor entertainment industry, yielding nearly 300 books and three television programmes. According to legend, in 1885 Bérenger Saunière was appointed parish priest of Rennes. One fine day he chanced upon a folded ancient parchment crammed inside the carved out hollow of a Visigothic pillar used as an altar in his church. This coded Latin text spoke of a treasure belonging to a seventh-century AD Merovingian king, Dragobert II (died AD 679).

Soon after this discovery, Saunière sped off to Paris with his 'treasure map' to seek scholarly advice, and is said to have returned home having purchased three paintings, including *The Shepherds of*

Arcady by Nicolas Poussin. Within this painting the shepherds point to an inscription on a tomb apparently resembling one still standing at Arques, a few kilometres east of Rennes. Part of Saunière's deciphered code was said to read 'Poussin holds the key'. So *The Shepherds of Arcady* was said to be a coded treasure map literally pointing the way to the treasure of Jerusalem.

The foundations of the Rennes Temple treasure legend were laid by the Abbé Saunière's extraordinary building programme, initiated in 1891. Out of nowhere this man of the cloth somehow found the funds to set up new statues, rebuild much of the village and provide it with a new water supply and access road. Oddly for a man of sworn humility, the priest also built himself a luxurious villa alongside the church with elaborate gardens, an orangery and a mysterious locked tower. On his deathbed in 1917, Saunière's final confession was apparently so shocking that the priest who heard it is said never to have smiled again for the rest of his life. Where did this humble parish priest, overseeing a small village of some 300 inhabitants, get the funds for these ambitious renovations?

Perhaps the most fascinating intrigue surrounding the myth of the Rennes-le-Château treasure is the character of Noel Corbu, founder and proprietor of the Tower Hotel in Rennes, and self-styled biographer of Saunière and his bizarre antics. Corbu claimed that the priest accessed treasure worth 18.5 million francs, but later raised his estimate to a staggering 4,000 billion francs. When Corbu first exposed the tale of the treasure, the story was dynamite. The hotelier quickly invited a journalist called Albert Salamon to visit Rennes and record his testimony.

Salamon, and hundreds of other devotees, swallowed Corbu's story hook, line and sinker. But beneath the edifice of Templar knights, Jewish treasure and secretive priests, something stank of fraud. In 2003 Bill Putnam and John Edwin Wood convincingly lifted the lid on the truth in *The Treasure of Rennes-le-Château. A Mystery Solved*. Noel Corbu, it turned out, was not a quietly dedicated local historian. He was an entrepreneur who had written his own detective story and dabbled in the black market. Most of his historical narrative was a literary invention designed with one specific aim in mind: to put the area on the map and bring fame and fortune to his humble hotel.

Saunière's own book-keeping shows that his building renovations actually cost 193,000 francs, the equivalent of about £1.5 million today. While this is a considerable sum for a rural parish priest to get his hands on, it is hardly a vast fortune. The priest did have good reason to behave secretively, but this had nothing to do with the discovery of the long-lost treasure of Jerusalem, but everything to do with pious fraud. Quite simply, Saunière was trafficking masses for the dead, personally celebrating fifty-five masses a day and also taking payment for services not rendered. Ecclesiastical law set the limits of saying masses for the dead at three a day. The priest was keen for his illicit moonlighting not to come to light. There is no doubt that Putnam and Edwin Wood are correct in calling the links between the Rennes-le-Château story and the Jerusalem treasure pseudo-history and 'fantastic in the extreme'.

So far, everything I had read about previous attempts to find the Temple treasure of Jerusalem could be comfortably excluded. In terms of scientific accuracy it wasn't worth the paper it was written on.

12

Dead Sea Treasures

IF THE TEMPLE treasure isn't under the Temple Mount of Jerusalem, in the Vatican or tucked away in Rennes-le-Château under the watchful guard of a knight of the Priory of Sion, where on earth is it? Of all the weird and wonderful scenarios, the curious case of the Copper Scroll offers the most tantalising reason for optimism to date. Without doubt the most unusual of the Dead Sea Scrolls, this document has courted controversy ever since it was found propped against the inner wall of Cave 3 at Qumran on 14 March 1952. For a year and a half its mysterious contents remained sealed, although the unique copper medium generated more curiosity than hope of an innovative read. If the other 850 Dead Sea Scrolls were anything to go by, this was expected to be no more than another biblical tract or community rulebook. As it turned out, nothing could have been further from the truth.

The first hints that something strange lurked within the folded leaves of the scroll emerged in 1953. After staring at some uncleaned, obscure letters scratched on to its eroded copper surfaces through a glass museum showcase in Jerusalem that September and October, an obsessed German professor, K. G. Kuhn, arrived at the fantastic conclusion that the scroll was nothing less than an inventory of buried treasure, perhaps deposited 2,000 years ago by the Essenes, a pious Jewish sect who lived in the secluded wilderness around the western Dead Sea. As John Marco Allegro later recalled in *The Treasure of the Copper Scroll* (1960), 'Some blamed the heat of the Jerusalem summer, others the strength of the local *'arak*, few took the learned professor seriously.'

Nobody would really be sure about the scroll's contents, however, until it was opened and translated, a precarious job that stood every chance of shattering the brittle metal. Certainly no suitable laboratory facilities existed in the Middle East. So in summer 1955 John Allegro arranged for the copper to be opened at the College of Technology in Manchester, England, with precision saws designed to cut through human skull bone in brain surgery. The operation proved a success and revealed three plaques about one millimetre thick and 29 centimetres high, riveted together to form a unique 2.4-metre-long document.

Even though formal publication had been allocated to the Polish scholar and former priest Józef Milik, of the Dominican Ecole Biblique in Jerusalem, Allegro couldn't contain his excitement. Soon after the opening he broke academic protocol by personally translating the text and, in the process, confirmed that the scroll was indeed an inventory of buried treasure. In October 1955, Allegro wrote to inform Lankester Harding, director of the Jordanian Department of Antiquities, that 'These copper scrolls are red hot . . . Next time you're down at Qumran, take a spade and dig like mad by the airhole of the iron smelting furnace . . . there should be nine of something there.'

Despite facilitating the opening in Manchester, and thus being the key to the Copper Scroll's stunning revelations, Allegro soon found himself sidelined. Roland de Vaux, the Head of Jerusalem's Ecole Biblique and editor-in-chief of the Dead Sea Scrolls international team, informed Allegro by letter that he found his reading of the text inaccurate, and somewhat haughtily thanked him for 'making transcriptions in case an accident should happen'. Perhaps these more cautious elder statesmen of archaeology had good reason to dampen down Allegro's enthusiasm. Privately they were aware that he was a controversial figure, a maverick who could not be trusted to stick to professional scholarly ethics. After all, this was the man who would even tell the BBC that his interpretation of the commentary of the Book of Nahum from Cave 4 at Qumran suggested that the Essenes had worshipped a 'Teacher of Righteousness', who was crucified by Gentiles and was expected to rise from the dead. Sound familiar? Allegro's theory that Christianity's own messianic worldview was derived from the highly religious Essene Jews was considered an unqualified smear against the Church. A hornets' nest of public resentment had been stirred up.

Allegro's frustration at being unable to publish details about the Copper Scroll continued to simmer. In 1958 his *The Dead Sea*

Scrolls: A Reappraisal went into a second edition and, as he boasted in a letter to the German scroll specialist Hunno Hunzinger, if he could update it with the spectacular results from Cave 3 at Qumran 'It would sell another million . . .' Other than the odd comment, however, he reserved his translation and interpretation for a major new book, treading a fine line by publishing *The Treasure of the Copper Scroll* in 1960, the same year that Milik's official report on the scroll appeared in the *Annual of the Department of Antiquities in Jordan.* Allegro got his exclusive by effectively gazumping the official publication team.

For the first time, the Englishman's impressive translation exposed the full wonders of this 'treasure map'. Here was a formulaic description of sixty-one buried items listing types of wealth, quantities and locations. For instance, Items 1 and 7 read respectively:

> In the fortress which
> is in the Vale of Achor, 40
> cubits under the steps entering
> to the east: a money chest and
> its contents, of
> a weight of
> 70 talents.

> In the cavity of the
> old House of Tribute, in the
> platform of the Chain:
> 65 bars of gold.

Over the last forty years the Copper Scroll has been dissected and debated in hundreds of articles and specially related conferences. Yet, other than the facts that the scroll dates to the Roman period, is written in proto-Mishnaic Hebrew, and is a list of sixty-one buried items of varying monetary value, a dense fog still envelops the text. The scroll is unique in metallic composition, palaeography, language, content and genre, and even though the text is extremely well preserved, scholarly opinion remains as wide as the Grand Canyon. The doyen of Dead Sea Scrolls studies, Professor Frank Cross of Harvard University, identified the script as a late Herodian substyle of the 'vulgar semiformal' hand of AD 25–75. The official publication by Józef Milik, on the other hand, favoured a far wider potential date range of AD 30–130.

Today, most scholars accept the Copper Scroll treasure as real. But as to who owned it, why it was concealed, and under what historical circumstances, everyone seems to have their own favourite theory.

1. The scroll was an inventory of treasure of the Essene bank, hidden by members of the Qumran community either before or during the revolt of AD 66–70 and recovered afterwards. The treasure represented tithes collected by Essene priests.

2. The treasure is so great that, if real, it can only have consisted of easily transported objects, removed from the Jewish Temple of Jerusalem destroyed in AD 70 and hidden by its priests.

3. The Essene community of Qumran was destroyed in June AD 68, and reoccupied by the Zealots (Jewish patriots named after Greek *Zelotai* famous for their suicidal last stand against Rome at Masada). The Copper Scroll records sacred materials, tithes and tithe vessels sanctified by dedication or actual use in God's service that the Zealots had plundered from the holy places for money and to buy food. The scroll was written and hidden in Cave 3 during the three months of Zealot occupation at Qumran before the settlement fell to Rome.

4. The treasure was money that the Zealot general, Eleazor ben Simon, captured during a battle with the Roman governor Cestius Gallus in autumn AD 66; Cestius' baggage had been transporting public funds.

5. The scroll was a record of accumulated funds that were still systematically collected after the destruction of Jerusalem in AD 70 for rebuilding and maintaining a new Jewish Temple at some future date. The funds were deliberately hidden away to await the arrival of the day of redemption.

6. The treasure comprises redemption funds accumulated as religious taxes and tributes. Because Jerusalem was inaccessible owing to the Roman siege (and later its destruction), the tribute had to be deposited in *genizas* (sanctified synagogue storerooms) between the First and Second Jewish Revolts against Rome, pending the rebuilding of the Temple. As imminent disaster approached around AD 135 with the failure of the Second Jewish Revolt, the positions of the inventory were registered in the Copper Scroll.

7. The scroll is a record of treasure hidden by Simon Bar-Kokhba during the Second Jewish Revolt in autumn AD 134.

One piece of evidence, seven incompatible interpretations from some of the world's greatest minds. Even the magnitude of the Copper Scroll treasure is open to debate. John Allegro could be a loose cannon at times, but to his credit he possessed extremely perceptive powers of observation and was a brilliant scholar. Calculating the volume of treasure was a simple process, or so he thought:

> Silver — 3,282 talents, 608 pitchers, 20 *minas* and 4 staters
> Gold — 1,280 talents
> Vessels of unknown precious metals — 619

The quantities certainly impress, but are misleading because nobody has successfully worked out the equivalent weight or value of the talent in first-century AD Israel. This was clearly not the talent of rabbinical literature or of Old Testament times because, if true, the 80 talents of gold stored in two water pitchers listed in Item 33 would have weighed 1.5 tons, an impossibility for clay pitchers measuring less than 20 centimetres in height. The mathematics simply do not balance.

Allegro concluded that the talent concerned was close to the Greek *mina* of 12 ounces, yielding an overall comparative value for the treasure of about $1 million (in 1960). Elsewhere, the Copper Scroll's treasure has been estimated at between 58 and 174 tons of precious metal. On the basis of another Dead Sea scroll, 4Q159, where the talent equates to 6,000 half-shekels, the 5,000 talents of the Copper Scroll have been equated to a staggering $3 billion.

Although the jury clearly remains out on the exact value of the Copper Scroll treasure, majority opinion accepts that this document refers to money and religious objects originating in the Second Temple of Jerusalem. If correct, the physical evidence lay somewhere in the stifling heat of the Dead Sea wilderness.

Vespasian, commander of the Roman
forces in the First Jewish Revolt,
AD 66–70, and founder of the Flavian
dynasty, appointed emperor of Rome
in AD 69

Vespasian left his son, Titus, in charge
of razing Jerusalem and plundering the
treasures of the Jewish Temple

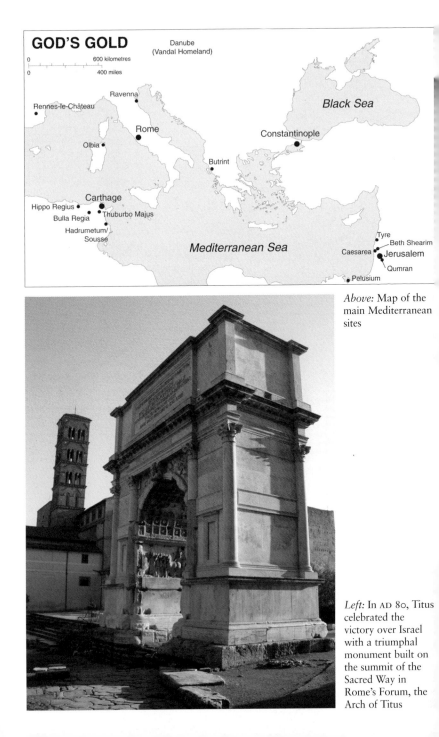

GOD'S GOLD

Danube
(Vandal Homeland)

0 ——— 600 kilometres
0 ——— 400 miles

Ravenna

Rennes-le-Château

Rome

Olbia

Butrint

Black Sea

Constantinople

Carthage

Hippo Regius
Bulla Regia
Thuburbo Majus
Hadrumetum/
Sousse

Mediterranean Sea

Tyre
Beth Shearim
Caesarea
Jerusalem
Qumran

Pelusium

Above: Map of the main Mediterranean sites

Left: In AD 80, Titus celebrated the victory over Israel with a triumphal monument built on the summit of the Sacred Way in Rome's Forum, the Arch of Titus

A relief on the Arch of Titus shows the greatest symbols of Judaism paraded along the streets
of Rome in Vespasian and Titus' Triumph of AD 71: the seven-pronged gold candelabrum
and the gold and bejewelled Table of the Divine Presence, with a pair of silver trumpets tied
to its front (from left to right)

Rome's 50,000-seat Colosseum, the greatest entertainment facility of the ancient world, built
in AD 72 with spoils looted from the Temple of Jerusalem

King Herod's Temple Mount in first century AD Jerusalem; the Sanctuary rises on the right

Royal spoils looted from Lachish, Israel, by Assyrian soldiers in 701 BC, including two cylindrical cult stands. The menorah described in Exodus, and used in King Solomon's Temple, would have resembled this form

By 165 BC, the menorah in the Temple of Jerusalem had evolved into the seven-pronged form: the type seized by Titus in AD 70, complete with pedestal adorned with 'pagan' images of eagles and sea monsters

An eagle on the side of a second-to-third century AD sarcophagus at Beth Shearim, in the Galilee, corresponding to eagles on the base of the Arch of Titus menorah pedestal

A soldier with a menorah on his head in Beth Shearim's Roman catacombs. The candelabrum's knotted central shaft replicates the Tree of Life

The bronze Judaea Capta coin series, struck by Vespasian from AD 71. The reverse shows a mourning Jewess alongside a conquered Jew with tied hands, a palm tree, the symbol of Judaea, and conquered enemy armour

Above: Model of Imperial Rome by Italo Gismondi (Museo della Civiltà Romana), showing the highlights of the route of the Triumph of AD 71. Top left: Marcellus' Theatre in the Field of Mars. Bottom left: the Circus Maximus. Middle right: the Colosseum and, to its left, the Temple of Peace

Right: 'Madam Lucretia' in the Piazza di San Marco, Rome, is probably the original cult marble statue of the Egyptian goddess Isis

On the morning of the Triumph, Vespasian and Titus offered prayers at the Pantheon, in the Field of Mars, Rome

The arched Porticus of Octavia, Rome, across which Vespasian's Triumph paraded in AD 71

13

Castles in the Air

AGAINST A BACKDROP of forbidding dark brown mountains nestles Qumran, a sprig of green relief and peaceful oasis in the wilderness. The ancient settlement sits halfway up the mountainside, straddling a plateau with spectacular views of the Dead Sea's flat desert hinterland below, here and there interrupted by islands of date plantations. On clear days the Jordanian hills are framed dramatically against the eastern skyline. For both seclusion and security Qumran occupies a perfect setting. But a perfect setting for what purpose: a religious retreat or well-defended stronghold?

By examining the ruined settlement near which the Copper Scroll was found in 1952, I wanted to confirm certain key points that would determine whether or not this document held the secret to the lost Temple treasure of Jerusalem. In particular, was Qumran a monastic settlement inhabited by the Essenes, the most pious Jewish sect of the ancient world, or was it, as the latest research favours, the site of a wealthy manor house owned by a rich and Romanised Jewish member of the ruling class of Judaea?

This question is crucial. If Qumran was not an Essene retreat, then there would be no reason to attribute the Dead Sea Scrolls to this sect. And if this was true, then the Essenes were not necessarily either the authors or secret owners of the precious texts concealed in the nearby caves. Ruling out the Essenes also opens up the possibility that the Copper Scroll does not describe their wealth at all, but could have been written by priests from the Temple of Jerusalem. In which case, as an official map of Temple treasures, it would be a remarkably valuable document.

Qumran is one of the most famous archaeological sites in the world and also one of the most controversial. The settlement was thoroughly excavated between 1953 and 1956 after the same type of pottery recovered from the nearby caves containing the Dead Sea Scrolls was spotted overlying Qumran, leading to speculation that the scrolls were the concealed belongings of these mysterious inhabitants.

History has not been kind to Qumran's excavator, Roland de Vaux, the director of the Ecole Biblique et Archéologique in Jerusalem. On the one hand he successfully supervised rapid excavation, turning out detailed preliminary reports. On the other, his scientific methodology was dubious by modern standards and his leap of faith between the physical evidence and interpretation somewhat creative. But what troubles modern scholars are the thousands of small finds and pottery: uncovered in three different chronological phases, these have never been fully published, so we remain unclear about which coins and finds relate to which periods of the site's history. Without this level of knowledge, the story of Qumran will remain jumbled and incomplete.

Consequently, Qumran has become all things to all men. De Vaux was a man of the cloth, a French priest with his own singular mindset and background. Living in a communal environment in Jerusalem, it is hardly surprising that he saw in the ruins a form of monastic life based on agriculture, stock-rearing and low-level industry. Clay inkwells found amidst the ruins conjured up images of a *scriptorium* of the type common in medieval monasteries. No doubt, it was here, postulated de Vaux, that the Dead Sea Scrolls themselves were written.

The identification of Qumran and its caves as an oasis of Essene monastic life was based on what in the 1950s seemed to be a watertight holy trinity: de Vaux's excavations; the nearby scrolls, whose mystery gripped the imagination; and vivid descriptions of Essene life around the western shore of the Dead Sea.

The most influential factor was the Essenes – loaded dice in the story of the Qumran enigma. As a youth, the first-century AD historian Flavius Josephus was so obsessed by this sect that he spent three years living with one of its most pious members, Bannus, who ate nothing but wild plants, wore clothes made of tree bark, and frequently immersed himself in cold water for purposes of ritual cleanliness. Back in the Eternal City, having helped Rome crack the First Revolt, Josephus wrote at length about this Jewish sect, for whose extreme and unwavering religious observance he had a profound respect.

The Essenes were not fun-loving. They rejected pleasure as evil and considered the conquest of passion virtuous. Rather than marry, Josephus tells us that the cult leaders 'choose out other persons' children, while they are pliable, and fit for learning . . . and form them according to their own manners . . . they guard against the lascivious behaviour of women, and are persuaded that none of them preserve their fidelity to one man.'

Personal possessions were renounced by the Essenes, who were renowned for their white robes, which were worn until they literally dropped off their bodies. Of all Jewish sects, including the Sadducees and the Pharisees, Josephus considered the Essenes the most religiously observant. After sunrise, he records, 'they are sent away by their curators, to exercise some of those arts wherein they are skilled, in which they labour with great diligence till the fifth hour. After which they assemble themselves together again into one place; and when they have clothed themselves in white veils, they then bathe their bodies in cold water.' Purification conditioned the movements of everyday life.

Of key interest to the archaeological discovery of the Dead Sea Scrolls is Josephus' testimony that the Essenes were unusually studious and secretive. The sect studied the writings of the ancients dutifully, and newly recruited members swore 'to communicate their doctrines to no one . . . and will equally preserve the books belonging to their sect'. This religious integrity eventually impressed even the Romans, who mercilessly tortured captured Essenes in AD 68 to try and force blasphemy from their lips or to make them eat non-kosher food. Sect members responded by smiling at their pain and laughing at their tormentors. In Essene doctrine the body was corruptible but the soul immortal.

Following de Vaux's excavation at Qumran in the 1950s, his picture of an Essene settlement remained common currency for over thirty years. Here, an extremist Jewish sect shied away from society, wrote the Dead Sea Scrolls and hid them in the surrounding caves when the fearful tramp of Roman boots echoed along the desert roads during the First Jewish Revolt. The imprint of the Essenes was everywhere: the inkwells from a *scriptorium* linked the thoughts of a studious people to the physical scrolls themselves; the dominance of water systems and *mikvehs* (ritual baths) proved their obsession with ritual purity through cleanliness; while their pottery workshop reflected a self-sufficient economy closed to the outside world.

Confronted with such staggering physical remains, and before the scrolls and ruins of Qumran were fully studied, most scientists of the day would have arrived at precisely the same conclusions as Roland de Vaux. And though he remains an easy target because he never published a final excavation report, he was a meticulous recorder. Today, sixty years on, the vast body of diaries and artefacts he left behind have prompted an archaeological revolution in thinking on the mysteries of the 'Qumran Triangle'.

The traditional picture of Qumran as a quiet 'monastic' Essene outpost has recently been shattered by Professor Yizhar Hirschfeld of the Hebrew University. Hirschfeld has jettisoned the Essene–Qumran theory wholesale. His forceful new argument envisages the site as a manor house set within a wealthy estate – similar to the setting of a medieval castle – and owned by one of the king's favourite 'knights'. Here a wealthy aristocrat and his estate manager and slaves reaped the riches from highly specialised produce: dates, bitumen and balsam. Qumran, then, was the local version of a Roman villa, but with a tower and reinforced outer walls to defend against regional insecurity. In Judaea such fortified manor houses were known as *baris* in antiquity. Hirschfeld believes the Essenes lived not at Qumran but at Ein Gedi in a cluster of huts he has excavated on a mountainside 200 metres above the ancient town. Such a remote shanty town, he believes, is a far more appropriate setting for pious, non-materialistic Jews.

Even though 'knights' and 'manor houses' smack somewhat inappropriately of medieval Europe and feudalism, and the theory thus requires a leap of faith across the chasm of time and place, Professor Hirschfeld's study has done 'Qumranology' a great service. The site is now out of its closet. Qumran does only make sense in a wider regional context. Contrary to today's image of the Dead Sea as a barren no man's land, the lowest place on earth was a bustling hive of activity in antiquity. Forget the relentless sun that can fry an egg. Ignore the lack of fresh spring water and the poor nutritional resources that suggest (according to anthropological studies based on Qumran's ancient cemetery) that only 6 per cent of adult males lived beyond the age of forty (compared to 49 per cent at Jericho). Set aside the superficial uselessness of the Dead Sea as a maritime resource.

The truth is that in the Hasmonaean and Roman periods the oases of the Dead Sea were organically linked to Nabataea in modern Jordan by small ports strung along its shore. Here man overcame matter and a hostile environment to turn this wilderness into the equivalent of an ancient Silicon Valley. The region's unique geography may have supported extremely limited industry, but these operations were highly coveted and notably lucrative. Most appealing were the royal date plantations King Herod bequeathed to his descendants.

Judaean dates were world famous both as delicacies and for their medicinal qualities. In the Bible Jericho was known as the 'town of dates' (Deuteronomy 34.3) and in his *Natural History* Pliny the Elder remarked that the 'outstanding property [of Judaean dates] is the unctuous juice which they exude and an extremely sweet sort of wine-flavour like that of honey'. Two thousand years ago the shores of the Dead Sea were evidently carpeted with oases of sweet-smelling date plantations, stretching at least from Jericho in the north to En Boqeq on the southern shore, where hundreds of date pits from a first-century AD processing plant have been unearthed. New research suggests that the so-called 'wine press' at Qumran, as well as its satellite farm at Ein Feshkha, actually specialised in date honey.

If dates were the mainstay of the economy, traded the length and breadth of the civilised Roman world, the Dead Sea was also renowned for two other specialist products, balsam and bitumen. An inscription on the mosaic floor of a mid-fifth-century AD synagogue at Ein Gedi mysteriously refers to the 'secret of the town' that must be guarded from outsiders. The mystery that made Ein Gedi such a wealthy oasis in the middle of a wilderness was almost certainly balsam. The second-century historian Galen wrote in *De Antidotis* that this plant 'is called *Engadinne* after the place where it grows most abundantly and is most beautiful, being superior in quality to that which grows in other parts of Palestine'. Although balsam no longer grows along the Dead Sea, this large shrub, whose bark, shoots and twigs yielded resin and juice coveted across the Roman world for perfumes and medicine, was used to treat headaches, eye disease, cataracts and myopia. In the mid-third century AD, the medical writer Solinus knew about *opobalsamum* from the Dead Sea, and Statius described how *Palaestini liquores* were used to scent corpses in embalming.

In the Roman world perfumes were a luxury item that permeated the whole of society and many aspects of everyday life. Pliny tartly recorded how

> their cost is more than 400 *denarii* per pound . . . We have even seen people put scent on the soles of their feet . . . somebody of private station gave orders for the walls of his bathroom to be sprinkled with scent . . . this indulgence has found its way even into the camp . . . using hair oil under the helmet. (*Natural History* 13.20–23)

Various ancient historians, ranging from Josephus to Diodorus Siculus, Pliny and Strabo, all agree that Judaean balsam was the finest in the world. And securing the balsam plantations and local economic interests was the key that drew the might of Rome to this isolated part of Israel in AD 68. So valuable were the resources of the Dead Sea and its balsam groves that the area was subjected to a scorched earth policy during the First Jewish Revolt.

Base as it may sound, the overpowering reason for Rome's invasion of the Dead Sea wilderness was money. In this Rome was highly successful, seizing and subsequently controlling the balsam plantations of the Ein Gedi region. As Pliny confirmed to his Roman readership,

> The balsam tree is now a subject of Rome and pays tribute together with the race to which it belongs . . . the immense value of even the cheapest part of the harvest, the wooden lopping, fetched only five years after the ravages of war of the destruction of the Temple, 800,000 *sesterces*. (*Natural History* 12.118)

Balsam tells you all you need to know about nurture bullying nature to develop the western Dead Sea in the Roman era. The economic importance of the area is commemorated in Roman coins issued by Vespasian and his sons after their victory in the Jewish War, depicting a handcuffed Jew standing against a palm tree beneath which sits a mourning Jewess and a pile of discarded armour. The date farms of Palestine were now controlled by Rome.

Was Qumran somehow involved in the lucrative production and trade of dates and balsam, perhaps as a centre of cultivation in its own right? If so, this would surely disprove the contention that the settlement was a centre of Jewish learning. Strong grounds exist to argue thus. Even though Qumran's own small date press probably only served the estate community, the industrial complex at its farm, Ein Feshkha, was a far bigger affair, most probably specialising in date honey. A thick burnt level excavated at Ein Feshkha, and attributed to the First Jewish Revolt, as well as the subsequent appearance of Roman tiles stamped with the logo of the Roman army, certainly fits the pattern of a deliberate imperial takeover in AD 68.

Today we can be certain that the settlement of Qumran – allegedly the home where the Dead Sea Scrolls were written by dedicated Jewish scribes – was not the isolated monastic settlement envisaged by Roland de Vaux. One clinching piece of evidence is the rich array of 679 ancient coins the site has yielded, 94 dating to the period of the First Jewish Revolt (AD 66–70).

The large cluster of coins recovered creates a headache for enthusiasts of the Essene theory, given that Josephus was explicitly fascinated by the non-materialistic character of a sect which forsook all earthly pleasures to serve God. Emphatically, he notes that

These men are despisers of riches . . . Nor is there any one to be found among them who has more than another; for it is a law among them, that those who come to them must let what they have be common to the whole order – insomuch, that among them all there is no appearance of poverty or excess of riches, but every one's possessions are intermingled with every other's possessions. (JW 2.122–3)

Science also casts a long shadow over the idea that whoever occupied Qumran was truly reclusive. It has long been assumed that the settlement's clay pots were produced for exclusive use at Qumran and the surrounding caves. This image fitted neatly with the idea of Qumran as an Essene settlement because in-house production ensured that the sect need not deal with the outside world and would guarantee that their pots were not rendered ritually unclean by the handling of Gentiles or menstruating women.

However, samples of pots from both Qumran and the surrounding scroll caves have recently been examined by Neutron Activation Analysis (NAA), a process that identifies the unique chemical 'fingerprint' of the clay using nuclear chemistry. The results show that only about 33 per cent of the pottery was local to Qumran, with the rest imported from Jericho. More disturbingly, the so-called scroll jars weren't even crafted from a clay source local to Qumran. The link between the people of Qumran and the Dead Sea Scrolls has thus been fully severed. Whoever lived there, it was certainly not the exclusive sect of pious Jews known to Josephus.

But what about the eight Jewish ritual baths that dominate the surface of Qumran, the largest concentration of *mikvehs* in Israel — surely these are certain proof of extreme Jewish piety at Qumran? Even this time-honoured assumption is no longer clear-cut. Just how efficient can these baths have been in such an arid part of the world? Qumran is not fed by natural springs and, in antiquity, relied on the meticulous channelling of water during the few occasions when winter flash floods swept the area. Even with the capture of this rainfall, Qumran would still only have received a miserly 50–100 millimetres of rain each year. Ensuring the continued flow of fresh water for purposes of ritual purity was thus impossible.

If Qumran was occupied by a pious Jewish community undertaking ritual immersion several times a day, this behaviour would have been wholly counter-productive. With no constant means of replenishment, the water within the pools must have stood stagnant for up to nine months between rains. Full body immersion in such disease-ridden waters, or even the simple washing of the hands and face, would have been sufficient for the bather to contract the parasites *Ascaris lumbricoides* (roundworm) and *Trichuris trichiura* (whipworm) or other entero-pathogenic micro-organisms that are friends of cholera, hepatitis A and shigellosis. The notion that the occupants of Qumran would have exposed themselves to such a harmful environment is absurd and opens up the possibility that these water features were more about spectacle and social prestige than religious observance.

Even though a full answer to the riddle of Qumran remains unresolved, the Essene model becomes increasingly hard to justify. The site can only have been owned and controlled by a wealthy Jewish landlord, a member of the Rome-loving ruling class of Judaea. The current 'keeper' of Qumran (artefacts, diaries and master plans), Jean-Baptiste Humbert, believes that Qumran is more reminiscent of a Pompeian villa than a rural estate. The eastern extension may have been a *triclinium* (dining room) with flashy plaster decoration and fancy tiles. In this he perhaps pushes the picture too far.

So where does this leave the Copper Scroll as a possible map identifying the hiding places of the Temple treasure of Jerusalem? With the Essenes out of the picture, the probability opens up that the scrolls were not their property at all. Instead, they could represent ancient wisdom accumulated in Jerusalem and relocated to the Dead Sea to escape the wrath of Rome.

Today we know of fifty-seven caves holding ancient cultural remains within a network of 279 caves and crevices that honeycomb the mountainside at Qumran. The 850 scrolls are also hugely diverse in subject matter and date, spanning a period from the end of the third century BC to AD 68 or later (the Copper Scroll is the latest deposit). And this massive body of writing could hardly have been the work of a few scribes toiling at one site like Qumran: palaeography points to the hands of 500 different scribes. The only place on earth that could have produced and stored such a scholarly collection in the first century AD was Jerusalem.

So, if the Copper Scroll was not a list of hidden Essene treasure, and if the majority of the Dead Sea Scrolls originated in Jerusalem, surely this makes the likelihood that the Copper Scroll describes the wealth of the Temple more than plausible? Not exactly: nothing is ever simple with Qumran and the Dead Sea Scrolls.

There are clear objections to the Copper Scroll/Temple treasure theory. If your most prized possession was on the verge of being seized by an enemy force, such as the Romans in Jerusalem, would you calmly pour yourself a glass of wine and set about the laborious process of writing a shopping list of all your earthly belongings? The Copper Scroll bears no resemblance to a list hastily jotted down on a memo pad. Its formality is more akin to that of an official document today, requiring a specialist in calligraphy and a properly equipped office. And incising on copper rather than writing on papyrus must have been at least ten times slower. If the threat was immediate, you would surely have made some rapid notes on a scrap of paper and run for the hills. The desperation of the Jews in Jerusalem and the meticulous record keeping of the Copper Scroll are incompatible.

Also, why resort to laboriously etching on copper when ink and papyrus would have been far simpler and swifter? John Allegro sheepishly cut the corner on this crucial problem by proposing that copper made the document ritually clean. But this makes no sense at all because it assumes that the rest of the Dead Sea Scrolls were ritually impure.

Furthermore, if the treasure was so sacred, why conceal it in locations that can at best be described as temporary hiding places? Many of these 'secret' places were random and wholly unsuitable for even short-term concealment. Thus, 42 talents were hidden in a salt pit under some steps; others were placed in cavities, fissures and the spur of a rock in a cistern. Untithed goods and 70 talents even ended up in a wooden barrel in an underground passage. Equally temporary was the dam sluice and wine press pit holding 200 talents of silver. But perhaps most desperate of all was the decision to hide wealth beneath corpses in graveyards, a very strange practice for observant Jews. Thus, Item 55 reads:

> In the grave of the
> common people who (died)
> absolved from their purity
> regulations: vessels for tithe or
> tithe refuse, (and) inside them,
> figured coins.

The scroll text also suggests that the innovator was not planning for a long-term eventuality. The descriptions of the hiding places are very vague, and it is highly questionable whether even a native intimate with the local landscape could have identified the place names from the scroll itself. Even more strange, most of the topographic citations are not complete names but coded mnemonic indicators, highly abbreviated references to places only comprehensible to a select inner circle. Would Jewish High Priests really have relied on such ad hoc descriptions to conceal, and more importantly to recover, the most important treasures known to man?

The incompatibility between the enduring copper medium of the scroll and the relatively uninspired hiding places cited has led to forceful arguments that the Copper Scroll describes Jewish taxes rather than Temple treasure. As soon as the scroll was translated, John Allegro quickly pointed out that various terms in the document indicated tithes. Temple economics were based on an annual half-shekel poll tax levied throughout Israel and amongst the Jews of the Diaspora, which was used to maintain the Temple and its services. Israel also levied a cattle tithe for feast days in Jerusalem, while charity monies for the poor were collected every third year. For John Allegro, at least some of the wealth in the Copper Scroll represented this kind of basic taxation.

If the Copper Scroll's wealth was real, the tax interpretation makes the best sense. Certainly, the geopolitics of the First Jewish Revolt and the pattern of treasure interment remain completely illogical. Why preserve something on copper for perpetuity when its supposedly invaluable contents refer to materials hidden in places meant to be known only to a few select insiders, but which were nonetheless relatively easy to locate? Use of the copper medium denotes a desire to preserve memory of the concealed treasures long term. Yet the scroll's style and the nature of the hiding places could realistically have permitted only short-term deposition and reliance on the obscure place names listed. The scroll is a confusing paradox.

The dubious character of the Copper Scroll is cemented by its mysterious final entry:

> In the Pit
> adjoining on the north, in a
> hole opening northwards,
> and buried at its mouth: a copy
> of this document, with an
> explanation and their measurements,
> and an inventory of each thing, and other things.

Such text is surely the stuff of a fictitious treasure hunt. In reality, not one item on the Copper Scroll inventory has ever been found even though Israel has undergone one of the most intensive periods of excavation in recent history. In the golden age of excavation in the 1990s, the country possessed the largest number of archaeologists per capita in the world. You might have expected at least a slither of silver to have materialised. But nothing has emerged – apart from the Dead Sea Scrolls themselves, which begs one final question: if the caves of

Qumran were such reliable hiding places, why didn't the author of the Copper Scroll hide his treasures within them?

A passionate John Allegro, convinced he had deciphered the modern locations of the ancient names listed in the scroll, even led expeditions to Jerusalem, the Vale of Achor and Qumran between 1960 and 1963 to uncover the legendary treasures. Despite the support of King Hussein of Jordan, the team returned to England empty-handed.

Nothing in the enigma of the Copper Scroll adds up. It can't have been Essene wealth because this sect shunned material goods. It clearly didn't comprise precious Temple treasure because such poor hiding places would never have been selected. And nowhere are the gold candelabrum, silver trumpets and other chief instruments of Jewish worship in the Second Temple of Jerusalem mentioned.

If the treasure was ever real, then it can only have been tax collected after the Temple of Jerusalem had been razed to the ground. Just as many Jews today still devotedly save money in a tin labelled 'For Jerusalem', so it would seem that within the decades after the First Jewish Revolt the Temple tax was privately reintroduced. But rather than plans for a new Temple coming to fruition, the iron fist of Rome gripped the province of Palestine ever more tightly. Finally, Judaea exploded into the Second Revolt under Simon Bar-Kokhba (AD 131–5). Once again Jerusalem and the Dead Sea were flooded by troops, leaving no alternative but to conceal the Temple taxes in the most convenient hiding places. Perhaps no treasure has ever turned up because Rome tortured Jewish priests into disclosing these places.

To me this interpretation is still highly optimistic. I prefer the opinion of Józef Milik, the official expert on the Copper Scroll, who denounced the document as ancient Jewish myth-making, an inspirational fiction mourning for a brave old world destroyed and doomed to oblivion. Typically, in *Ten Years of Discovery in the Wilderness of Judaea* (1959), he writes that the scroll

> contains a list of about 60 deposits of treasure, hidden in various sites scattered over the Palestinian countryside, but mainly concentrated in the region of Jerusalem, near the Temple and in the cemetery of the Kedron valley. The total of gold and silver said to be buried exceeds 6,000 talents, or 200 tons – a figure that obviously exceeds the resources of private persons or of small communities.

CASTLES IN THE AIR

In addition to these quantities of gold and silver, the roll mentions incense and precious substances which are said to be stored in vessels also made of valuable materials . . . All these motifs recur in other folkloristic works that give clues to buried treasure. An example of such folklore is found in Egyptian Arabic literature, the *Book of Buried Pearls and Hidden Treasures*, which Ahmed Bey Kamil published in Cairo in 1907.

A non-literal interpretation of the Copper Scroll has also been backed by T. H. Gaster, who proposed in *The Dead Sea Scriptures* (1976) that the scroll was humorous literature, a literary invention addressed 'to hearts and minds of men who were looking to an imminent restoration of the past glories of Israel'. In other words, once the Temple fell under the might of Rome in AD 70, such folklore was written with the intention of reminding Jews living in the Diaspora of a faded golden age and, more importantly, to offer hope for a future revival of Jewish fortunes within Israel. As fascinating and multi-layered as the Copper Scroll undoubtedly is, the document certainly takes us no closer to the truth behind the fate of the iconic objects in the Temple treasure of Jerusalem.

Temple Treasure

14

Divine Light – The Menorah

THE DISAPPEARANCE OF the vast collection of art and money that Rome plundered from the Temple of Jerusalem is easily explained. Vespasian systematically liquidated the bulk of the Jewish treasure into ready cash for the imperial coffers exhausted by his predecessor, Nero. The fate of the greatest symbols of the Jewish faith, however, is far more circuitous. The Arch of Titus displays the looted gold menorah, the gold Table of the Divine Presence and a pair of silver trumpets. But what did these objects mean to Judaism and Rome, and were the images depicted on the Arch real or imagined?

In modern Judaism the menorah is the ultimate symbol of faith. Most Jewish households own a Hanukkah menorah in the same way that a cross typically hangs on the walls of Christian homes. It is a calling card that announces the owner's religion and asks the respective divinity to protect a family. The menorah is also the most characteristic and prevalent motif of ancient Jewish art, recorded 216 times within Israel and in 270 other locations across the Mediterranean basin. Wherever ancient great cities are excavated, the menorah is seen to have flourished.

This symbol was also adopted by Israel in 1948 as the official insignia of state, which, in an act of supreme irony, adopted the image from the Arch of Titus in Rome. Quite simply, this was considered a faithful representation of the original menorah from Jerusalem's Temple. So a depiction commissioned in the Eternal City by a pagan emperor, and emblazoned on one of its greatest victory monuments as a graphic expression of Israel's destruction, ended up resurrected by twentieth-century conquerors, a phoenix rising from the ashes. But is the Arch of Titus menorah an accurate depiction of the Temple candelabrum, and what did this object really mean to Judaism?

The menorah carried aloft by celebratory hands on the Arch of Titus was Rome's ultimate prize. What may seem to us today a simply designed object of limited function, restricted to Temple worship in Judaism, had a far deeper value to the conquerors. This 71-centimetre-tall form of primitive lighting was far more than a piece of gold booty. Rome was fully aware that the candelabrum was impregnated with symbolic importance beyond the physical and functional. For this was the very light of the Jewish people extinguished.

Both the post-Hellenistic and modern image of the menorah in art is conservative, always comprising a one-piece base and central shaft flanked by six branches divided symmetrically into two sets of three. The arms of the candelabrum usually rise in semi-circular fashion (although less frequently more angular with a V-shaped anatomy). Light fixtures traditionally holding sacred oil and lit with wicks were fitted on to the ends. This is the earliest form of the menorah depicted in ancient art and represented on the Arch of Titus, and allegedly the form that graced the Holy of Holies in Herod's Second Temple.

However, a careful look at the 486 artistic representations of the menorah, and an examination of the literary texts, reveals a dizzying array of different shapes and styles potentially used in Temple times. But which one illuminated Jerusalem in AD 70? Was this an original Solomonic antique dating back a thousand years or a later form? What type of menorah does Israel accuse the Vatican of imprisoning in its vaults?

The major reason for the menorah's spiritual mystique is its immense antiquity as a religious concept and object. From the pivotal moment of revelation, when God carefully instructed Moses how to create a menorah on Mount Sinai, until the dark days when Rome looted the Second Temple, like its people the Jewish menorah suffered a tortuous history. The prototype described in Exodus was a pre-Israelite design crafted and used in the desert after Moses led the flight from Egypt across the Red Sea, if you accept the biblical tradition. As with all aspects of Jewish worship, not least the plan of the Temple itself, the Bible furnishes precise regulations about the requisite shape of the prototype:

You shall make a lampstand of pure gold. The base and the shaft of the lampstand shall be made of hammered work; its cups, its calyxes, and its petals shall be of one piece with it; and there shall be six branches going out of its sides, three branches of the lampstand out of one side of it and three branches of the lampstand out of the other side of it; three cups shaped like almond blossoms, each with calyx and petals, on one branch, and three cups shaped like almond blossoms, each with calyx and petals, on the other branch – so for the six branches going out of the lampstand.

On the candelabrum itself there shall be four cups shaped like almond blossoms, each with its calyxes and petals. There shall be a calyx of one piece with it under the first pair of branches, a calyx of one piece with it under the next pair of branches, and a calyx of one piece with it under the last pair of branches – so for the six branches that go out of the lampstand. Their calyxes and their branches shall be of one piece with it, the whole of it one hammered piece of pure gold. You shall make the seven lamps for it; and the lamps shall be set up so as to give light on the space in front of it. Its snuffers and trays shall be of pure gold. And see that you make them according to the pattern for them, which is being shown you on the mountain. (Exodus 25.31–40)

At the end of the period of the exodus, dated between 1250 and 1200 BC, this candelabrum shone in the Tabernacle, a temporary tent-like sanctuary, and its oil-lamps were burnt from evening to morning before God (Exodus 27.21) as a 'statute for ever throughout your generations' (Leviticus 24.3).

When King Solomon built the first permanent Jewish Temple in Jerusalem between 965 and 925 BC, he is credited with equipping the Holy House with a multitude of 'lampstands of pure gold, five on the south side and five on the north, in front of the inner sanctuary; the flowers, the lamps, and the tongs, of gold' (1 Kings 7.49). To complicate the picture further, Josephus, doubtless exaggerating wildly, claims that Solomon crafted 10,000 candelabrums according to the laws of Moses, retaining one dedicated specifically to Temple worship 'that it might burn in the daytime, according to the law' (AJ 8.90).

In the days of the wandering in Sinai, when the oil necessary to keep the Tabernacle menorah burning was a rare commodity, the lamp was understandably lit only between sunset and sunrise. The tenth-century BC King Solomon, however, commanded immense wealth and lush agricultural lands throughout Israel, especially in the Galilee. Abundant sacred olive oil could now be pressed not only to keep the holy menorah burning around the clock, but to create an immense spectacle by displaying a host of additional burning lamps on golden stands. The Judaic concept of the perpetually lit lamp was born.

Despite the detailed commandments handed to Moses on Mount Sinai, the question of the shape of the Tabernacle and Solomonic menorah remains a matter of intense speculation. Rabbinical scholars maintain that the modern shape emerged fully formed and seven-branched. To sceptical academics, however, Exodus is nothing more than a priestly legend of dubious historical content edited in the sixth or fifth century BC as a tool to legitimise and rationalise later religious practice. In other words the priests fabricated a Jewish foundation myth to validate the centrality to Judaism of Temple worship based on sacrifice in Jerusalem.

A major problem that continues to obscure the matter is the absence of physical evidence. Of the 486 ancient artistic images recorded, not one dates to the periods of the Tabernacle or Solomonic Temples. Even though casual graffiti were relatively less common in these periods, lavish royal art still adorns ancient temples, palaces and tombs across Egypt, Iran and Iraq. The absence of traditionally shaped menorahs in these contexts is distinctly strange because Judaism would have based its prototype on current fashions.

Contrary to the modern assumption that the style of the Arch of Titus candelabrum, and the menorah of modern Judaism, stretches back into the mists of time, the earliest forms were unmistakably different in concept. Archaeological research conducted throughout the Near East leaves no doubt that lamps shaped like a seven-branched menorah did not exist during the desert wanderings of the proto-Israelite exodus in the Late Bronze Age period (1400–1200 BC).

Dozens of ancient settlements, tombs and temples of this period have been excavated across the Near East and Egypt, revealing a wealth of religious paraphernalia, but nothing resembling the traditional menorah. The modern mind has created a major misconception by approaching Exodus with a preconceived image. Another underlying problem are flaws in biblical translation. The term 'base and shaft' is a mistranslation that should read a 'base-forming shaft' or 'thickened shaft' because the Hebrew word employed, *yerakh*, derives from the anatomical term for a thigh. The image implies a cylindrical object flaring at its base, not a branched object at all.

Whereas candelabra with branching arms are entirely unknown in this period, cultic stands used to support incense bowls, libation vessels, offering tables and sacred ritual objects were common. The Tabernacle candelabrum of the Late Bronze Age can only have resembled this form. At the time Egypt was the dominant political and cultural superpower, and it is south towards the fertile banks of the Nile that we should look for the menorah's original artistic inspiration. This river was the source of all life to Egyptians, and so all things Nilotic were elevated to the sacred plane and mirrored in contemporary art and architecture. At least one element of the vegetal symbolic decoration of the Tabernacle menorah was inspired by Egyptian culture.

If the lamp of the Late Bronze Age Tabernacle sanctuary was a tall flaring cylindrical object, did the seven-branched form evolve under the Early Iron Age inspiration of King Solomon? Contrary to tradition, once again this is improbable. The fully formed Jewish candelabrum remained a design of the future, yet to be invented. Instead, cult lamps of this era tended to be flat based, or slightly convex, with seven spouts rather than seven branches. Such an oil-lamp bowl would have sat atop a cylindrical cult stand, numerous examples of which have been excavated across the Near East. This configuration dovetails neatly with a contemporary Temple lamp description handed down by the Prophet Zechariah who, in a dream, saw a 'lampstand all of gold, with a bowl on top of it; there are seven lamps on it, with seven lips on each of the lamps that are on the top of it' (Zechariah 4.2). The cylindrical candelabrum remained the dominant shape beyond the reigns of Kings David and Solomon, the period of the United Monarchy, and is clearly depicted on wall reliefs preserved in the royal palace of Nineveh in modern Iraq. Here looters cart off various religious objects from the city of Lachish in Palestine, including a cylindrical cult stand, during King Sennacherib's conquest of Judah in 701 BC.

Historically, like all world religions Judaism has consciously sought umbilical links to create a continuity between the religion that emerged in the wilderness years of the Sinai and religious practices of the modern day. Just as Greek myth crucially transmitted 'historical' explanations for the imponderable perplexities of life to a predominantly illiterate society – how the planet was formed, the origins of life, love and culture – so Jewish symbols of the post-Roman era served as psychological reminders that, despite the destruction of Jerusalem and life in the Diaspora, not all links with the past were severed. The menorah offered hope for the future. To some Jews a flickering light keeping the messianic dream on a low burn, to others it was a daily reminder of the divine presence.

As uncomfortably as the truth may sit with modern Judaism, however, the pre-eminent physical image of faith did not exist throughout much of the Old Testament. If the Second Temple menorah immortalised on the Arch of Titus bears no physical resemblance to the lamps of the Tabernacle or Solomon's Temple, what exactly is the antiquity of this holy vessel?

Both 2 Kings (24.13–15) and Jeremiah (52.17–23) emphatically describe the plunder and destruction of the Temple treasures by King Nebuchadnezzar's henchmen in 587/6 BC, when the Jews of Israel were expelled to Babylon. Although Old Testament tradition subsequently records some Temple vessels being returned to Jerusalem by King Cyrus of Persia for use in a new Temple, there is no tangible proof to confirm this wishful thinking. Once again, priests writing centuries after the event tried to spin history to legitimise, and to an extent mythologise, the Jewish present – not for political reasons linked to territorial wrangling, but simply to bolster the historical and religious substance of biblical Judaism. Such revisionism typifies the foundation myths of all religions across the globe.

The earliest appearance of the traditional seven-armed menorah in art turns up on coins struck by Mattathias Antigonos, the last king and High Priest of Judaea's Hasmonaean dynasty. The reverse side of issues struck in the years 40–37 BC featured a seven-branched lampstand with a triangular base. Just how long the form had graced Temple worship is uncertain, but one specific moment in time demands attention.

In 168 BC Antiochus Epiphanes attacked Jerusalem with a strong force and desecrated the Temple. At this time of anguish the Bible specifically confirms that 'He arrogantly entered the sanctuary and took the golden altar, the candelabrum for the light, and all its utensils . . . Taking them all, he went into his own land' (1 Maccabees 1.21–4). The reality of their looting is confirmed by Josephus (*AJ* 12.250). Three years later Jerusalem was reconquered by Judas Maccabeus, who purified and renovated the Temple. For this occasion a new menorah was crafted (1 Maccabees 4.48–50; *AJ* 12.318), according to the Babylonian Talmud from melted down weapons. After a lapse of two years without sacrifice and worship, the lamp was once again relit on 25 Kislev 165 BC, a major historical episode of joy in Judaism that led to eight days of celebration, a tradition commemorated today as the winter festival of Hanukkah, the Festival of Lights.

A century later, when Pompey the Great and his military entourage violated the Holy of Holies in 63 BC, a single sacred menorah was seen alongside many other wonders. All these treasures were left in their original locations. In all probability it was this gold candelabrum – already an object more than a century old, and crafted under the inspiration of Judas Maccabeus – that Titus would seize from Herod's Temple in AD 70. By the time the sacred Jewish menorah reached Rome a year later, the most precious symbol of Judaism was already over two centuries old.

However, the story does not end there. A perplexing feature adorns the Arch of Titus menorah, a highly elaborate base consisting of a two-tiered octagonal pedestal that remains a subject of great controversy for one very good reason: it is covered with highly conspicuous 'pagan' figures in the form of sea monsters and eagles holding a wreath in their beaks. With the Old Testament's fierce prohibition against precisely this kind of artistic idolatry, many historians forcefully reject any notion that this specific lamp was the Second Temple original. So could the fancy artwork of the Arch of Titus menorah expose the object as nothing more than a fantastic product of the mind of a Roman sculptor?

With arguments and counter-arguments spinning through my mind, I decided to go to the one place I knew where the problem could be resolved once and for all: the ancient Jewish underground cemetery at Beth Shearim in the Galilee.

15

Hunting Graven Images

BOTTLE-SHAPED BETH SHEARIM nestles in a shallow wooded basin of the Lower Galilee, peering out westward towards the Jezreel Valley and the far-off Mediterranean Sea. For the home of the greatest Jewish necropolis of ancient Israel, this hill of death is remarkably tranquil. Perhaps the shaded terrain and geographical seclusion becalmed the atmosphere to form the perfect spot for intellectual thought and the rabbinical academy that evolved within its peaceful pine forest.

In the second century AD, the Jewish town of Besara – House of the Gates in Hebrew – became home to the Sanhedrin, the highest legislative body of Jewish Palestine and its supreme judicial council. With its fertile foothills and opportune location at a crossroads linking the cities of the Galilee and the Jezreel Valley with the Mediterranean coast, over time the settlement flourished to become rich in mind and pocket, especially renowned for its giant glassworks. Even today echoes of the ancient town's proud inheritance stud the hillside, across an area measuring 500 by 200 metres, in the form of ruins including a giant press for producing exportable olive oil and a nine-ton slab of glass, imperfectly cast and abandoned 1,600 years ago. Following extensive excavations initiated in 1936, the ruins of Beth Shearim are today one of the country's most important heritage sites, although local Israelis and Bar Mitzvah boys studying their ancestry as part of their initiation into manhood tend to frequent the ruins more than overseas tourists.

By far the most startling remains, however, are underground. Over the course of 300 years both local celebrities and the rich and famous of the Diaspora chose Besara as the favoured Jewish burial place in the Mediterranean basin. The honeycombed hill of underground tunnels and funerary chambers were to Roman Jews what the Mount of

Olives is in the modern era. Today, Israel's military leaders, politicians and public figures all lie united in view of Jerusalem's Temple Mount awaiting the appearance of the Messiah. Many Jewish magnates and dignitaries who found fame and fortune overseas also prefer the Mount of Olives as their final resting place.

Inscriptions found at Beth Shearim, written in Hebrew, Greek and Palmyrene, reveal a remarkably similar interment pattern for antiquity. Epitaphs speak of the burials of the head of the Council of Elders of Antioch and his family, and the leading rabbis of the synagogues of Tyre, Sidon and Beirut. Rubbing shoulders with the great and good were the finest families of Byblos, Palmyra and Messene in Babylonia, all shipped back to the heartland for perpetual rest: from Atio, the daughter of Rabbi Gamaliel who died still a virgin aged twenty-two, to Rabbi Judah Ha-Nassi, who established the Sanhedrin at Beth Shearim and edited the Jewish Mishnah. With Jerusalem out of bounds following the destruction of Jerusalem, Besara served as a surrogate cemetery – Judaism's most prestigious burial place. Catacomb 20 alone, cut through 75 metres of limestone, accommodated 125 sarcophagi (burial coffins) and about 200 burials.

With its elegantly sculpted and arched façades and landscaped courtyards, Beth Shearim is a gem of design and engineering. Beneath the ground the dark tunnels, monumental sarcophagi, and inscriptions in many tongues create an eerie, macabre atmosphere. A third-century AD Aramaic inscription warns that 'Anyone who shall open this burial upon whomever is inside it shall die an evil end.' Reluctant as I was to descend, this underworld I hoped held the key to the mystery of the Arch of Titus menorah.

All the evidence conspired to suggest that the golden candelabrum originated in the Hellenistic period, seemingly crafted by Judas Maccabeus. But with its eagles, lions and sea monsters, I wasn't convinced that the decorated pedestal could have been crafted in Jerusalem either in the second century BC or when King Herod built and furnished the Second Temple. A string of scholars have vehemently denounced the Arch of Titus menorah and its sacrilegious base as nothing more than an abominable product of imperial Rome.

Wandering around the hillside sloping down to this Jewish underworld was, for me, a trip down memory lane. In 1992 I had managed to contract Tick-Borne Relapsing Fever (TBRF) here. A rare condition more commonly known as Cave Fever, TBRF has the genetic ability to vary its surface antigens, leading to repeated stimulation of the immune system. In other words, the symptoms are like malaria, with relapsing fever endemic for years afterwards. Only 10 per cent of caves in Israel are infested by Cave Fever's offending ticks, but in the Lower Galilee, where Beth Shearim lies, this figure soars to 55 per cent. Hence, my reluctance to revisit these catacombs.

However, I soon refocused on the menorah's fancy pedestal base and recalled the lines of the Ten Commandments that Moses carried down Mount Sinai on two tablets:

> You shall not make for yourself an idol, whether in the form of anything that is in the heaven above, or that is on the earth below, or that is in the water under the earth. You shall not bow down to them or worship them; for I the Lord your God am a jealous God, punishing children for the iniquity of parents, to the third and fourth generation of those who reject me. (Deuteronomy 5.8–9)

This edict was emphatic and, if taken verbatim, then the base of the Arch of Titus menorah clearly broke Israel's covenant with God. Equally damning were the high emotions provoked when King Herod dramatically bolted the figure of a golden eagle over the entrance to the Temple in Jerusalem. Two of the most celebrated interpreters of Jewish law of this period, Judas son of Saripheus and Matthias son of Margalothus, considered this an act of sacrilege violating God's commandment. Josephus vividly recalls these two ancient academics inciting the youth of Jerusalem to

> pull down all those works which the king had erected contrary to the law of their fathers . . . for that it was truly on account of Herod's rashness in making such things as the law had forbidden, that his other misfortunes, and this distemper also, which was so unusual among mankind, and with which he was now afflicted, came upon him: for Herod had caused such things to be made, which were contrary to the law . . . for the king had erected over the great gate of the temple a large golden eagle, of great value, and had dedicated it to the temple. Now, the law forbids those that live according to it, to erect images, or representations of any living creature. (AJ 17.150–51)

Jerusalem's rebellious teenagers didn't need further prompting to rip down the eagle in broad daylight and hack it to pieces with an axe. Would the Jewish necropolis of Beth Shearim confirm this prohibition against graven images? If it did, I would be back at square one again with the Arch of Titus menorah. If the lamp's base wasn't Jewish art, then perhaps the entire representation was the fabrication of Roman imagination. Trying not to think about evil ticks and Cave Fever I ducked through the triple-arched entranceway cut through the Eocene limestone into the distant past of my ancestors.

The light abruptly died, the air became damp and heavy, the temperature plummeted by at least twenty-five degrees – the perfect playground for ghouls. An icy breeze hovered over the hallowed halls. As my eyes adjusted to the darkness, ghostly shapes of centuries gone by veered into sight. This city of the dead was impressively planned. Arched ceilings and narrow corridors of soft, white limestone led to discrete chambers containing family tombs. The deceased were laid to rest in massive stone sarcophagi, and it was these that intrigued me most. Just how these highly observant ancient Jews chose to adorn their tombs would bring me closest to the realities of Temple law and to the precise styles of decoration acceptable in the Bible Lands.

Although underground Beth Shearim is something of a menorah city, with dozens of representations incised into walls and even sculpted out of the living rock, other weird and wonderful images, equally conspicuous, came as a shock. The sarcophagi are all alike: simple rectangular limestone boxes about 1.5–2 metres high and 3 metres long, with corresponding lids whose edges are sculpted into horns resembling ancient altars. Was this a deliberate replication of Temple ritual, I pondered, with the deceased offering his or her soul to God?

While most of the stone coffins I came across were simply adorned with plain circular roundels and rosettes, several others were remarkably elaborate. Stylised lions with hungry large eyes and sharp teeth made sense as symbols of the Lion of Judah. In the early Iron Age, for instance, King Solomon adopted this beast as the symbol of royalty:

The king also made a great ivory throne, and overlaid it with pure gold. The throne had six steps and a footstool of gold, which were attached to the throne, and on each side of the seat were arm rests and two lions standing beside the arm rests, while 12 lions were standing, one on each end of a step on the six steps. The like of it was never made in any kingdom. (2 Chronicles 9.17–19)

Why some of the Beth Shearim lions were aggressively chewing an ox, however, was a completely different matter. This composition didn't seem particularly holy to me. But even more perplexing was to follow. The front of yet another sarcophagus blatantly displayed two flying Nikes alongside a pillar. Long before she was elevated to shoe manufacturer's paradise, the perfect brand image, Nike was a Roman goddess of Victory: you couldn't get closer to an archetypal pagan symbol.

The apparent contradiction between the law of God and earthly reality continued. I hardly had time to draw breath, and mull over the meaning of the weird and wonderful images of Beth Shearim, before Deuteronomy 5.8–9 was profaned yet again. In front of me stood the remains of a sculpted soldier with a menorah standing on his head, a scene that could have been lifted straight out of the sketchbook of the Jewish artist Marc Chagall. The candelabrum was typically seven-branched with a common three-pronged base. Its shaft was elaborately adorned with the twisted knot of a tree. Clearly the deceased had personally commissioned a highly original piece of mortuary art. As the symbol of eternal light, the menorah in this composition was an obvious divine plea for enduring life in the afterworld.

Figurative art is traditionally considered an abomination in Judaism. Any image in human form detracted from the omnipotence of God, and hence was prohibited. So much for theory. In reality, from the Hellenistic period onwards the Near East was flooded with vivid images drawn from the broad panorama of paganism. Initially a source of religious tension, it didn't take long for ideas and images to be absorbed into local culture and be given new meaning. Irrespective of historical age or religious context, this is one of the immutable laws of human behaviour. Unless you live in a ghetto, it is impossible for people to be unaffected by changing cultural tastes and fashions.

By the early Roman period – contrary to the view of many modern historians – there can be no doubt that Judaism was evolving culturally with the changing times. What we would traditionally term 'graven images' became mainstream Jewish symbols, with alternative layers of meaning tailored towards the doctrines of the user. This is especially true for the great golden Temple menorah itself, whose symbolism is heavily based on a primitive Near Eastern cult stretching back to the dawn of time.

Stepping gingerly along the corridors of death, an uninvited guest, I considered the reality of Second Temple Judaism. Because it lies underground and was forgotten to man for 2,000 years, the necropolis of Beth Shearim is amazingly well preserved. And if the observant Jews of the headquarters of the Sanhedrin were allowed freely to decorate their tombs with figurative art, then any Jewish community across the Diaspora must have enjoyed the same liberty.

Abruptly, two sets of images of my old friend the eagle, ripped from the entrance to Herod's Temple, peered at me from the sides of further sarcophagi and I knew I had absolute proof for the authenticity of the base of the Arch of Titus menorah. The destruction of Herod's eagle had been a political act, not driven by religion. Herod may have been many despicable things, but he was no fool. Why spend a king's ransom on a spiritual home for Judaism and then antagonise its people? Ipso facto, this candelabrum and its base adorned with eagles and sea monsters was indeed the original sacred one, the perpetual lamp from Herod's Temple. Though stylised, there was no mistaking the beak, outspread wings and talons of this lord of the birds confronting me in Besara's catacombs.

The evidence that I needed safely procured, I scrambled out of this hole in the ground, scrubbed my hands and face at length in the hope of ridding myself of any residual mould, and walked up to Besara's ancient synagogue to collect my thoughts. Arches and walls spring from the living bedrock of this house of prayer.

My trip to Beth Shearim had revealed watertight proof that Judaism in the Roman period had no aversion to figurative art as long as the images emitted the right religious message. Take the eagle, for instance, which is a primary symbol of the Old Testament. The eagle of ancient Judaism was clearly not the bloodthirsty, meat-eating bird of prey that topped the military standards of Roman soldiers marching into battle. If anything, Rome stole this image from the Near East where, as early as the third millennium BC, the thunderbird represented the sun in Mesopotamia.

The biblical eagle has manifold meanings: the symbol of God and his protection of the chosen people; a sign of royalty; an expression of immortality. In Exodus (19.4), God reminds Moses of his protective powers: 'You have seen what I did to the Egyptians, and how I bore you on eagles' wings and brought you to myself.' Further, Deuteronomy (32.11–12) reveals how the Lord watches over Israel, 'As an eagle stirs up its nest, and hovers over its young; as it spreads its wings, takes them up, and bears them aloft on its pinions, the Lord alone guided him.'

Perhaps even more graphic were the dreams of the exiled prophet Ezekiel in Babylon, which confirm the eagle as a divine symbol in Judaism. One particularly vivid dream explains the presence of both the eagle and the ox in Jewish art:

> As I looked, a stormy wind came out of the north: a great cloud with brightness around it and fire flashing forth continually, and in the middle of the fire, something like gleaming amber. In the middle of it was something like four living creatures. This was their appearance: they were of human form. Each had four faces, and each of them had four wings. Their legs were straight and the soles of their feet were like the sole of a calf's foot; and they sparkled like burnished bronze. Under their wings on their four sides they had human hands . . . As for the appearance of their faces: the four had the face of a human being, the face of a lion on the right side, the face of an ox on the left side, and the face of an eagle. (Ezekiel 1.4–10)

All three of these animals through which God chose to appear to Ezekiel turn up in the Jewish necropolis of Beth Shearim, and the eagle, of course, is conspicuous on the base of the Arch of Titus menorah. As the symbol of God, the heavens and immortality, its existence in Second Temple Jewish art makes complete sense. For the same reason, the eagle remained popular in the Late Roman and Early Byzantine period, featuring above the door of the synagogue at Capernaum in the Galilee and standing behind the figure of Orpheus playing his lyre on a wall relief in the third-century AD synagogue of Dura Europos in Syria.

So Judaism's allegedly strict ban on figurative decoration turned out to be a modern myth perpetrated by orthodox Jews imposing their own narrow interpretation on antiquity. Their view is understandably myopic; it is the belief of a group firmly stuck in the shtetls of early modern eastern Europe. Today archaeology exposes a very different truth, and even a careful reading of Late Roman rabbinical sources reveals all kinds of figures displayed in Jerusalem at the time of Herod (except human beings), even 'dragons' with smooth necks: exactly the kind of sea monsters that turn up on the pedestal of the Arch of Titus menorah.

16

The Tree of Life

IDLING ON A wall in Beth Shearim's ruined Roman synagogue, I conjured up images of Jews sitting on the synagogue benches 2,000 years ago praying and chatting about the town's latest olive harvests and shiploads of raw glass sent to their Jewish brethren in Tyre. After all, the ancient synagogue wasn't just a pious house of worship, where reverent voices spoke in hushed tones. These places were also community centres where businessmen haggled, people congregated for social events and kids got up to trouble round the back.

Somewhere within its confines, Besara's synagogue may well have possessed a menorah like the Temple original. Not merely a means of producing light, all of the town's Jews would have been aware of the object's historical symbolism. They would have incorrectly assumed that the seven-branched shape dated back to the days when Moses crafted the first Tabernacle menorah in the wilderness of Sinai. The fateful destruction of Solomon's lamp by King Nebuchadnezzar would have been imprinted on their memory. And Judas Maccabeus would have been celebrated as a superhero who rekindled the Temple ritual in the second century BC, an event celebrated in the depths of winter as Hanukkah, the Festival of Lights. Every time Vespasian and Titus were mentioned, their memory would have been cursed.

After studying the Arch of Titus menorah base, however, I came to realise that modern history has forgotten the elementary symbolism of the ancient Jewish candelabrum. My walk in Beth Shearim's valley of the dead revealed that the pedestal symbols were specifically chosen to reflect God's control over the entire world. As a bird of the skies who soars closest to God's throne, at one level the eagle represented the heavens. Conversely, the sea monster or *ketos* stood for the depths of the sea. In this sense, the base designed for the Second Temple rather neatly advertised in one quick glance the extent of God's omnipotence. But this was just the veneer of a far deeper symbolic cosmology.

Other than evoking curiosity and amusement, the scene in the ancient cemetery of the soldier 'wearing' a menorah on his head left me bemused. I felt I had missed a crucial clue in this composition, a small detail that held the key to a completely different meaning of the ancient Jewish menorah. I replayed the images just taken on my digital camera without inspiration. What was I missing?

Straining to stir my imagination, I stared at the blue skies overhead. The answer was all around me, laughing in the light breeze – trees. What had bothered me beneath the ground was the central shaft of the soldier menorah, which had clearly been designed to resemble the knotted body of a tree.

The Tree of Life is the central spine of all Near Eastern creation myths. It is perhaps the most powerful symbol of all time, an image that unites rather than divides world religions across time and place. The earliest human symbol of fertility, eternal life, salvation and the divine presence, the sacred tree is a rarity that makes nonsense of sup-posed differences and antagonisms between religion. What remains is a startling truth: all religions evolved from the same trunk.

The Tree of Life is best known from Genesis, where it stood at the centre of the Garden of Eden at the dawn of civilisation. The same motif, however, is a far older image first known from the epic tale of Gilgamesh, an historical king of Uruk who lived in Babylonia along the River Euphrates (modern Iraq) around 2700 BC. In ancient Mesopotamia this divine tree grew in Dilmun (Paradise) at the source of the Water of Life. Here, the cosmic world tree is described as having its roots in the underworld and its crown in heaven. An almost iden-tical myth prevails in Judaism, as is clear from a medieval record retained by Jewish communities of the Diaspora:

In Paradise stand the tree of life and the tree of knowledge, the latter forming a hedge about the former. Only he who has cleared a path for himself through the tree of knowledge can come close to the tree of life, which is so huge that it would take a man 500 years to traverse a distance equal to the diameter of the trunk . . . From beneath it flows forth the water that irrigates the whole earth, parting thence into four streams, the Ganges, the Nile, the Tigris, and the Euphrates. (*Legends of the Jews* I.321)

All across the ancient Near East the sacral ruler responsible for temples and holy groves was also the traditional guardian and caretaker of the sacred tree. God's appearance to Moses in a burning bush on Mount Horeb in modern Jordan would thus have made complete sense to someone living in Bronze Age Palestine, where even cities tended to be named after the sacred tree. The 'lighting' of the bush symbolised life, in this case God's anticipated liberation of his people from Egypt. Especially famous was the Canaanite city of Luz where Jacob dreamed about climbing a ladder to heaven. Luz translates as 'City of Almond', and one cannot help but wonder whether the 'ladder' on which Jacob dreamt he climbed to heaven was actually the branches of an almond tree.

Although this is little more than educated conjecture, the relation of the almond to the Tree of Life and Exodus' description of the menorah is clear and crucial to my investigation. From time immemorial the almond tree and its fruit have been blessed with major potency in early religion. Its modern botanical term, *Amygdalus communis*, incorporates the biblical term Luz, which also meant Great Mother in the ancient Near East. Not only was the insignia of the Bronze Age sacred ruler a rod or sceptre made from a branch of the Tree of Life but, at least in the Bible, the most powerful staffs were cut from the almond tree.

Thus, during the power struggle between the twelve tribes of Israel in the wilderness of Sinai, Moses was instructed by God to take twelve staffs from the tribes, one for each ancestral house, and to inscribe them with the name of the head of each. Rather like drawing lots, only the staff of Aaron of Levi 'put forth buds, produced blossoms, and bore ripe almonds' as a sign of his divinely appointed leadership (Numbers 17.8). It is with this deep history and symbolism in mind that the almond was chosen to be the central motif of the golden menorah and Temple worship, which had to possess 'cups shaped like almond blossoms, each with calyx and petals' on each branch (Exodus 25.33).

So, what is so outstanding about the almond tree? Quite simply, it is the first tree to herald the arrival of spring in the Near East, when it blossoms in glorious white petals, and also the last to shed its leaves. For communities intimate with nature, and whose everyday existence was precariously bound to the seasons, such a long-lived cycle provided an ideal model of life, stability and resurrection. For this reason, according to Jewish rabbinical legend, Paradise could only be reached though a hole in an almond tree, where the angel of death's power was neutralised. For similar, if more scientific reasons, as well as being a food delicacy and a product with potent medicinal qualities, *luz*, the biblical term for the almond, also in ancient pathology denoted the indestructible bone where the neck meets the spinal column.

At its core, therefore, the symbolism of the Jewish menorah is inextricably linked to the Tree of Life in the ancient Near East. It is an object representing God's eternal dominance over the heavens, earth and the sea, and also the very life force of Judaism. The images of the eagle and sea monster on its base merely reinforce this symbolism.

Nowadays, it is largely forgotten how profound has been the inspiration of the Tree of Life in all world cultures. One of the earliest and most remarkable examples of organised religion in Britain also revolved around a tree: in 1998 a circular henge was exposed by coastal erosion at Holme-next-the-Sea in Norfolk, consisting of fifty-five wooden posts enclosing the lower trunk and roots of a large oak tree weighing two and a half tons. Erected in the Early Bronze Age, just before 2000 BC, the oak had deliberately been placed in the henge with its roots exposed upside down, as if it were protecting worshippers from the dark underworld beneath and channelling the life force from its roots into the realm of man.

Over time, the primitive memory of the Jewish menorah's symbolism evaporated to be replaced by more scientific interpretations. From the Late Hellenistic period onwards, many Jewish scholars focused instead on numerology. The lamp's magical seven branches replicated the seven planets known in antiquity, over which God's shining light literally ruled supreme. Thus, Philo of Alexandria equated the menorah's six side branches and position in the Temple to planetary inspiration:

> The candlestick he placed at the south, figuring thereby the movements
> for the luminaries above; for the sun and the moon and the others run

their courses in the south far away from the north. And therefore six branches, three on each side, issue from the central candlestick, bringing the number up to seven, and on all these are set seven lamps and candle bearers, symbols of what the men of science call planets. For the sun, like the candlestick, has the fourth place in the middle of the six and gives light to the three above and the three below it, so tuning to harmony an instrument of music truly divine. (*On Moses* 2.102–3)

Medieval Jewry took the Kabbalistic mystical power of the number seven even further, claiming that Solomon's ten menorahs furnished seventy burning lamps. This value symbolised the seventy nations over whom, so tradition asserted, the great king held sway. Even today, Jewish brides encircle their husbands-to-be seven times in Jewish marriage ceremonies, to demonstrate a will to make a home as fine as the world God created in seven days.

The Jewish menorah's most potent inspiration, however, is not numerology, but the Tree of Life, a universal symbol that has touched all major world religions. When the True Cross of Christ was captured in Jerusalem by Sasanian forces in AD 617, Christian commentators compared their loss to the death of the Tree of Life. Even the modern Christmas tree and its electric lights is a faded memory of the Jewish Temple candelabrum and the same Tree of Life. The most primeval of Near Eastern images is also the root of the Buddhist stupa cut in stone, Chinese wooden layered pagodas, South American totem poles and the British maypole. There is no escaping the Tree of Life as the source from which all creation emanates. We may not notice it today, but the symbol continues to shine all around us.

17

Bread of Heaven

IF IT SHOULD ever surface at public auction, the gold menorah from King Herod's Temple – the pre-eminent symbol of Judaism – would command an immense price and shatter all records for an antiquity. By comparison, the Table of the Divine Presence is a lesser known object of worship, and little regarded in mainstream Judaism today. Yet until the second century AD it was venerated as the central symbol of faith.

After the Ark of the Covenant, the Divine Table was the second most important vessel created to God's command by Moses at the foot of Mount Sinai as an instrument of worship and offering. When the Ark of the Covenant was destroyed by the marauding forces of Nebuchadnezzar in 586 BC, historically the Table became the most valuable piece of Temple furniture. Only from the fourth century AD onwards did the menorah assume a central symbolic role in the Jewish Diaspora, largely as a visual counterpart to the cross: the symbol of emergent Christianity, the dominant religion of the Mediterranean basin.

As with the golden candelabrum, God's instructions to Moses for crafting the Table were strict and precise:

> You shall make a table of acacia wood, two cubits long, one cubit wide, and a cubit and a half high. You shall overlay it with pure gold, and make a moulding of gold round it . . . You shall make for it four rings of gold, and fasten the rings to the four corners at its four legs . . . You shall make the poles of acacia wood, and overlay them with gold, and the table shall be carried with these. You shall make its plates and dishes for incense, and its flagons and bowls with which to pour drink-offerings; you shall make them of pure gold. And you shall set the bread of the Presence on the table before me always. (Exodus 25.23–30)

Equally specific was the ritual of stocking the Table and its position within the Tabernacle sanctuary in the wilderness and later Temples. Twelve loaves were baked using choice flour, with two-tenths of an *ephah* allocated to each. The finished product was stacked on the gold table in two rows, six to a row, alongside pure frankincense. In the wilderness of Sinai, hot bread was placed on the Table every Sabbath by Aaron 'before the Lord regularly as a commitment of the people of Israel, as a covenant for ever' (Leviticus 24.8). Table and bread stood in the Tabernacle tent to the north, immediately outside the Holy of Holies (Exodus 40.22–3).

By the Second Temple period the Showbread Table had become far more ostentatious and was most probably crafted entirely of pure gold. Cost was hardly an issue, and solid gold had the added advantage of being far easier to maintain than a decaying acacia wood table covered with cracked gold leaf. During the Triumph in Rome of AD 71, Josephus described the Table simply as golden and weighing many talents (*JW* 7.148). Elsewhere, he expanded on this description, labelling the object one of the 'most wonderful works of art, universally renowned', and confirmed that the Herodian version was not entirely plain, but was like 'those at Delphi' with feet 'resembling those that the Dorians put to their bedsteads' (*AJ* 3.139).

Measurements based on the comparative proportions of human figures adorning the Arch of Titus relief conjure up an image of a Table measuring 52 centimetres in height, and the artwork reinforces the view of an elaborate piece of furniture. Despite the Arch's false perspective (which fails to depict the back of the Table in order to give pride of place to the silver trumpets tied across its front plane), the Table is either hexagonal or more probably octagonal, with six to eight corresponding legs.

An extraordinary account of a Table of the Divine Presence crafted in Egypt by order of King Ptolemy II Philadelphus (285–247 BC) is preserved in a letter allegedly written around 270 BC by Aristeas, an influential diplomat in Philadelphus' court. This letter, addressed to his brother, describes an Egyptian embassy dispatched to Eleazor, the High Priest of Jerusalem, to try and patch up relationships with the Jews following a generation of persecution in Egypt.

Ptolemy II Philadelphus is credited in this work as liberating 100,000 Jewish captives, and ordering the Hebrew law to be translated into Greek to foster racial equality in Alexandria. To this end the king sent a diplomatic treasure chest to Jerusalem containing 50 talents of gold, 100 talents of silver, 50 gold and silver bowls and 5,000 blocks of stone for Temple renovations. In return, Egypt invited six elders from each tribe 'who have led exemplary lives and are expert in their own law' to come to Alexandria and translate the Torah (Jewish teachings).

Aristeas specifically claimed that the Showbread Table crafted in Egypt was 'of pure gold and solid on every side; I mean, gold was not overlaid upon other material, but a solid metal plate was put in place'. The border around the Table was a handbreadth wide with a rope, egg and fruit design and a revolving rail, in which precious stones were secured with golden pins. An egg pattern with precious stones was set along the upward-slanting border.

The main plane of the Table was even more spectacular:

> On the surface of the table they worked a meander pattern in relief, with precious stones of many sorts projecting in its midst, carbuncles and emeralds and also onyx and other species of outstanding beauty. Next to the arrangement of the meander there was placed a marvellous design of open net-work, which gave a rhombus-like effect to the middle of the table; inlaid into this were rock-crystal and amber, affording spectators an inimitable sight.
>
> The legs were made with capitals of lily shape, the lilies making a bend underneath the table, and the upright leaves being the part in view. The base of the leg which rested on the floor was entirely of carbuncle, a handbreadth high and eight fingers in width . . . And they represented ivy intertwined with acanthus growing out of the stone and encircling the leg, together with a grapevine and its clusters, all worked in stone, right up to the top; the style of the four legs was the same. All the parts were carefully made and fitted, the ingenious art corresponding to truth to such a superlative degree that if a breath of wind blew the leaves stirred in their place; so closely was every detail modelled on reality. (*Letter of Aristeas* 66–70)

Towards the close of his letter, Aristeas concluded, 'You have the story, my dear Philocrates, just as I promised. I believe such an account will afford you greater pleasure than the books of the romancers.' Despite

Aristeas' protestations that his description was factual, and not a work of romance like so many doing the rounds in Alexandrian literary salons of the era, readers would have recognised the genre as a contemporary work of historical fiction written between 132 and 100 BC, some 150 years later than when the story is set. Regrettably, this testimony about the Table of the Divine Presence must be largely thrown out of court, although there is every reason to suspect it is based on contemporary records and thus contains at least a kernel of truth. In an era of such creative ability and skill, the Table of Jerusalem is far more likely to have resembled Aristeas' elaborate affair than the prototype of Exodus.

To increase the complexity surrounding the ritual use of this object, a series of tables were used in the Showbread ritual at the Jerusalem Temple. When freshly baked bread was carried into the sanctuary, it was placed initially on a marble table to the side of the porch. Opposite stood a gold table on to which old bread was removed. With its gleaming white purity, marble was appropriate for fresh offerings; gold reflected the divine presence in which the bread had stood and been blessed by God. Both tables 'promote what is holy to a higher status and do not bring it down', according to the Mishnah. Finally, the gold Table of the Divine Presence stood inside the sanctuary with its bread offerings, according to the Mishnah, baked and administered in the Second Temple period by the House of Garmu.

How can we be certain that the Table was venerated more highly than the menorah? Between AD 132 and 135, at the height of the Second Jewish Revolt, the Jewish military leader, Simon Bar-Kokhba, struck silver coins showing the façade of the destroyed Temple sanctuary alongside the inscription 'Jerusalem'. The reverse of the coin displayed a *lulav* (palm branch) and *etrog* (citron) and the inscription 'Year One of the Redemption of Israel'. Four columns support a schematic view of the entrance to the Temple, and at its centre stands the Table of the Divine Presence visible from its narrow side, with raised and arched ends. None of these coins depicted the candelabrum.

The minting of this money had little to do with economics and everything to do with propaganda. Small and mobile, coins travelled swiftly across great distances from pocket to pocket and were thus the perfect 'advertising board' for promoting ideologies. With the silver series of AD 132–5, Bar-Kokhba was trying to stir up trouble and incite sedition against Rome. His highly potent message was the equivalent of dropping thousands of paper flyers over Iraq during the First and Second Gulf Wars as part of the softening up process to create a sympathetic atmosphere ripe for toppling Saddam Hussein. Here, though, the Jews were expressing their intention of vanquishing Rome and renewing sacred Temple service around the central symbol of the Table. The *lulav* and *etrog* symbolised a desire to restore the three pilgrimage festivals, particularly Sukkoth, while the Table symbolised the restoration in perpetuity of the Temple ritual itself. Once again, Bar-Kokhba was instructing Jews the length and breadth of Israel to be brave, strong and to anticipate the renewal of Temple worship; God would continue to feed his people.

In Temple times the Table of the Divine Presence was an intensely symbolic religious apparatus, a divine message from God to his people. In one of the earliest and most important commentaries on the books of the Bible, Philo of Alexandria was intrigued by the ritual. His enquiry led to a simple explanation:

> The loaves of bread are symbolic of necessary foods, without which there is no life; and the power of rulers and peasants by the ordering of God [consists] in the necessities of nature, [namely] in food and drink. Wherefore He adds 'before me continually thou shalt place the loaves of bread', for 'continually' means that the gift of food is continual and uninterrupted, while 'before' means that it is pleasing and agreeable to God both to be gracious and to receive gratitude.

Despite his convoluted writing style, often described as ingenious, fanciful and even perverse, Philo is a crucial source for understanding Second Temple Judaism. Born around 20 BC, when King Herod's Temple was spanking new in Jerusalem, not only did he live through some of the most turbulent years of Jewish history, he was also a major player in these events. Around AD 39–40 Philo accompanied an Alexandrian embassy dispatched to Rome, where the emperor Caligula was petitioned about controlling religious persecution back home. His *Questions and Answers on Exodus* were written as an ancient version of Bunyan's *Pilgrim's Progress* or Dante's *Divine Comedy*, to set forth and interpret the history of the human soul.

Philo correctly exposed an obvious message. Bread was the primary life force of antiquity. By demanding constant exposure to fresh bread, an eternal reminder was circulated for farmers to tend their fields 'religiously'. By blessing the Showbread, God favoured the fields of Israel and its farmers. While bread stood within the Temple sanctuary of Jerusalem, Israel's agricultural wellbeing was guaranteed and divinely protected. The importance of bread was etched into the Jewish psyche from the period of the Exodus, when, in their haste to escape the pharaoh, bread had insufficient time to rise. The Jews' lucky escape was later ritualised in the festival of Passover, when all bread is thrown out of homes and replaced with unleavened Matzah.

When Titus plundered this Jewish symbol in AD 70, he knew exactly what he was doing. The gold value or artistic brilliance of the object didn't concern him. What interested Rome was the message conveyed – once the empire possessed the Table of the Divine Presence, it also controlled the fields, farmers, crops and economy of Israel. This was a statement of intent that spoke volumes to Jews across the world: now we are your masters and if you want protection and prosperity you must answer to Rome. As we see on the Arch of Titus, the Table was given pride of place at the head of the Triumph of AD 71, a perpetual reminder of these facts.

For these reasons bread retains particular significance in Judaism. Every Shabbat Jewish families will enthusiastically buy *chala*, special Shabbat bread. After the genocide and starvation of the Second World War, many Jewish families adopted a private habit of buying fresh bread every day as a reminder of former atrocities and as a sign of a return to health and prosperity. And as bread remains a central symbol of Judaism, so the biblical ritual of the Showbread metamorphosed over time into the Catholic communion. Today's grab and go society tends to take for granted just how central wheat remains to life, but it is around us every day as we fly from meeting to meeting – in the buns of our burgers and the bases of our pizzas.

18

Trumpeting Messages

WHETHER THE OCCASION was the appearance of God in a clap of thunder, a cry to battle or Temple worship, music was a constant tool of inspiration in the Old Testament. Amongst the biblical orchestra of lyres, cymbals and singers, the silver trumpet was the noblest instrument. From Exodus to the Arch of Titus and beyond, as the announcer of pageantry in medieval and modern royal courts, the trumpet's special status is secure. But what exactly was so special about the two silver trumpets of Herod's Second Temple that compelled Rome to parade them in the Triumph of AD 71 and depict them both on the Arch of Titus tied to the Table of the Divine Presence? Were they an example of the wealth of the House of God or vanquished symbols now rendered impotent?

The trumpet evolved from the *shofar*, the earliest wind instrument used in the ancient Near East. Derived from the Akkadian word *shapparu*, a wild goat, this natural instrument was originally a goat's horn, but was quickly replaced by a ram's horn in early Judaism. Even though the *shofar* survives today as a symbol of redemption blown in the festivals of Rosh Hashanah (New Year) and Yom Kippur (Day of Atonement), certainly by the time of King Solomon and the First Temple period it had been replaced by the trumpet in everyday Jewish ritual and worship.

Along with the menorah and Table, the trumpets were the last of the key religious items that God commanded Moses to create on Mount Sinai:

> The Lord spoke to Moses, saying: make two silver trumpets; you shall make them of hammered work; and you shall use them for summoning the congregation, and for breaking camp . . . The sons of Aaron, the priests, shall blow the trumpets; this shall be a perpetual institution

for you throughout your generations. When you go to war in your land against the adversary who oppresses you, you shall sound an alarm with the trumpets, so that you may be remembered before the Lord your God and be saved from your enemies. Also on your days of rejoicing, at your appointed festivals, and at the beginnings of your months, you shall blow the trumpets over your burnt-offerings and over your sacrifices of well-being; they shall serve as a reminder on your behalf before the Lord your God: I am the Lord your God. (Numbers 10.1–10)

Unlike the golden lamp, the silver trumpets may well have existed in this biblical form from the very beginning. Archaeologists generally attribute the emergence of Israel within Canaan to the Late Bronze Age, placing the historical period of the Exodus towards the middle of the thirteenth century BC. The stunning discovery in 1922 of the tomb of Tutankhamun, the Eighteenth Dynasty Pharaoh of Egypt, leaves no shadow of doubt that such trumpets graced this period. Tutankhamun ruled from 1334 to 1325 BC and his military trumpet was a cylindrical tube of bronze, silver and gold inlay terminating in a flaring bell depicting the king wearing the Blue Crown of Egypt and holding the crook sceptre.

Whether we accept the flight from Egypt in Exodus as a physical truth, or only believe in the reality of close political and economic ties between the pharaohs and Late Bronze Age Canaan, there is very good reason to locate the inspiration for Moses' silver trumpets south in Egypt – as with the decorative scheme adopted for the menorah.

Following the discovery of Tutankhamun's trumpets, Egypt's Antiquities Service in 1939 agreed to allow a bandsman from a British Hussar regiment to play the silver trumpet. Against a backdrop of intermittent power failure in Cairo, which prompted fears of the resurfacing of the boy-king's curse, Tutankhamun's trumpet was broadcast live by the BBC to an estimated global audience of 150 million people.

This wonder of the age of the ancient pharaohs, however, was nothing short of a mirage. Bandsman Tappern's rendition of the Grand March from *Aida* and the Posthorn Gallop may have produced gasps of amazement at the time, but he did enjoy a little help from modernity. Tappern had quite normally, and in all innocence, inserted his own movable mouthpiece into the end of Tutankhamun's trumpet, enabling the instrument to be manipulated like a modern version. Unfortunately, pharaonic musicians had access to no such advantage.

Both the trumpets of Tutankhamun and of biblical Temple worship would only have been able to produce three notes. The lowest was dull and poorly centred; the middle one was excellent and would have travelled audibly across any battlefield; the upper note, however, would have been useless, requiring extreme pressure that would have damaged the player's lips. Thus, in effect the silver trumpet was a one-trick pony.

The natural trumpet lacking valves, slides or pistons dominated history into the eighteenth century and, as the Baroque trumpet, was especially popular in royal circles in the period 1600–1750. Only in 1815 would Heinrich Stölzel and Friedrich Blühmel invent the modern-day version equipped with valves. The prototype, however, was never intended to be a musical instrument. Sounding the ram's horn, the *shofar*, was a cry to God for relief and help. Its sound combated evil and averted catastrophe (war, pestilence and locusts); it was, in short, a loud noise that frightened away spirits in the same way that church bells protected Christian communities in medieval Europe.

The elongated trumpet, crafted from the medium of silver denoting truth, held greater religious sway in the Old Testament. The elongated trumpet emitted a purer note than the ram's horn. The biblical silver trumpets were blown almost exclusively by a guild of seven priestly trumpeters at times of daily burnt offering, celebration, feasts and at the beginning of each month. Thus, when Solomon dedicated the Temple in Jerusalem:

> Then the king and all the people offered sacrifice before the Lord. King Solomon offered as a sacrifice 22,000 oxen and 120,000 sheep. So the king and all the people dedicated the house of God . . . Opposite them the priests sounded trumpets; and all Israel stood. (2 Chronicles 7.4–6)

After the return from exile in Babylon, silver trumpets replaced the *shofar* for most cultic activities within Judaism. The priestly trumpet sounded three times every morning to mark the opening of the Temple gates; nine blasts accompanied morning and evening sacrifice; and the start of the Sabbath was announced by a threefold trumpet blast from the top of the Temple.

The pair of trumpets profiled in the Arch of Titus relief measure 71.5 and 80 centimetres in length and conform to Josephus' description of these holy vessels: 'a narrow tube, somewhat thicker than a flute, but with so much breadth as was sufficient for admission of the breath of a man's mouth: it ended in the form of a bell, like common trumpets' (*AJ* 3.291). Both closely resemble Tutankhamun's trumpet and also a pair depicted on the revolutionary coins of Simon Bar-Kokhba during the Second Jewish Revolt of AD 132–5. Of all the Temple treasure (menorah and Table), the silver trumpets remained the least altered over time and essentially standardised into the eighteenth century.

After the fall of the Temple in Jerusalem, however, the trumpet disappeared from Jewish worship. In a deliberate search for individual cultural identity, early Christianity avoided the trumpet. Where the instrument does feature in the New Testament it is always as an allegory of peace and tranquillity; to the Christian God the trumpet was idolatrous, a cry of war. Thus, in the eighth book of the second-century AD *Sibylline Oracles*, Christianity was described as vastly different to pagan and Jewish worship:

> They [Christians] do not pour blood on altars in libations or sacrifices. No drum sounds, no cymbal, no flute of many holes, which has a sound that damages the heart, no pipe, which bears an imitation of the crooked serpent, no savage-sounding trumpet, herald of wars.

Similarly, in his *Paedagogus* (*The Tutor*), Clement of Alexandria (*c.* AD 150–215) advised:

> Leave the syrinx [Greek trumpet] to the shepherds and the flute to the superstitious devotees who rush to serve their idols. We completely forbid the use of these instruments at our temperate banquet.

But the trumpet's legacy will not die. The biblical Book of Revelation still promises Christians that seven trumpets blown by seven angels will announce the destruction of man:

> And the fifth angel blew his trumpet, and I saw a star that had fallen from heaven to earth, and he was given the key to the bottomless pit . . . and from the shaft rose smoke like the smoke of a great furnace . . . Then from the smoke came locusts on the earth, and they were given authority like the authority of scorpions of the earth. (Revelation 9.1–3)

For Judaism, redemption and the second coming of the Messiah will also be heralded by the brassy sound of the trumpet.

> The Messiah will have Elijah blow the trumpet, and, at the first sound, the primal light, which shone before the week of the Creation, will reappear; at the second sound the dead will arise . . . at the third sound, the shekiah [sunset] will become visible to all; the mountains will be razed at the fourth sound, and the Temple will stand in complete perfection as Ezekiel described it. (*Legends of the Jews* IV.234)

Once in the hands of Rome, however, no temple stood and no messiah could come. The empire had not just imprisoned Judaism in the present, it now owned its future too.

Revolution

19

City of Unbrotherly Love

Now that I understood what the Temple treasure meant to Judaism, a logical extension was to fathom the spoil's value to Rome — monetary windfall or symbol of eternal victory? Was the torching of the Temple coldly premeditated or the result of fast changing circumstances on the ground? The answer lay hidden amid the causes of the First Jewish Revolt. Rarely triggered by a single event, wars are invariably the culmination of inter-related provocations. The First Jewish Revolt was a snowball rolling down a mountainside, starting slowly and inconspicuously, but eventually accumulating uncontrollable mass and speed. An ugly crash was inevitable.

Josephus' account of the slippery descent into war is a saga of great complexity and bloodshed that resonates profoundly with the modern Arab-Israeli conflict. The intriguing art on the Arch of Titus is not the simple representation of ancient Jewish treasure worth hundreds of millions of pounds but a reflection of one of the most devastating battles of antiquity. It shows the ambitions of Rome and its military machine in action, the inner workings of the mind of an emperor. Contributing to it was a string of tragic and selfish decisions made by a small minority of megalomaniac Jewish politicians, who were responsible for the tragedy that subsequently befell Judaism — expulsion into a dark Diaspora and far-off lands, and the eventual evil of the Second World War.

The fate of the Temple treasure of Jerusalem makes little sense dislocated from its historical setting. But the tale is a maze of complications and only the principal events can be summarised here. Today, scholars package the First Jewish Revolt not so much as a war against Roman colonialism and culture but as an internal class struggle between Judaea's peasantry and ruling class. However, while the destruction of Jerusalem was admittedly paved by Jewish factional infighting and hatred, the roots of the fall lay in the imposition of Roman values that led to the suffocation of local religion.

The first fifty years of the first century AD were precarious years for Israel. Ever since King Herod had assumed the throne as a client king of Rome in 40 BC, the Jewish ideal of a land ruled by a wise leader of esteemed ancestry had faded. The two-faced Herod could not be trusted. Despite being the brains and purse behind the Second Temple of Jerusalem, one of the architectural wonders of the age, Herod forfeited the people's trust. This half-Jew of Edomite extraction – an isolated group not recognised by mainstream Judaism – lacked morals and wisdom, preferring to court status and wealth by playing politics for high stakes.

Herod may have paid lip-service to Jewish values, but his soul had been bought by Rome. In return for keeping the peace, controlling Israel's Jews and collecting taxes for the empire's coffers, Herod was granted the rule of a fertile land ripe for the picking. With the construction of the port of Sebastos at Caesarea in the late first century BC, Israel suddenly became linked to a commercial revolution that was sweeping the former backwaters of the eastern Mediterranean. Wine, oil, glass, wheat, purple dye and dates found a highly receptive market across the empire, bringing unparalleled wealth to the rulers and middlemen of Israel. As lord of all he surveyed, everything was available for royal taxation. Eager to be more Roman than the Romans, Herod grew filthy rich on the sweat of his subjects. His introduction of athletic festivals, musical contests, wild beast fights and gladiatorial combat to Jerusalem fuelled local antagonism to the new culture.

To the Jews of Israel the Roman dream was a shock and an affront. But nobody could have predicted just how destructively the old and new worlds would collide. After all, Rome's model of puppet kings and taxation was a tried and tested formula. From Britain to Syria the imperial war machine had annexed the known world by military strength and political stealth. Contrary to the image of popular history, the empire did not court perpetual war. Instead, she shrewdly selected sympathetic local rulers to serve as puppet kings. It was an easy sell: join the greatest political and economic union the Western world had ever seen, merely offer a daily prayer to Rome while retaining your old domestic gods, and grow fat on the fruits of globalisation. The alternative: a toxic cocktail of poverty, enslavement or death. The opulent mausoleums scattered across the pre-Saharan fringe of Roman Libya remind us today that even the primitive tribal Garamantes bought into the new world view. In the end, everyone signs.

With the Jews of ancient Israel, however, Rome had made a serious miscalculation – they would not blindly enter the wolves' lair. In AD 6 the emperor Augustus established the new Roman province of Judaea over land formerly ruled by Herod. From the very start, might was right. Rome failed to acknowledge the deep sensitivities of the local Jewish population.

From the day Pontius Pilate controversially carried Rome's legionary standards into Jerusalem, and dipped into the sacred Temple funds to build an aqueduct, violence was only ever one provocation away. The new coins minted in Israel carried pagan symbols of sacrifice, a source of daily revulsion to Judaism. Rome behaved just as she wished, with Felix Antonius, a lowly ex-slave forced by the emperor Claudius to turn procurator (AD 52–60), stealing the Herodian princess Drusilla from her husband and marrying her without converting to Judaism. The painful truth is that Roman aristocrats considered Judaea the soft option on the path to political promotion. Most governors were appointed through favour and patronage, not on merit. Lacking skills of negotiation and an understanding of Near Eastern customs, after serving in Judaea most governors like Pilate, Cumanus and Festus quickly disappeared from the pages of history. Most proved to be rotten eggs.

Yet these were minor complaints compared to the provocations of the megalomaniac emperor Gaius Caligula who, in AD 40, demanded that the High Priests erect his statue inside the Temple of Jerusalem as a living god. To enforce his demand, the emperor ordered Publius Petronius, governor of Syria, to march from Antioch to Jerusalem with three legions and Syrian auxiliaries. The full might of Rome was heading south. To the Jews this was a direct attack on monotheism and thus absolutely non-negotiable. To no avail they pointed out that sacrifices were already offered to Caligula and Rome twice a day, and grimly promised that 'if he would place the images among them, he must first sacrifice the whole Jewish nation' (*JW* 2.197). Caligula was unforgiving, and ordered anyone opposing his demands to be slain. Outright war was only avoided by the emperor's timely assassination in AD 41.

For a short time the inevitable was merely delayed. During Passover a Roman soldier guarding the Temple 'pulled back his garment, and cowering down after an indecent manner, turned his breech to the Jews' (*JW* 2.224). The Jews responded in time-honoured fashion by stoning the Romans, and in the subsequent Temple riot 10,000 Jews were trampled underfoot. Not long after, a soldier at Beth-Horen tore up a copy of the Jewish book of prayer, the Talmud, and threw it into a fire — shades of Nazi Germany 2,000 years later.

During the reign of the emperor Nero (AD 54–68) the Jews started to fragment into various seditious sects to combat the Roman presence. In particular, the Sicarii, knife-wielding assassins who killed for money, arose in Jerusalem with a deadly reputation for mingling with crowds during festivals and slaying people by stealth before silently vanishing back into the crowd. The Jewish revolution was born; the seditious called for Jews obeying the Roman way of life to be killed. The houses of great men were plundered and villages set on fire 'and this till all Judaea was filled with the effects of their madness' (*JW* 2.265).

Finally, in AD 66 Gessius Florus, Roman procurator of Judaea, 'blew up the war into a flame', according to Josephus, by seizing 17 talents from the sacred Temple treasure. When the inevitable anti-Roman riot erupted, Florus got his excuse to march on Jerusalem, where he plundered houses and killed the inhabitants of the Upper Market Place. Some 3,600 men, women and children were slain, according to Josephus, but Rome had now made its final irreversible mistake. These Jews included noblemen of the Roman equestrian order, previously allies.

Now the empire would have to contend with not just the mob, but also the more resourceful citizens of Judaea. Israel's Jews stopped paying tribute to Rome, a sign of a complete breakdown in political relations. Josephus is quite clear on the effects of these actions: 'And this was the true beginning of our war with the Romans; for they rejected the sacrifice of Caesar on this account' (*JW* 2.409).

In a wonderfully comic cameo in the Monty Python film, *Life of Brian*, a group of Jewish revolutionaries quietly plot against Rome in Jerusalem's amphitheatre when they are rudely interrupted by the hero and messiah-in-waiting, Brian, peddling Roman fast food: otters' noses, wrens' livers and badgers' spleens. In hushed, reverent tones, Brian enquires whether the schemers are the Judaean People's Front. The response is incredulous, with the leader literally spitting, 'We're the People's Front of Judaea.'

Although written for humorous effect, this scene faithfully reflects the confusion and tragedy that befell Jerusalem in AD 67–70. Fiction mirrors the sad reality of a Holy City fragmented into a web of hostile Jewish revolutionary groups. Each swore by its own High Priests, disregarding the legal line of succession. Over time inter-group alliances collapsed and re-formed, so when Titus arrived to besiege Jerusalem four sets of Jewish revolutionaries were locked in open warfare on the streets of the Holy City. Personal ambitions made a mockery of centuries-old tradition and loyalty. As Josephus explained, this was 'a sedition begotten by another sedition, and . . . like a wild beast grown mad, which from want of food from abroad, fell now upon eating its own flesh'. Internal revolution went a long way to weakening Israel militarily and politically, making Rome's task much easier. The empire could sit back and save energy while Jewish zealots slit Israel's wrists.

How did such an ungodly situation arise? With revolution quashed in the Galilee, Jerusalem's Jews were only too aware of the enemy might heading their way. New stories of Roman atrocities filtered into town by the hour. One logical response to such military pressure might have been to combine forces for a final showdown. Yet as gleaming Roman armour appeared on the horizon, the chasm dividing Jerusalem's Jews simply widened. This was not mere gentlemanly disagreement but entrenched civil war.

The direct seed of the Revolt in Jerusalem was the green-eyed monster – personal greed. In the 50s AD, members of the ruling class of Judaea exploited countrywide anarchy as an opportunity to increase their personal power at the expense of their friends. By AD 62 various gangs, such as the revolutionary party, the *poneroi*, led by the former High Priest Ananias, roamed Jerusalem like medieval warlords surrounded by their own court and private army.

The three most extreme factions dividing Jerusalem were controlled by Eleazor ben Simon, Simon ben Giora from Gerasa, and John of Gischala. For a year from spring 68 to 69, the city was run by a coalition of John, Eleazor and the Idumaeans, descendants of the Edomites forcibly converted to Judaism by the Hasmonaean kings. Eleazor may have been from solid priestly stock, but was removed from office by the High Priests and so subsequently joined the Zealot leadership. Unwilling to share power, however, he later split from the central Zealot group and set up a new camp within the inner court of the Temple, hanging his weapons over the holy gates in a public display of defiance.

John of Gischala was equally partisan. With a force of 6,000 men, 20 commanders and the support of a further 2,400 Zealots, he pursued a reign of terror between the Temple and as far south as the Ophel and the Kidron Valley.

Despite an acrimonious split with Eleazor, John eventually forced his old ally to reunite factions. During the Passover of AD 70, John's armed men managed to sneak into the Temple Mount and overpower Eleazor. But by now their constant bickering had allowed a third revolutionary to take over Jerusalem.

Simon was a splitter from the Zealot faction, whose reputation had been cemented when he successfully attacked the rearguard of Cestius Gallus, governor of Syria, in AD 66 and seized the imperial baggage. Through this display of courage he attracted the respect of establishment figures. He quietly trained up an army in the citadel of Nain and amongst the cave networks of Pheretae in the Judaean Hills. By October AD 66, Simon controlled 10,000 men and 50 commanders backed up by a further 5,000 Idumaeans. His anarchic band of men terrorised the Upper City of Jerusalem and the Acra district of the lower city. To the general Jewish population Simon and the Zealots were 'a greater terror to the people than the Romans themselves' (*JW* 4.558). Between spring AD 69 and the destruction of the Temple in the summer of AD 70, he forged a position as the leading commander of an independent State of Israel.

The general populace of Jerusalem was disgusted by the chaos in its midst. Thus, Jesus son of Gamala denounced the revolutionaries:

The scum and offscourings of the whole country, after squandering their own means and exercising their madness first upon the surrounding villages and towns, these pests have ended by stealthily streaming into the holy city: brigands of such rank impiety as to pollute even that hallowed ground [the Temple], they may be seen now recklessly intoxicating themselves in the sanctuary and expending the spoils of their slaughtered victims upon their insatiable bellies. (*JW* 4. 241–3)

Such was the anarchic madness polluting Jerusalem when Titus arrived at the gates of the city in spring AD 70. Three different leaders, three different armies dividing the Jews, one faith. Within six months the ambitions of all three warlords would be strangled by Rome; John would be sentenced to life imprisonment and Simon executed in the Eternal City the following year.

20

Turning the Screw

B Y THE TIME Titus was ready to strike, Jerusalem badly needed a respite. Families were bitterly divided by factional infighting, father pitted against son. Bloodshed coated the ancient city. Now, with morale low, the exhausted Jewish armies were about to receive a rude reality check.

The battle for Jerusalem was amongst the bloodiest in recorded history. The Jewish revolutionaries proved immensely stubborn, refusing honourable surrender and Rome's hand of peace. More crucially, the eyes of the world were focused on the Holy City. Vespasian may have been dispatched to Israel with a reputation for hard dealing and for bringing troublesome provinces to heel, but by the time of the siege of Jerusalem he was emperor of the entire Roman Empire. Priorities had changed. Vespasian was back in Rome sweet-talking the Senate and putting the imperial house in order after years of abuse under Nero. Titus, alone, was left to mop up Jerusalem.

The Flavian dynasty now on the throne had been elevated to power by nothing other than diligence. Farmers by background, Vespasian's ancestors had no military pedigree, no aristocratic history. So the new emperor desperately needed a foundation myth to solidify his claim to fame. And Israel, with the huge prize of Jerusalem and the Temple of the Jews, was the perfect opportunity for a propaganda coup. Time and circumstance had dealt the Jews an unlucky hand of cards. With a shattering victory essential, Titus marched out of the coastal port of Caesarea with four legionary forces, bolstered by Syrian auxiliaries familiar with the local terrain. The sight of the greatest force ever assembled in ancient Israel must have been terrifying.

In theory, the logistics of taking Jerusalem were a nightmare. The city was protected by three walls and built on two hills divided by

a valley. Even if he managed to punch a hole through these fortifications, the invader still had to contend with the daunting Antonia
Tower, the brainchild of King Herod to protect the Temple and his
own palace complex. The tower was impenetrable, perched 25 metres
up a rocky precipice and built of seamless, polished stone to complicate assault. Four towers protected the fort's corners, one soaring 35
metres into the heavens.

Poorly led and disenchanted, the divided Jews were unprepared for
a long siege. Once again, Titus could rely on Josephus' inside information on the city's layout to draw up battle lines. Since offering his
military and geographic knowledge to Vespasian after being captured
during the battle for Jotapata in the Galilee in July AD 67, the former
Jewish commander had proved invaluable to his new masters. Rome's
engines of war – enormous platforms equipped with battering rams
and archer emplacements – were instruments of pure fear. Some 25
metres high and iron-plated, they went about their mischief, pounding walls with a torturous thud day in, day out. The first city wall fell
after fifteen days, the second wall only five days later.

With the military operation proceeding to plan, Titus started the
psychological war. His soldiers caught, whipped and crucified up to 500
Jews a day. From rage and spite, Roman soldiers amused themselves by
nailing the prisoners in different positions until so many bodies lined
the approach to the old city that wood for crosses ran out. Next Titus
ordered the hands of prisoners to be cut off and sent to John of Gischala
and Simon ben Giora, now united in fighting Rome. These brutal
measures had one main objective: to scare the city into surrender.

Once the outer walls were levelled, only the Antonia Tower stood
between Rome and the ultimate goal, the Temple, the beating heart of
Israel and Judaism. Four mighty siege banks were built against the tower
to the north. Jewish forces retaliated by undermining the banks and
smearing the timbers with inflammable pitch and bitumen, only then
burning down the siege ramps which had taken the Roman engineers
seventeen days to complete. For the first time, the Roman troops were
downcast. The tower would not yield, so Titus changed tack and
decided to play the waiting game. If he couldn't get into Jerusalem, the
Jews would not get out. He started building a new city wall guarded by
thirteen towers. The townsfolk were now prisoners in their own city.

Inside Jerusalem, dignity was in short supply. Daily survival was a battle. Even at the start of the siege stacks of corn had been worryingly low. The Roman army scorched Israel's wheatfields, and the Jews did themselves no favours by setting fire to the city's grain reserves during factional infighting. The grip of Rome intensified and famine incited grim tragedies of survival. Jewish revolutionaries tortured the lower classes into revealing their secret stashes of food, while mothers snatched morsels from the mouths of their own babies. Old men were dragged through the streets, and fellow citizens stabbed with sharp stakes until they revealed the location of any food they may have concealed. Josephus condemned this behaviour particularly strongly, concluding:

> no other city ever endured such miseries, nor since the world began has there been a generation more prolific in crime. Indeed they ended up actually disparaging the Hebrew race . . . and owned themselves, what indeed they were, slaves, the dregs of society and the bastard scum of the nation. It was they who overthrew the city, and compelled the reluctant Romans to register so melancholy a triumph, and all but attracted to the temple the tardy flames. (*JW* 5.442–4)

If Josephus was reporting fact – and both historical and archaeological evidence exists to back up his testimony – then the actions of the rebel mob during the siege of Jerusalem marked a terrible descent into barbarity. The city turned into an endless 'kind of deadly night'. Multi-storeyed houses became charnel houses for the dead. The distress of the famine turned the town crazy. Some Jews staggered through the streets like mad dogs in search of sustenance. Others searched the sewers and dunghills for scraps of food, gratefully chewing even a blade of grass like cattle. When even these scraps ran out, belts, shoes and leather became fair game.

Even this desperation seemed tame compared to one particular atrocity, whose notoriety resonated across the entire Roman Empire. Mary, the daughter of Eleazor from the village of Bethezuba, fled into Jerusalem from her rustic villa as the wrath of Rome swept south. Because she was renowned for her good family and fortune, the Jewish rebels lost no time plundering her home in Jerusalem and raiding her kitchen every day, almost as if in sport. Rather than kill her, though, her tormentors preferred to toy with her by demanding daily meals. When stocks were exhausted, she committed the ultimate sin. Believing that 'famine is forestalling slavery, and more cruel than both are the rebels', she slew her infant son and roasted his body.

After eating half she saved the remainder for the rebels, who were paralysed with horror at the evil they had inspired. Soon the city was abuzz with the latest tale of urban atrocity. Titus was appalled to learn of this cannibalism. There and then he swore to bury this accursed memory beneath the ruins of the country 'and would not leave upon the face of the earth, for the sun to behold, a city in which mothers were thus fed' (*JW* 6.217). Such was the psychological reality of the war raging in battleground Jerusalem, AD 70.

With such terror and bestiality tearing apart the fabric of society it is hardly surprising that Jewish revolutionaries occasionally lost their grip on the bigger picture. At one such moment of vulnerability, twelve Roman soldiers, a trumpeter and a standard bearer from the Fifth Legion crept into the Antonia Tower and cut the throats of the Jewish guards.

Titus lost no time ripping out the tower's earthen defensive banks to forge a safe passage for the Roman army to the very edge of the Temple. Once again, the Romans attacked the Temple guards by night. Four banks were thrown up over the corners, gates and cloisters. From here, the capture of Jerusalem literally hinged on the lighting of a match. Titus and his generals chose to smoke out the Jews: the Temple gates were far too heavy to succumb to Rome's battering rams. Swords drawn, the soldiers waited to pounce while silver door-plating melted around their sandals.

Josephus dated the final assault on the Temple of Jerusalem to 30 August, traditionally the day when Solomon's Temple was burnt to the ground by the Babylonians in 586 BC. The implication is that the end was fated: a Roman soldier, without orders, 'but moved by some supernatural impulse', flung a burning timber through a low doorway leading to the northern side of the sanctuary. The Temple blazed, the Roman troops enthusiastically plundered its treasury, and the Jewish army was decimated. All the priests could do was tear golden spikes off the sanctuary wall and hurl them pathetically at the Romans. The air was thick with the war cries of legions, the howls of the rebels and the shrieks of the dying. Finally, the people of Jerusalem were all reduced to the same class and status. As Josephus confirmed, 'No pity was shown for age, no reverence for rank; children and greybeards, laity and priests alike were massacred' (*JW* 6.271).

The Temple, spiritual heart of Judaism, was lost. The Romans carried their standards into its court and offered sacrifices; Titus then gave his troops permission to burn and sack the city. The Archives building went up in smoke and with it hundreds of years of Jewish history. A similar fate befell the council-chamber and the palace of Queen Helena, a Jewish convert and ruler of the kingdom of Adiabene in Mesopotamia.

Finally, the Jewish forces deserted the impregnable Acra Fortress in the Upper City and its huge towers, Hippicus, Phasael and Mariamme, whose walls were so thick that they were capable of defying every engine of war known to man. On 26 September, AD 70, Titus was master of all Jerusalem and raised Rome's standards along the towers. From this lofty height, the belly of Jerusalem was exposed beneath him. The strength of the towers, the size of their masonry and the accuracy of their seams amazed Titus. While he gladly burnt the rest of Jerusalem to a crisp, the Roman warlord left the Acra towers standing as a symbol of Rome's omnipotence.

21

Death of a Temple

THE 140-DAY SIEGE of Jerusalem changed the face of the world. By feeding the fires of sedition and civil war, Israel fell on its own sword. Upper-class avarice and arrogance brought a tidal wave of death and destruction to the land. Between 600,000 and 1.1 million Jews are said by Tacitus and Josephus to have been killed during the fighting. Another 17,000 were dispatched to a life of hard labour in Egypt's mines and a further 700 shipped to Rome as stage props for the Triumph of Vespasian and Titus and a grim end in the amphitheatre.

Rome's razing to the ground of Jerusalem was meticulous. Gone were the Temple, religious sacrifice, the homeland. The legend of the wandering Jew was born, and the stereotype of the Jewish people as easy prey and social scapegoats would endure until the United Nations voted to recognise Palestine as the State of Israel in 1948. Early Christianity, the son of Judaism, was also flushed out of the land, relocating to the shores of the River Tiber in Italy, where it would establish deep roots to become a global religion. Without the fall of Jerusalem, Christianity would never have been free to soar to such lofty heights.

In April 2005, I stared across Jerusalem from the top of the Acra Tower in the Upper City. Of its original three towers, only Phasael still stands. This sole beacon is the only major ancient landmark to survive the events of AD 70. Tracing the excavated outline of the first-century AD Jewish city wall, my eye was caught by a dense cluster of stone ballista catapult balls abandoned in the fortress corner. The landscape and atmosphere of AD 70, however, is long gone.

Jerusalem has been intensively explored since the nineteenth century, from Edward Robinson's discovery in 1838 of an arched pier at the southern tip of the western Herodian Temple wall to Professor

Nachman Avigad's excavations of the Jewish Quarter in 1969–83. All this fieldwork has exposed one clear truth: Titus really did impose a scorched earth policy on Jerusalem, devastating the old city with fire. Today hardly a vestige remains of Herod's Temple Mount.

From the summit of the Acra Fortress I surveyed the same battle lines as Titus examined in September AD 70. From here Titus gave the order to raze the city to its bones. The rectangular box-like girdle that surrounded the Temple Mount in the first century AD still dominates Jerusalem, but within these walls not one piece of masonry survives from the Second Temple. I turned towards Robinson's Arch and the street it used to span, a main thoroughfare once abuzz with markets, shops and screaming urchins. The original paving slabs of the street have been uncovered and above them the silent witness of Titus' resolve: three-ton blocks of white stone thrown down from the Mount by Roman engineers systematically dismantling the hulking exterior of the Temple. These stones are taller than men and offer a hint of the Temple's former splendour.

Beyond Robinson's Arch, along the outer edge of the southern perimeter Temple wall, Professor Benjamin Mazar exposed the main staircase entrance sweeping up towards the Huldah Gates, still visible today as ghostly blocked doorways with semi-circular arches. A series of first-century AD *mikvehs* reminds us where Jews were obliged to purify their bodies before approaching God's Temple. Although immaculately landscaped today, an appropriate collage of Jewish, Christian and Islamic monuments, the bustle of life 2,000 years ago is sadly long gone.

From my vantage point I enjoyed a perfect spring day. A light breeze licked the flag of Israel planted on top of David's Citadel, fluttering across the city. Israeli schoolchildren ran along the fortress walls, apparently more interested in playing at Crusaders than Judas Maccabeus, Flavius Josephus or Simon ben Giora. It was time to leave Israel, but one question still disturbed me: why did Titus go to such lengths to put Jerusalem to the torch?

In general, Rome didn't believe in the wholesale erasure of foreign civilisations. Using a friendly local king, they preferred to crucify and enslave a few leaders, but to leave the infrastructure of state intact to serve the long-term interests of the empire. Josephus ascribed the destruction of the Temple to an appalling mistake by an ill-disciplined, over-eager soldier.

Resting in his tent at this time, Titus is said to have sprinted to the Temple like a man possessed. Amongst the din of clashing swords and burning timbers, the soldiers pretended not to hear his order to extinguish the flames, but continued slinging firebrands into the Temple. Liberalius, the centurion of Titus' bodyguard of lancers, was even ordered, allegedly, to restrain his men with clubs. Jerusalem in summer was a tinderbox and the fire was uncontrollable. While Titus was trying to restrain his forces, a soldier shoved a firebrand into the Temple gate hinge. 'Thus, against Caesar's wishes, was the temple set on fire,' concluded Josephus.

Rome had nothing to gain by decapitating Israel. The land was geographically diverse and immensely fertile, rich in wheat, olives and grapes. The Sea of Galilee yielded exquisite fish and the Dead Sea lands all manner of luxury produce. By restoring order, Rome could encourage specialised production and collect a massive slice of the pie. Exactly like today, taxation greased the wheels of society and was the foundation of domestic and foreign policy. So why burn Jerusalem to a crisp?

On no less than five occasions during the siege Titus allegedly called a halt to the clash of steel and offered Jerusalem's Jewish leaders the hand of peace. At one stage Josephus himself was sent out to deliver a diatribe about the futility of resistance against an invincible force, stressing that the legacy of Judaism stretching back to the Exodus from Egypt was now in jeopardy. Quoting common Roman policy, Josephus reminded his people that 'the Romans are but demanding the customary tribute . . . Once they obtain this, they neither sack the city, nor touch the holy things, but grant you everything else, the freedom of your families, the enjoyment of your possessions, and the protection of your sacred laws' (*JW* 5.405–6).

During a conference of war with his six generals, many Roman commanders expressed their opinion to Titus that, being used as a base for warfare, the Temple was technically a fortress and thus fit for legal attack. Despite these logical appeals, again we are told that Titus refused to 'wreak vengeance on inanimate objects instead of men, nor under any circumstances burn down so magnificent a work' (*JW* 6.241).

The image of Titus as a sympathetic commander cornered into action has filtered down over the centuries. Once the Temple was razed, the emperor's son was solemn rather than relieved:

> contrasting the sorry scene of desolation before his eyes with the former splendour of the city . . . he commiserated its destruction; not boasting, as another might have done, of having carried so glorious and great a city by storm, but heaping curses upon the criminal authors of the revolt, who had brought this chastisement upon it: so plainly did he show that he could never have wished that the calamities attending their punishment should enhance his own deserts. (*JW* 7.112–13)

If the destruction of the Jewish Temple, one of the wonders of the ancient world, brought Titus no pleasure, how did he feel about the treasure inside? The fledgling Flavian dynasty's attitude to this prospect would prove to be a completely different matter.

22

Flavian Spin

THE JEWS OF first-century AD Israel had personally induced the collapse of their biblical world by exercising a lack of social, political and religious flexibility. Josephus presents Titus and the Roman military machine as bending over backwards to offer the besieged Jews the chance of an honourable surrender and of preserving their former lifestyle. But the fate of the Holy City was really sealed because Simon ben Giora, John of Gischala and Eleazor refused to accept the same terms of peace offered to all other citizens of the vast Roman world stretching from Britain to Arabia – a fatal loss of vision and judgement. They also failed completely to manage the Roman threat by selfishly playing internal power games, which reduced the land to anarchy and civil war.

Under normal circumstances we can be sure that Rome would not have destroyed such a central symbol of religion as the Temple of Jerusalem. This was not how the empire played foreign politics. Their objective was control, not ethnic cleansing. The years of the First Jewish Revolt were strange times, however. To begin with, Rome made a profound mistake in assuming that Israel and its Jewish ethnic majority would follow the way of other nations. In this the empire failed to gauge how deeply religion and culture permeated society and just how incompatible was the doctrine of monotheism with Rome's own pantheon of different gods, who could be shuffled about to deal with all manner of situations and circumstances.

Of all the nations eventually conquered by Rome, only two cultures clashed terminally: the Jews of Israel and the far smaller demographic group of druids in Gaul and Britain. The emperor Tiberius outlawed druidism by decree, forcing its long-bearded priests into hiding and to preach from caves and woods. Rather like the Jews, whose Sabbath rituals and laws of purity were alien to many Mediterranean people, the druids were accused of carrying out human sacrifice and of being cannibals. In reality, they were teachers and interpreters of Celtic law and experts in philosophy and astronomy. Within traditional European Iron Age society, the druids were the principal teachers of wisdom and the judges responsible for legal interpretation and arbitration – just like Israel's High Priests.

Despite this cultural incompatibility, Rome's textbook procedure was always to restore the peace, encourage and control the economy: tried and tested imperial house cleaning. But plead as Titus did, the Jewish revolutionaries would not agree to peaceful coexistence. No alternative was left him but the eradication of the Land of Israel and its major troublemakers. So were the destruction of the Second Temple and the seizure of its treasures inevitable?

———◆———

On a Friday morning in April 2005 I left the crazy circus of Jerusalem and headed west towards the coast. I had a nagging suspicion that the final days of the siege were not as arbitrary as Josephus claimed. Did the freak throw of a burning firebrand really destroy the Temple; was it really lost by the saddest of accidents? Something didn't add up.

My destination was Caesarea, the chief maritime gateway into ancient Israel between the late first century BC and the early seventh century AD. This was where I believed the Temple treasure was kept under heavy guard until it was exported to Rome from the city's majestic quays. With its ruined Roman aqueducts marching into town from the north and the submerged port lying 10 metres beneath the waves – a casualty of seismic subsidence – the site of ancient Caesarea is endlessly fascinating and romantic. Each year a little more of the city is excavated and another chapter in the port's great history written.

Driving along the Sharon Plain, ancient Judaea's roaming wheat lands, I imagined the lie of the land in AD 70. As far as the eye could see, a ragged exodus would have been under way, a scene that would echo down the ages to be replayed across the killing fields of Europe from the early 1930s to 1945. Long lines of Jews, impoverished, emaciated and dispossessed, shuffled across the horizon. The great Temple of Jerusalem was razed to the ground, families had been brutally torn apart, and now the people of Judaea had been exiled from their own heartland, expelled from Jerusalem. To the thin hill air and fragrant fields of the Galilee the dispossessed marched towards a new home, where spiritual wounds would be licked and slowly healed over time. At the right hand of his father Vespasian, Titus had not only killed thousands of zealots, he had wiped out one of the most learned and sophisticated cultures of antiquity – or so he believed.

I swung west off the Tel Aviv to Haifa highway and noted how great swathes of coastal sand dunes had been chewed up by urban development since my last visit. Caesarea is one of Israel's most buoyant playgrounds for the rich and famous, just as in antiquity, and each year its villa quarter encroaches a little further on the ancient ruins.

This was the modern economic reality, but I wanted to explore the economics of ancient Roman Caesarea. Ditching my hire car by the Byzantine esplanade, where headless statues of emperors preside over a fifth-century AD marketplace, I walked down to the beach through the Crusader gateway, past colossal columns and sprawling Roman warehouses.

Sebastos, the port of Caesarea, was the world's first artificial harbour, a state-of-the-art facility into which Herod poured much of his life's savings. It would certainly have been the largest and most reliable port city from which to dispatch spoils of war. Titus' reliance on Caesarea as his naval base in the battle for Israel is also implicit in Josephus: 'On the return of Caesar [Titus] to Caesarea-on-sea, Simon was brought to him in chains, and he ordered the prisoner to be kept for the triumph which he was preparing to celebrate in Rome.' If the human cargo intended for the Triumph was already in Caesarea, there is every reason to expect the Temple treasure to have passed through the city. Having just demolished Herod's Temple in Jerusalem, Rome was now using his port to ship the loot and symbols of a vanquished state west to the Eternal City.

Sitting on the end of the breakwater I stared out over the Mediterranean. Arab fishermen idled the day away in the forlorn hope of a catch. There is little chance here: the fishing grounds were over-exploited before the 1960s and have never recovered. By contrast, in the first century AD Vespasian knew Israel to be ripe for the picking and must have made a pact with his son whereby the destruction of Jerusalem was inevitable. The burning of the Temple was probably regretted in Rome, but the looting of its treasuries was coldly calculated and deliberate.

What started as misfortune ended in personal glory for Vespasian. He is alleged to have got the call to lead the Roman forces against Israel by bad luck. Having committed the ultimate sin of falling asleep during one of Nero's poetry performances, he was refused permission to pay his respects at the palace the following day. Soon after, he found himself shipped off to an uncertain future in the mosquito-infested backwaters of the eastern Mediterranean. Little could he have guessed how fate would unfold.

Vespasian was born in a small hamlet in the Sabine countryside, the hill country north-east of Rome renowned for olives, herbs and cattle raising. His lineage was far from noble, and throughout his life he would be teased about his rustic accent. Even though one descendant, T. Flavius Petro of Reate, had fought as a centurion for the Republicans at Pharsalus in 48 BC, he had been reported for cowardice in fleeing the battlefield. At best, Vespasian's father, T. Flavius Sabinus, may have achieved the post of leading centurion in a military legion. Sabinus was also something of an entrepreneur, a moneylender in the Helvetian region of Lake Geneva, into which Rome was fast expanding and where new opportunities were arising. Commercial awareness would later stand his son in good stead.

Vespasian was hardly an eager political player in his early years. His elder brother had long received the *latus clavus* (broad tunic stripe), the 'badge' of membership of the senatorial order. But Vespasian was indifferent to politics, and only got his act together when his mother teased him for becoming his brother's footman.

During his early political career he served on the so-called Board of Twenty, probably in the unglamorous but practical position of head of street cleaning in Rome. At this stage of his career the emperor Gaius Caligula noticed thick mud in an alley and ordered it to be thrown over Vespasian's toga for his failure to do his job properly. New ambitions started to burn in the face of such public humiliation.

At the age of twenty-four Vespasian stood for senatorial office before being sent to Crete. By the age of thirty-nine he was elected to the praetorship, and now had the right to command armies. Yet even as he was progressing up the political ladder, money worries forced him to return home to work in the family mule business. His nickname, the 'muleteer', gave little indication of his future imperial aspirations. In AD 41, Vespasian's career took him abroad to the Rhine and then Britain.

Despite an impressive portfolio of experience, Vespasian continued to pull the short straw. On drawing lots in AD 62 for his proconsulship he landed the unpopular tenure of Africa, where turnips were thrown at him at Hadrumetum in Tunisia for failing to prevent a food shortage. However, by the time he was commanding three legions in Judaea, the Flavian dynasty was enjoying significant power and prestige. His brother was also Prefect of Rome.

When Vespasian went to command the complicated but winnable war in Israel, he was simply a servant of the empire; a few years later he would return as the most powerful man in the world. The end of the 60s AD were years of confusion and tyranny. After the dreaded Nero committed suicide, Servius Sulpicius Galba, governor of Hispania Tarraconensis in Spain, was appointed his successor. But before Vespasian could even send his son, Titus, back to Rome to salute the new emperor, Galba was butchered in the middle of the Roman marketplace and Marius Salvius Otho, governor of Lusitania in Portugal, had seized power. Simultaneously, Aulus Vitellius Germanicus, commander of Germania Inferior, proclaimed himself emperor and the empire was at war in turmoil and disorder. After losing the battle of Betriacum, Otho committed suicide. Never before had Rome experienced anything like the Year of the Four Emperors in AD 68–9.

Not far south of where I sat by the sea at Caesarea stand the hulking walls of a Roman amphitheatre. Here the first-century Roman garrison took up residence, and it was probably here that Vespasian was declared emperor by his commanders and soldiers in AD 69. The empire was in chaos and needed a stable and strong ruler to take the reins. With his humble background Vespasian initially refused the offer. When his commanders drew their swords and threatened to kill him unless he agreed, Vespasian reluctantly accepted.

This startling turn of events may sound fortuitous, but imperial ambitions had awoken in Vespasian soon after he arrived in Judaea. His accession was well planned and immaculately timed. In reality, he was first proclaimed emperor in Alexandria on 1 July, AD 69, with the support of its governor, Tiberius Alexander, and his two legions. With its copious wheatfields, Egypt was crucial to Rome; control Egypt and you possessed the breadbasket of the empire – and the allegiance of its people. It was only ten days later that the supposedly spontaneous proclamation was made at Caesarea, 535 kilometres north of Alexandria. By 15 July all of Syria had hailed him as emperor. By the last week of December, AD 69, Vespasian was back in Rome on the imperial throne and Vitellius the pretender decapitated. The commander of the First Jewish Revolt was now lord of the inhabited world.

Even though Josephus portrays these events as due merely to the throw of the dice, Vespasian and his cronies had harboured these ambitions for many months. How did this dramatic turn of the tide affect Israel, and what instructions were left with Titus for dealing with Jerusalem? The two Flavians must have engaged in dialogue deep into the night, no doubt right here in Caesarea from where Vespasian then sailed to Rome and from where Titus marched to bring Jerusalem to its knees.

For Vespasian and Titus there were two pressing priorities: the need of the new dynasty for a propaganda coup and hard cash. With no ancestral history to reinforce the Flavians' claim to the throne, a great military victory was required. Vespasian had the support of the army and, with his humble no-nonsense background, also of the populace. But this would not be enough to establish a dynasty and to see his sons accede to the throne in later years. Suddenly, events in Judaea were crucial to the Flavians – the destruction of Jerusalem and the Temple would legitimise their right to rule down the generations. Every leader has his own defining moment – 31 BC and the battle of Actium for Octavian (the future emperor Augustus), 1066 and the battle of Hastings for William the Conqueror, and 1805 and the battle of Trafalgar for Horatio Nelson and England. The battle for Jerusalem would be Vespasian's ultimate claim to fame.

The Roman historical commentator Tacitus described the times preceding the rise of Vespasian as 'rich in disasters, terrible with battles, torn by civil struggles, horrible even in peace'. Once on the throne, however, he added that the new emperor 'purged the whole world of evil'. Despite his slow start in life, and possibly because of the wealth of military and commercial experience accumulated on his journey, Vespasian was not only an accomplished military general, he was also an astute politician.

Modern politicians consider themselves the masters of political spin, spending fortunes on advertising campaigns that spread subliminal messages and soundbites across the land into the front rooms of the electorate. Perhaps they might be humbled to learn that Vespasian cracked this art 2,000 years ago. With his proclamation as emperor, the Flavian propaganda machine swung into action. Vespasian, and hence the Flavian dynasty, would be 'branded' as the team that harnessed chaos and brought *pax*, peace, to the world.

Soon after 1 July, AD 69, Vespasian ordered coins be struck bearing the words PACIS EVENTVS (The Coming of Peace). The Roman Empire enjoyed a global economy, and the same coins used in London were common currency as far away as the Jordanian port of Aqaba, gateway to the Red Sea. This was Vespasian's way of broadcasting his message and intent. By the middle of his reign, the emperor's coins simply stated PAX. Peace had arrived, and with a bust of Vespasian on the coin's reverse, the world knew who was responsible.

Throughout the first century AD, the Roman Empire had tackled several irritating insurrections in Britain, Germany, Gaul and Syria. All were suppressed without any of the fanfare of the First Jewish Revolt. But the sack of Jerusalem would be the Flavians' major claim to fame, and the defeat had to be packaged as something much more than a bare-knuckle fight. The destruction of the Jews had to be portrayed as a global event orchestrated by great leaders. Suetonius tells us that Vespasian famously boasted to the Roman Senate that 'My sons will succeed me or no one will', and the First Jewish Revolt would be the dominant argument for Flavian rule and succession.

This was bad luck for the Jews, who found themselves troublemakers in the wrong place at the wrong time. Vespasian pursued a sweeping set of measures to boost the Flavian image, not least ensuring that his accession was presented to the world as fated. Among the eleven supernatural explanations given by Suetonius for Vespasian's claim to power was the tale of a statue of Julius Caesar on Tiber Island, Rome, that turned from west to east, pointing towards the region from where the new ruler and peace would emanate.

Yet, at least in the short term, the most effective piece of propaganda was the minting of a remarkable series of silver coins bearing a bound Jewish prisoner in front of a palm tree, symbol of Judaea, his arms tied behind his back, with a Jewish woman crying at his feet. Arms and armour of the defeated Jew lie abandoned in the background. The Latin text inscribed around the scene reads JUDAEA CAPTA: Judaea Captured. This popular piece of Flavian propaganda, minted continuously over a twelve-year period, left no member of the empire unaware of where peace originated and who created it.

Stage-managing propaganda was one matter, implementing a grand strategy quite another. Without a massive injection of cash to pay for the new image, the Flavian brand would remain hollow. Where could Vespasian get his hands on a king's ransom? The issue was elementary for the imperial schemers, as father and son discussed the matter 2,000 years ago at Caesarea while enjoying the same view as me. Both knew from various government reports that the Temple of Jerusalem was loaded. It had to fall.

In his *Natural History*, Pliny the Elder, a contemporary of Vespasian, described Flavian Rome as a city enjoying

> the immeasurable majesty of the Roman peace, a gift of the gods, who, it seems, have made the Romans a second sun in human affairs. And all the wonders of the world have been matched in Rome itself over its 800 years' history: the buildings it has accumulated are enough to make another world, and of these the culmination is the Temple of Peace itself. (*Natural History* 27.3)

In other words, Vespasian and the Flavian dynasty transformed the architectural face of Rome. This was another essential strategy. By AD 67 the greed and poor financial acumen of the emperor Nero had bankrupted the Eternal City. War in Asia Minor from AD 54 to 63 and in Britain during AD 60–61 had diminished the imperial gold reserves. The army was behind in paying its soldiers – a fatal omission. To make matters worse, Rome itself looked tattered, its marble veneer streaked black by the great fire of AD 64. Despite this serious predicament, Nero had continued to please himself with gross extravagance: costly leisure pursuits, a tour of Greece, theatrical performances, racing, and palace building. His selfish pursuit of personal gratification traversed the Mediterranean, where he ransacked provinces in search of the finest works of art, which he imported for his palace in Rome for his own pleasure, not for the entertainment of the people.

To finance his public relations campaign and the rebuilding of Rome, Vespasian needed to raid the Temple of Jerusalem. As many assets as possible had to be liquidated – and fast. The new emperor estimated that 4,000 million sesterces were required to restore the state's fortunes, the equivalent of about £2.25 billion in today's terms. The annual taxation of the provinces yielded 800 million sesterces (£452 million). Thus, the equivalent of five years' revenue was urgently needed. Back in Italy, Vespasian was already liquidating public property and increasing rates of taxation. New census programmes were initiated in Egypt and Gaul to determine the empire's productive capability, and mines previously considered exhausted were reopened as imperial concerns, especially in gold- and lead-rich Spain.

In Judaea, Vespasian continued the asset stripping. Rich Jewish estates were sold to the highest bidder and the Jewish tax that previously went to the Temple authorities was now diverted as an annual poll tax, the *fiscus judaicus*, to the Temple of Capitoline Jupiter in Rome. Free Jewish males aged between twenty and fifty, women up to sixty-two years of age and children aged three or more, paid 8 sesterces. If the Jewish population across the Roman Empire totalled five to six million, a new tax windfall of 40–48 million sesterces was created (£22–27 million).

Despite these swift initiatives, there was still nothing like enough cash. The Temple treasure of the Jews, however, was a godsend, the answer to all Vespasian's prayers. A demand for ready cash was the main reason why, ultimately, Jerusalem had to fall. Titus' overtures for a peaceful surrender were honest; the Jews' inflexibility cost them their lives, liberty and homeland. Titus had no preconceived plans to burn down the Temple and raze it to the ground. The Temple treasure, however, was another matter. Rome needed the Jewish treasure chest – this was non-negotiable.

Caesarea was the main witness to this budgetary policymaking: the base of the Roman army; the headquarters of Vespasian and Titus; the port from where the Temple treasure – and, with it, the extinguished hopes of a lost people – sailed over the horizon to Rome. As I stared out to sea, I picked out dark shadows deep offshore: the submerged and subdued Roman breakwaters that sank beneath the waves 2,000 years ago. Caesarea was built along a seismic fault line, a geological problem of which King Herod was ignorant. In the end it didn't matter how much money he threw at the world's first purely artificial port in 22 BC. The project was doomed from the very beginning. The sea sighed at the futility of Herod's soured dream.

Similarly, Vespasian and Rome would realise that it is in the nature of civilisations that all crests of the wave are succeeded by deep troughs. However much money Vespasian lavished on sculpting his dreams and honing his image, a fall was brewing over the distant horizon. Would the Jewish Temple treasure of Jerusalem, one of the greatest artistic and spiritual legacies of man, survive that fall? Or, in a fit of economic desperation, were the gold menorah, the Table of the Divine Presence and the silver trumpets to be thrown into the melting pot, crudely liquidated to help build a new Rome?

Before looking so far ahead, I needed to focus on the immediate fate of the Temple treasure in AD 71.

Imperial Rome

23

Walking with God

ITALY IN SPRING is an absolute delight with its alluring sunshine, flowers in bloom and lightly caressing winds – the scents of promise. As my plane banked over Rome's Campiano airport in May 2005, a smattering of blood-red poppies stained motorway lay-bys, quarry edges and back yards, welcoming us to Arcadia. Rome's ancient agricultural ideals reverberate in the modern day in the form of giant circular haystacks lying idly between runways like huge organic column drums. Gypsies kicked a football across the ancient cornfields, where they were encamped close to the primary artery of communication. The geography mirrored that of Rome's ancient foreigners, who dwelt along the southern banks of the River Tiber, the bustling 'airport' of antiquity, where wooden ships served the role of modern aeroplanes.

My plans for Rome were simple, but ambitious: to try and reconstruct the route of Vespasian and Titus' Triumph in AD 71 (would any of the ancient landmarks even survive, I wondered?); to get a sense of the atmosphere, gravity, excitement and sorrow of that fateful day; to find out what it was like to be a foreigner in ancient Rome, an alien in an imperial society defined by its oppression of barbarians; and to locate the Temple of Peace, where the emperor Vespasian put Jerusalem's Temple treasure on show as war booty and an eternal expression of Rome's status as the global superpower. In truth, I was not especially confident. After all, no one had taken on this daunting task for nearly two thousand years.

The quest would succeed or founder on my ability to relocate several key monuments, major ancient highlights of the spectacular Triumph described in Josephus' original text: the Temple of Isis; Octavian's Walks; the Gate of the Pomp; a cluster of theatres; the

Temple of Jupiter Capitolinus; and finally the Temple of Peace. Each ancient landmark illuminates a path to a subsequent clue. With my copy of Josephus' *Jewish War*, medieval and modern maps, and numerous photocopies of scholarly literature, I wasted no time before pounding the streets of Rome.

•—◆—•

The Triumph of the emperor Vespasian and his son, Titus, was the greatest of the 320 or so that Rome ever celebrated. The event was a meticulously planned piece of theatre, deliberately staged around moments of high drama and spectacle steeped in symbolism. As I explored the back streets of Rome, piecing together the route of the Triumph of AD 71, and as astonishing snapshots of the ancient Triumphal Way emerged from amongst the hybrid collage of Rome's architecture – the new recycling the old – I was bowled over by Rome's tight planning. Timing, locations, scenery and actors – nothing was left to chance.

Specific gods whose spirits hovered over the fourteen quarters of the city were courted in their temples of worship before celebrations could commence. Unlike modern cities, whose various districts are characterised primarily by function (retail, residential or municipal), the citizens of Rome referred to its individual quarters according to the nature of their resident gods. When the Triumph snaked boisterously across the Field of Mars, hugging the Capitoline Hill and then entering the Forum itself, the gods local to each district had to be appeased by prayer and sacrifice. In AD 71 this directive was adhered to as if the planners suffered from an obsessive-compulsive disorder. To neglect a god was to awaken and set loose harmful spirits. Similarly, the architects of the Triumph selected historical landmarks both for their visual impact and their symbolic effect on the expectant hordes enjoying a Roman holiday at the emperor's expense.

Although Vespasian and Titus were each technically entitled to separate Triumphs by decree of the Roman Senate, they chose to share the honour, cleverly realising that this would double the pomp and ceremony. The night before the great day, the formalities started. Josephus claims the entire city turned out, so that within its walls 'not one of the immense multitude was left'. The crowds had assembled over the course of the afternoon and early evening in the Field of Mars, ancient Rome's Region IX: the most appropriate setting for the event's First Act, the starting point from which to set in motion the celebration of a famous military victory. Mars, of course, was Rome's chief god of war, who had so potently cast his spell over the battlefields of Israel.

The Field of Mars (Campus Martius) was a vast swathe of open ground stretching some two kilometres from the Capitoline Hill to the River Tiber. Despite being susceptible to flooding due to its low-lying terrain, some of Rome's greatest monuments and finest craftsmen were found close to the banks of the river.

A snapshot of its character was captured by the great historian, geographer and philosopher Strabo (64/63 BC–AD 24). Although the Romans typically applied the term *strabo* to describe someone whose eyes were physically distorted or deformed, the scholar was actually a visionary, credited with compiling the first comprehensive geographical encyclopaedia of the inhabited world. On the basis of personal travels as far afield as Ethiopia and Egypt, he subsequently published his seventeen-volume *Geographia* between AD 7 and 18.

The *Geography* paints a lively picture of early Roman life in the wild open spaces of the Field of Mars:

> Indeed, the size of the Campus is remarkable, since it affords space at the same time and without interference, not only for the chariot-races and every other equestrian exercise, but also for all that multitude of people who exercise themselves by ball-playing, hoop-trundling, and wrestling; and the works of art situated around the Campus Martius, and the ground, which is covered with grass throughout the year, and the crowns of those hills that are above the river and extend as far as its bed, which present to the eye the appearance of a stage-painting – all this, I say, affords a spectacle that one can hardly draw away from. (*Geography* 5.3.8)

The district was also studded with hot sulphurous springs, ponds and lush wooded groves, all instilling a uniquely mystical atmosphere. With a dramatic and iconic background of such natural beauty and ancestry, it is no surprise that Vespasian chose the Field of Mars for the start of his Triumph. Historically, religiously and geographically, nowhere else would do.

But where precisely in the Field of Mars did the celebrations start? Josephus oddly confirms that the night before the great day, Vespasian and Titus purified themselves not at one of the great shrines of Rome, but at the place of worship of the mystery cult of Isis:

> Now all the soldiery marched out beforehand by companies, and in their several ranks, under their several commanders, in the night time, and were about the gates, not of the upper palaces, but those near the temple of Isis [Iseum]; for there it was that the emperors had rested the foregoing night. And as soon as ever it was day, Vespasian and Titus came out crowned with laurel, and clothed in those ancient purple habits which were proper to their family. (*JW* 7.123–4)

Why the Iseum? Wouldn't this have been a callous slap in the face of Rome's pantheon of established gods? The worship of Isis arrived up the Tiber in the first century BC on the ships of Alexandrian merchants keen to hang on to their tried and tested domestic gods. According to myth, the god Osiris had ruled over Egypt until his brother Seth severed him into dozens of pieces in a fit of jealousy at his sibling's power. A mourning wife, Isis, managed to recover Osiris' dissected body parts and carry them into her own body to give birth anew to her husband.

Even though the inner workings of this cult remain a mystery, new members certainly participated in initiation rites that replayed the ritual of death and rebirth. Isis was especially popular amongst slaves and freedmen through her virtue of resurrection, and she welcomed both female priests and the worship of women. Rather like the modern fascination with the Church of Scientology and the Jewish Kabbalah, the cult of Isis also encouraged material sacrifice and donations of wealth. The cult grew swiftly in Rome as Isis became a universal Mother Goddess. By the early fourth century AD she was Christianity's main competitor, and even today icons of the Virgin Mary bear more than a passing resemblance to Roman artistic depictions of Isis.

Mainstream acceptance was one thing, but imperial benediction during a Roman Triumph? This mystery nagged at me as I trudged past the Piazza Venezia and the Monument of Victor Emmanuel II of Savoy dedicated to the first king of a unified Italy in 1861. Earlier research had left me in little doubt that nothing still stands of Rome's Temple of Isis. So how do you find a building that was knocked down centuries ago and whose masonry was recycled century after century into medieval, Renaissance and Baroque buildings? Down-hearted and not a little frustrated, I racked my brain and set up office on the steps of the Victor Emmanuel Monument as statues of Victory and the Sea laughed at me from their comfortable perches above the city, smugly concealing their secrets.

Surrounded by papers, and my laptop sparked into life, the realisation began to dawn on me that even if the Temple of Isis is nothing more than a memory, its legacy lives on in a meandering trail of Egyptian sculpture. The first trace of this phantom temple is Madam Lucretia, the modern Italian name for the bust of a monumental Roman marble statue of a woman quietly abandoned in a urine-infested corner of the Piazza di San Marco. Cloaked in perpetual shadow, she surveys the daily flow of thousands of visitors gasping at the majestic sight of the Victor Emmanuel Monument across the road.

Lucretia was moved to this spot around AD 1500 and, despite her high monetary and artistic value as a museum piece, she remains a living icon. During festivals she is often painted and adorned with carrots, onions, garlands and ribbons. She remains a much-respected figure of the community, a knowledgeable stone known to 'speak' on important occasions. Thus, in 1799 she fell forwards on her face to reveal a black ink inscription on her back that declared 'I can't stand it any longer'. Rather than a despairing judgement on the degenerate nature of contemporary society, this exclamation reflected the political opinions of a failed attempt to oust the papacy and establish an independent republican government. Ancient Lucretia, it would seem, is a modern medium for social commentary.

This marble figure shows many scars of life's adversities, not least in her heavily eroded hair and facial features, and the lead staples that surgically pin her fractured rib cage together. Today she is something of a 'Renaissance woman', a symbol of unity standing immediately beside the entrance to the United Nations building. Her dress, however, suggests an altogether different ancestry as the Egyptianising goddess of Isis, possibly the actual cult statue that adorned her Roman temple in the Field of Mars.

Three minutes' walk away from the Piazza di San Marco I discovered that the Egyptian theme of this sector of the Field of Mars continued with the unlikely sight of an Egyptian obelisk carried on the back of a white marble elephant in the centre of the Piazza della Minerva. The 5.5-metre-tall red granite obelisk came to light in 1665 in the cloister of the Church of Santa Maria sopra Minerva, whose elegant façade casts a deep shadow across the piazza. Originally erected by the pharaoh Apries in the sixth century BC in Sais, a town of Lower Egypt, the emperor Caligula shipped it back to Rome for installation in the large temple on the Campus Martius dedicated to Isis and Serapis.

Soon after its discovery, Pope Alexander VII Chigi decided to display the obelisk publicly in the piazza in front of the church, entrusting the design of the monument in 1667 to the genius of the Baroque, Gian Lorenzo Bernini. The elephant was considered an image of great strength, and so symbolised the divine wisdom bestowed on a strong mind. An inscription on the statue base cites the personal philosophy of Alexander VII: 'a strong mind is necessary to support solid wisdom'. Over time this symbolism faded away, so that by the eighteenth century the elephant was more prosaically known as Minerva's Piglet due to a regrettable perceived resemblance.

In ancient Egypt, obelisks – from the Greek word for 'skewer' – were designed as physical manifestations of the sun god Atum-Ra. The apex represented the starting point of the sun's ray and the centre of the sun's power, while the base signified the formless matter that the divine light of the sun transforms into the cosmos. After being conveyed to Rome, their original religious function was lost as they became high-prestige artistic expressions of Rome's dominion over its provinces, peoples and their gods.

As is common in Mediterranean cities, towns and villages, the church of Santa Maria sopra Minerva in front of Minerva's Piglet sits on ancient foundations, in this case the Temple of Isis itself. Nothing of the temple survives today other than the bits of masonry and sculpture that once adorned it and come to light from time to time during building work in the church's precinct. Using a former building as a stone quarry for a later building, of course, is highly efficient and perfectly logical. Ever since the fourth century AD, however, early Christianity has deliberately rooted thousands of churches over former Roman temples to seal off and imprison paganism's rampant power. This was the ulterior motive for the destruction of the Temple of Isis.

Walking around the perimeter of the former temple, one sees that its entire structure has been completely devoured by the church, later Baroque-period tenement blocks and souvenir stores. Particularly popular are open-fronted shops peddling *gelati* – Isis abandoned in favour of ices. On the far eastern flank of the *insula*, the 5-metre-wide lane of the Via delle Paste is a haven for motor scooter parking. Here the first two courses of masonry above ground are distinctly Roman: were the raucous Germans knocking back their drink in the dark lane outside the Bar Miscellanea aware that this was once the south-east corner of the Iseum? Here waiters serve vast quantities of beer where the priests of Isis once chanted in mysterious tongues.

Just around the corner from the Piazza della Minerva the heavens opened and in a blinding flash of revelation the reason why Vespasian and Titus spent the night before the Triumph at this spot became blatantly obvious. Josephus, it seems, didn't do his research too well. True, there was a Temple of Isis at this spot 2,000 years ago, and as if to hammer home the point yet another Egyptian obelisk stands in the middle of the Piazza della Rotonda, a needle pointing heavenward. Only in this instance the power of Atum-Ra's fire-like sun is shackled by the ice-cold water from a fountain built around the base of the 6.3-metre-high obelisk taken to Rome from the Temple of the Sun in Heliopolis, Egypt, where it had peacefully stood since the thirteenth century BC. Giacomo della Porta's fountain was crafted in 1711 under orders of Pope Clement XI. But Isis and obelisks, I now realised, were a complete red herring.

What Josephus neglected to report, perhaps because the reality would have been so obvious to a Roman audience, is that the most important religious building of the Roman Empire stood next to the Temple of Isis. His reference to Isis was simply an elementary act of signposting, whose importance has become overstated across the centuries. Vespasian and Titus did not choose this spot to purify themselves the night before their Triumph; this location chose them. A gentle hill would have given a perfect view of proceedings for the gawping multitude pouring out of the city by the thousands. The open space would have comfortably accommodated the hundreds of soldiers polishing their armour, not to mention the fussy directors putting finishing touches to the Triumph's elaborately designed floats.

At the foot of the hill, today engulfed by vendors peddling handbags, sunglasses, leaning towers of Pisa and plastic guns firing bubbles that float around the 80-metre-wide piazza like messages from the gods, stands one of the most magnificent and important architectural monuments of classical antiquity, the Pantheon.

The Pantheon has stood undisturbed by the destructive hand of man for almost 1,880 years. The building planted on the site today owes its survival to the temple's conversion into the Church of St Mary of the Martyrs in AD 608. The earliest incarnation was commissioned by the Roman general and statesman Marcus Agrippa in 27–25 BC, only to be destroyed like much of ancient Rome by one of the great fires that plagued the city in AD 80. Domitian's subsequent rebuild fared even worse, being struck by lightning thirty years later and, once again, burning to the ground. The current temple is the handiwork of the emperor Hadrian, who rededicated the building to the original founder, Marcus Agrippa.

The Pantheon comprises a front porch annexed to a rotunda, in combination 60.5 metres long. Its pedimented classical façade is supported by Corinthian columns with monolithic shafts of Egyptian granite and by bases and capitals of white Greek Pentelic marble. A set of holes cut into the pediment once formed an eagle and wreath design, the attributes of Jupiter, crafted from gilded bronze. The porch below, today crammed with children from all over the world resting beneath monster marble columns two metres wide, originally housed statues of the emperor Augustus, Marcus Agrippa and of the god Mars. Another statue, of Venus, was famous for her earrings – made from a pearl once owned by no less a celebrity than Cleopatra of Egypt.

Although no one really knows how the Pantheon functioned in antiquity, it may well have been the 'seat' of all the gods, a Roman version of the Greeks' Mount Olympus. But more than this, Roman emperors also held court here, hearing petitions and handing out judgements. The Pantheon was thus a perfect symbolic choice from which to embark on the Triumph.

The majestic spectacle of that day emerged in narrow snapshots. The piazza is heavily built up, and the ancient view distorted in my mind by twenty-first-century hawkers crying 'uno Euro' for their tacky goods. An androgynous Sicilian in black shades and a coffee-and-cream shirt buttoned up to his throat played surreal elevator muzak on his electronic organ, while his wife and two toddlers looked on with bitter-sweet pride and hunger.

After offering sacrifices in the early morning sun, it is almost certain that on the great day itself it was from the Pantheon that Vespasian and Titus walked out in purple robes to the roar of the city. Tens of thousands of Roman citizens tightly packing the Field of Mars as far as the eye could see would have cheered on their heroes as the gods of war looked on in satisfaction. The stench of death on the streets of Jerusalem the year before would have seemed worlds away.

24

A Word from the Sponsors

ONCE THE PANTHEON of the gods and the ancestral dead had been respectfully appeased in the Field of Mars, a crucial formality awaited Vespasian and Titus before the triumphal parade could start to roll. Battles may have been won and lost through the strategic guile and bravery of these commanders-in-chief and the unconditional loyalty of their soldiers, but the business of war was the matter of the Senate, which was chief executive and treasury rolled into one. Naturally it had nervously followed the Jewish Revolt, voting for troop allocations and the supply of generous funds.

One false move and armies were known to turn against the Senate, and the city mob to grind more than its teeth if excessive funds were wasted on war rather than more prosaic tasks like cleaning stinking sewers. Vespasian had left Rome out of favour with Nero and returned an emperor. A man of humble beginnings, the new ruler was well aware of the Eternal City's political sensitivities.

Before the pageant of the Triumph could start, Vespasian and Titus thus received the blessing of the Roman Senate and the congratulations of their 'sponsors'. Josephus dwells on this morning meeting at some length, explaining how the commanders

> then went as far as Octavian's Walks; for there it was that the senate, and the principal rulers, and those that had been recorded as of the equestrian order, waited for them.
>
> Now a tribunal had been erected before the cloisters, and ivory chairs had been set upon it, when they came and sat down upon them. Whereupon the soldiery made an acclamation of joy to them immediately, and all gave them attestations of their valour; while they were themselves without there, and only in their silken garments, and crowned with laurel: then Vespasian accepted of these shouts of

theirs; but while they were still disposed to go on in such acclamations, he gave them a signal of silence.

And when everybody entirely held their peace, he stood up and covering the greatest part of his head with his cloak, he put up the accustomed solemn prayers; the like prayers did Titus put up also; after which prayers Vespasian made a short speech to all the people, and then sent away all the soldiers to a dinner prepared for them by the emperors. (*JW* 7.124–9)

The whereabouts of Octavian's Walks is lost in the mists of time, but can only have existed at one very special location. At the far west end of the Forum, just past the monumental Triumphal Arch of Septimius Severus, stands a well-preserved rectangular structure. Although the current incarnation dates to AD 283, the original building was devised as a Senate House (the *curia*) by Julius Caesar and completed by Augustus in 29 BC. Even though stylised images of the Senate on contemporary coins show a building more reminiscent of a Chinese pagoda than a Roman temple, this was one of the most powerful buildings of the empire. Inside its hallowed walls, lined with expensive Phrygian marble, 300 senators would congregate and debate matters of state. Three statues perched on the top of the façade's pediment, including a Winged Victory standing on a globe, guarded its doors.

The Augustan building was decorated inside with marble balustrades depicting on one side an anonymous emperor burning the book of debt and, on the reverse, a sow, ram and bull being led to sacrifice in the Forum and a scene of imperial benefaction. A similar *suovetaurilia*, animal sacrifice, almost certainly took place on the morning of the Triumph, but not in front of the Senate House. About 40 metres west of the *curia* lies the symbolic heart of Rome, the *Umbilicus Urbis* (Navel of the City) where, according to legend, Romulus dug a circular pit when he founded Rome. Here all new citizens arriving at the city traditionally threw in a handful of dirt from their place of origin, as well as the first fruits of the year as a sacrifice. The Navel of the City was also considered a gateway to the underworld, whose lid was prised open three times a year to liberate bottled up evil spirits and stop them brewing undue mischief for the empire.

Against this powerful political backdrop, Vespasian and Titus would have been received at the *rostra*, a massive rectangular orator's platform that still stands today. The podium dominates the Forum of Julius Caesar and would have been unmissable in AD 71 with its coloured panelling of pink-grey marble from Chios cut with vertical bands of black-red marble from Teos. Reinforcing the spectacle of power, the platform was decorated with the bronze rams (*rostra*) ripped off vanquished enemy warships.

Once the 'sponsors' had been appeased, Vespasian and Titus followed tradition by serving lunch to their troops as a sign of respect and a morale booster – a PR stunt repeated by George W. Bush when serving Thanksgiving dinner to troops in Iraq after the 2003 Gulf War. The entourage then moved into the suburbs of Rome to recoup forces before the main event. According to Josephus:

> Then did he retire to that gate which was called the Gate of the Pomp, because pompous shows do always go through that gate; there it was that they tasted some food, and when they had put on their triumphal garments, and had offered sacrifices to the gods that were placed at the gate, they sent the triumph forward, and marched through the theatres, that they might be more easily seen by the multitude. (*JW* 7.129–31)

This enigmatic passage offers little to go on. Our only clues are a Gate of the Pomp where Roman Triumphs started, which must lie in proximity to a cluster of theatres. Fortunately, the route of the Triumphal Way is relatively certain, starting at the Circus Flaminius in the Field of Mars and then passing through the Porticus of Octavia and between the Temples of Apollo and Bellona before heading for the ancient Vicus Jugarius by way of the Triumphal Gate (Gate of the Pomp) in the Republican-period city walls.

How many of these landmarks still stood to illuminate the final public procession of the mighty Temple treasure of Jerusalem? Would I be able to find the ruins of the Circus Flaminius, that monument which symbolised the completion of Rome's subjugation of the Jews?

25

Aliens in Rome

THE CIRCUS FLAMINIUS, laid out by C. Flaminius Nepos in 220 BC to the west of Rome, hugs the hips of the River Tiber close to Fabricius' Bridge. This Roman thoroughfare once led into the heart of the ancient city's foreigners' quarter, the *Transtiberinum* or Trastevere in modern Italian. The term 'circus', however, is something of a misnomer. From time to time emperors such as Augustus held Egyptian crocodile fights here, and the Taurian Games were a fixture organised every five years.

But on an everyday basis the open communal space of the Circus served as a lively venue for public meetings, markets, banking transactions and funerary orations. Here the state presented gifts and money to the army on special occasions – an emperor's birthday or after military victories – and enemy spoils of war went on public show. If the Forum was the administrative and political heart of the city, then the pulse of cosmopolitan Rome beat in the 260-metre-long and 100-metre-wide Circus Flaminius.

Making my way towards the main landmark of Rome's Region IX, I wondered what the mood around the Circus was like that day in AD 71, as chained Jews were herded in preparation for humiliation. The area would have been abuzz for days with officials putting up decorations, painting over graffiti and mounting security operations. From the Circus Flaminius the city's great foreigners' quarter sprawled across both sides of the Tiber. Certainly the Jewish community living along the riverside ghetto would have been in mourning behind closed shutters, but were the local Greeks, Gauls, Germans and Ethiopians appalled or enthralled by the pomp in their midst? Just how far did their sympathies stretch?

Trastevere remains fiercely independent today, so where better to mull over this question than from the far side of the river? I crossed the fast-flowing Tiber by the Pons Fabricius, the stone bridge thrown across the river in 62 BC by Lucius Fabricius, commissioner of roads, and passed over Tiber Island, a no man's land in the middle of the water once graced by a temple dedicated to the healing god Asclepius and by shrines to Jupiter Jurarius (guarantor of oaths), Gaia and Tiberinus (god of the river). Although peaceful today, covered with lush vegetation and evergreens, this part of suburban Rome would have been a hive of activity and babbling tongues in the first century AD. Here foreigners begged for menial jobs down by the docks and heaved sacks of North African grain and amphorae filled with Spanish oils into the city centre.

Today the Trastevere region is tranquil and bohemian, retaining something of the laid-back air of Paris's Rive Gauche. Students picnicked on the sloping stone revetment as the setting sun cast a gentle red glow across the water. Sipping local red wine and picking at salami, they animatedly discussed Nietzsche, Prime Minister Berlusconi and the latest crisis with the AS Roma football team.

Within the narrow streets of Trastevere, the city's insane traffic quietens. For the first time in Rome extensive graffiti covers the walls, declaring 'Morte il Fascio' (Death to the Fascists), 'Disonore ai Diffidati!' (Dishonour to the Doubters!) and 'Ciao. Sono per Lazio le do Merda' (Hello. I am for Lazio [football team], I Give you Shit). The rickety stone houses have a medieval flavour, while the piazzas emit a sense of great energy, warmth and intellectual endeavour, as if this district has spawned important philosophy, art and literature over the centuries. Small stalls peddle local crafts of leather and glass, turning their backs on the tourist tat sold outside the Pantheon.

In contrast to the imperial side of the river, little of the city's 2,000-year-old heritage survives above ground, although somewhere hides the tantalising ruin of Cleopatra's palace. You can feel the unsettled spirits of antiquity everywhere. For here lived the foreign populace that caused the Roman writer Lucan – himself a Spanish immigrant – to complain that his city was 'a glut with the scum of humanity'. Trastevere was home to the world's criminals driven from their homes, according to Sallust. Other writers dubbed Rome a sewer into which detritus flowed from all over the world.

To be a foreigner trying to scrape a living in imperial Rome could be daunting. The babble of Latin, the overpowering fascist architecture, and the marble masterpieces adorning almost every street corner can only have increased the sense of inferiority. Even today, as I took the lift to my hotel room by the Terminali railway station, the conspicuously framed Codified Text on the Sojourn of Foreigners in Italy (June 1931) still reminded visitors of their legal obligations under Articles 142–4:

> Foreigners must report within three days of their arrival in the State to the local police . . . The police is entitled at any time to ask foreigners to exhibit their identity papers in their possession and to give account of themselves . . . Wherever there is reason to doubt the identification of a foreigner the latter may be requested to undergo a personal examination . . . the Prefect may prohibit foreigners from residing in districts or localities of military importance for the defence of the State.

Xenophobia and class prejudice were without doubt rampant in ancient Rome, like any great cosmopolitan city past and present, but the extent to which it was institutionalised within society depends on which ancient voices you trust most. Even so the community must have felt deeply vulnerable peering through closed shutters at their Jewish brethren being dragged in triumph through the streets in AD 71. But did such oppression of 'others' really typify everyday life?

Certain lines of enquiry undeniably expose Rome's Jews as troublemakers who flaunted the law and needed suppressing from time to time. The earliest rumblings of disquiet date to 139 BC, when Gnaeus Cornelius Hispanus, the *praetor peregrinus* in charge of foreigners, expelled the Chaldaean astrologers and 'also compelled the Jews, who attempted to contaminate the morals of the Romans with the worship of Jupiter Sabazius, to go back to their own homes'. Even though Valerius Maximus, author of the *Memorable Deeds and Sayings* in which this reference appears, undoubtedly gets his religious wires crossed (Jupiter Sabazius was Phrygian, not Semitic), this event probably reflects a general clampdown on non-Roman religious activity. Valerius Maximus almost certainly also confuses Sabazius with observance of the Sabbath. Nevertheless, the cry of 'foreigners go home' was just as familiar on the streets of the Eternal City as in the West today.

Several emperors seem to have had it in for the Jews and their ghetto of 40,000 people amidst an overall urban population of some 1.2 million people (substantially larger than the modern community of 27,000 Jews). In AD 41, the mentally impaired Claudius forbade them the right of assembly, excluded them from the state's free wheat dole, and eight years later 'expelled from Rome the Jews who persisted in rioting at the instigation of Chrestus', according to Suetonius' biography of the emperor. The reason for this clampdown seems to have been a wave of missionary activity across the Mediterranean stirred up by the Jews of Alexandria, to whom Claudius penned a letter warning them not to 'stir up a general plague throughout the world'. Hadrian (AD 117–38) is acknowledged as one of the ablest and most enlightened of all Roman rulers, yet even he forbade circumcision and desecrated the site of the Temple in Jerusalem with a pagan sanctuary dedicated to Venus, the goddess of love.

References to Judaism crop up fairly regularly in the literary circles of post-Augustan Rome, painting a picture distorted by misinformation and prejudice. The prevailing attitude is generally one of amused contempt at the exotic and seemingly absurd customs of the Jews. A far harder line, however, had been taken in a speech delivered by the great orator Cicero in October 59 BC, in which he stated:

> Even when Jerusalem was still standing and the Jews at peace with us, the demands of their religion were incompatible with the majesty of our Empire, the dignity of our name and the institutions of our ancestors; and now that the Jewish nation has shown by armed rebellion what are its feelings for our rule, they are even more so; how dear it was to the immortal gods has been shown by the fact that it has been conquered, farmed out to the tax-collectors and enslaved. (*Pro Flacco* 69)

The philosopher Seneca objected to the Jews' observance of the Sabbath because they lost one-seventh of their lives to idleness, while the satirist Persius scorned the awed prayer of silently moving lips on the 'circumcised Sabbath'. Jewish abstinence from pork – a staple foodstuff reared on government farms – also puzzled the Romans; the satirical writer Petronius explained this behaviour as due to the Jews' veneration of the pig. Martial, the witty epigrammatist of the time of the emperor Domitian (AD 81–96), included in a catalogue of the unpleasant smells of Rome the odorous breath of the fasting Jew and, among the unendurable noisemakers of the city, the Jewish mendicant 'taught to beg by his mother'.

Uninformed and inaccurate commentary about the history of the Jews and their customs was evidently institutionalised, a reality reinforced by one of Rome's greatest historians, Publius Cornelius Tacitus, who also misunderstood their origins. Following legend he portrayed the Jews as fugitives from the island of Crete, where the mountain of Ida and the neighbouring tribe, the Idaei, came to be called Judaei 'by a barbarous lengthening of the national name'. Tacitus' take on Jewish origins, I suspect, should largely be ignored as little more than political propaganda geared towards discrediting the rich legacy of this people. The far younger history of mighty Rome, based largely on a dense web of myth, was not to be eclipsed.

The diffusion of hostile stories relating to the origins of Rome's Jews would resonate down the centuries. From his great Fascist residence at the Villa Torlonia in Rome, Benito Mussolini typically denounced the Jews as strangers lacking any ancestry in the Eternal City. Yet nine metres below his own villa and rolling gardens stretched the grave-lined chambers of an ancient Jewish cemetery haunted by the bones of the very people whose forebears he denied.

———◆———

In reality, much of the diatribe and Jew-baiting that dripped from the quills of Roman writers was a case of wishful thinking, a desire to keep foreigners at bay. Actually, many of the Jews of Rome enjoyed a special relationship with the political power-players of the empire that disposes once and for all of the myth of the Jews as slaves.

With his 'Magna Carta of the Jews', Julius Caesar (100–44 BC) bestowed special privileges which prevailed, on and off, for three centuries until the advent of Christianity. These decrees granted full freedom of worship and permission to raise money for communal purposes and to send the Temple tax to Jerusalem. It was Julius Caesar who decreed that Hyrcanus, the Jewish High Priest, could fortify Jerusalem.

Caesar similarly permitted Rome's community to try its own cases before a Jewish tribunal instead of the regular Roman courts. Modern Israel's exemption of its most observant Jewish population from compulsory military service is also nothing new. Surprisingly, this policy dates back to the reign of Julius Caesar and was initiated as a result of the impossibility of enforcing a compromise between enrolment, keeping the Sabbath and dietary laws. Little wonder Rome's Jews wept openly at Caesar's grave following his death at the hands of Brutus and the conspirators.

Religious toleration was especially relaxed during the reign of Augustus (27 BC–AD 14), when the greatest of emperors enhanced the Jews' privileges even further. In Jerusalem he donated costly gifts to the Temple and commanded that a burned offering be made there daily in perpetuity at his expense as a token of his homage to the supreme God of the Jews – or, at least, as a political gesture to bolster good relations with Herod.

Beyond the personal grief and deep empathy that must have consumed the Jewish community of Rome in AD 71, the outbreak of the insurrection in Palestine and the destruction of the Temple in Jerusalem triggered no political repercussions amongst the Jewish residents of Rome itself. Even though Israel had been wiped off the map, Jews' privileges in Rome and throughout the rest of the empire remained unchanged. As far as we know, no race riots ensued.

One significant exception to these tolerant domestic policies was the commutation of the Jewish Temple tax into a poll tax deposited in Rome's Temple of Jupiter Capitolinus. The collections of the *procurator ad capitularia Iudaeorum*, however, should not be seen as a punitive measure but rather as part of a broad taxation policy aimed at refilling the coffers of the national treasury that Nero had so expertly depleted. Yet during the reign of the Flavian emperor Domitian, this tax was brutally enforced with people even being stripped naked to check for circumcision. During the reign of Marcus Cocceius Nerva (AD 96–8), however, these abuses were wiped out. To commemorate the more relaxed conditions, a special coin was minted bearing the legend *Fisci Iudaici Calumnia Sublata*, 'Abolition of the Unjust Enforcement of the Jewish Tax', alongside a depiction of a palm tree as the symbol of Judaism.

A balanced examination of the historical sources leaves the impression that, as a body, the Jews of Rome were a powerful group whom emperors, ready to commit mass genocide elsewhere, would actively court. In 59 BC, the Roman aristocrat Lucius Valerius Flaccus was charged with extortion and misappropriation of the 'Jewish gold' (the Temple tax) collected in Asia Minor and destined for Jerusalem. During his trial held three years later, in reference to the Jewish community Cicero confirmed that 'You know how vast a throng it is, how close-knit, and what influence it can have in public meetings' (*Pro Flacco* 66). Such testimony is not much to go on, but when considered alongside the special privileges given to the Jews in Rome, this appeasement is reminiscent of American presidents visiting synagogues in the United States to curry favour and votes amongst the influential Jewish voting sector.

The Jewish 'mob' permeated society. At times it pursued an aggressive policy of securing converts, possibly including Nero's second wife, Poppaea, as well as the distinguished writer Caecilius of Calacte, the most important rhetor and literary critic of the Augustan age next to Dionysius of Halicarnassus. Hard work and due diligence also created deep-rooted respect amongst Roman society, which no doubt was the real reason for the satirists' wrath.

The basic tenets of Judaism even penetrated everyday life, with the Sabbath judged to be a sacred day, unfavourable for starting a journey but an opportune time to court a girl, according to the poet Ovid. Such influence was the true background to the spiteful sneers of those like the philosopher Seneca, who complained that by the mid-first century AD Judaism had become so widespread that 'the practices of this damnable race have already prevailed in every land. The vanquished have given laws to the victors.'

When it comes to putting flesh on these bones, however, the physical evidence is sorely lacking. For a city that boasts the survival of the most important standing ruins of antiquity, Rome refuses to give up the tales of its Jewish ghosts. Their homes and places of worship have long been consumed by the soils of the Eternal City. Ironically, the memory of ancient Jewish life only survives in death. Conclusive proof of a flourishing middle- and upper-class Jewish community between the first and fifth centuries AD is preserved in the physical

remains of over 530 inscriptions recovered from underground catacombs. These texts refer to between eleven and thirteen synagogues
scattered across the Roman town, all of which are destroyed today.

If Mussolini had studied his history properly, he might have heard
of Antonio Bosio, nicknamed the 'Columbus of the Catacombs' for
his successful subterranean explorations. As early as December 1578
Bosio stumbled across a Jewish catacomb at Porta Portese in the district of Monteverde Trastevere in the ancient foreigners' quarter,
where he noticed

> on practically every grave, the seven-branched candelabrum, either
> painted in red or imprinted on the stucco, a practice peculiar to the
> Jews . . . Notably, at the head of a dead-end corridor can be seen a
> large candelabrum . . . From the fact that we found no sign of
> Christianity in the cemetery and that we read on the fragment of one
> inscription the brief word 'synagogue' . . . we have decided and firmly
> believe that this was the particular cemetery of the ancient Hebrews.
> We are, however, ready to yield to any saner and better judgment.

A total of six Jewish catacombs containing 400 years of Jewish burials
have come to light in Rome since the sixteenth century. All but two
are utterly destroyed and none is accessible to the public today without
special permission.

To get an idea of what a Roman synagogue looked like, you must
go to Ostia, the port town of both the Eternal City and the empire at
large. Here fleets of merchant vessels unloaded the finest commodities
from all over the world, from Indian spices to Egyptian emeralds, virgin
oils, wild beasts for the theatre and the massive cargoes of Greek marbles
that infamously made the pavements of Rome crack under their
weight. Ostia also boasts Rome's only surviving ancient Jewish temple.

The port town's synagogue is a microcosm of the fate of Rome's
Jews. For one thing you have to be something of a detective just to
find the building, which is banished to the outskirts of town. In fact
it is the closest structure to the River Tiber and the furthest from the
heart of the town, locked well outside the safety of the gates of the
Porta Marina. Beyond Ostia's walls, the main Roman road peters out
to be replaced by a meandering track covered with dense vegetation
and a jungle of buttercups. The fragrant smells of wild lemon grass,

lavender and pine betray the former presence of the town's original herb garden.

Out on a social limb and on the periphery of all things Roman it may be, but inscriptions and excavated information leave no doubt that Ostia's synagogue was something of a trailblazer, the first building of its kind to put up *extra muros* and the last to stand centuries later. The earliest house of prayer opened its doors during the reign of the emperor Claudius (AD 41–54). A hundred years later, it was expanded to accommodate a congregation of 500 people, simultaneously being fitted out with mosaic floors and wall painting. An even greater refurbishment followed soon after AD 306, when a social meeting room, kitchen and a majestic Torah shrine approached by three stairs – the proverbial three steps to heaven – were added.

By this time Ostia's former glory as the main port of the empire had waned. But its fortunes lived on. While commerce dwindled, and the foreign merchants who had made the Jewish community feel so welcome took their skills elsewhere, the town was reinvented as the playground of Rome's senatorial class. Sumptuous new monuments now arose across the town and, curiously, the synagogue was towed along by these changes in prosperity and circumstance. To all intents and purposes it would have looked like a typical elite Roman building of the fourth century, on the outside constructed of herring-bone terracotta bricks, and on the inside boasting the finest marble veneer, with opulent mosaics even coating the sides of the ritual bath – the *mikveh* – one of Judaism's most holy types of structure.

In this juxtaposition of Judaism and classical Roman culture we have the most accurate picture of what Jewish life was really like in the Eternal City. On the one hand religious observance remained strict and central to identity. Yet, on the other, faith was expressed within a purely Roman architectural context – classical colonettes, but adorned with images of the menorah, *lulav* and *etrog*; mosaic floors, but decorated with Jewish iconography; imported slabs of white and purple marble, but cut with Jewish inscriptions.

Many scholars denounce the early fourth-century synagogue renovations as incompatible with the vital essence of Judaism's cultural symbols. More realistically, this shift in ideological-aesthetic taste shows precisely how the Jews of Rome fused the best of both worlds over time, just as they had in first-century Jerusalem and Beth Shearim. In worship they were largely left to their own devices and respected by mainstream society; and they felt sufficiently unthreatened to absorb central Roman styles of art and architecture. Uncompromising, yet pragmatic. If ever there was a happy medium, this form of acculturation was it.

26

Of Circuses and Artichokes

Aᴏ an afternoon exhuming all kinds of ghosts across the
river in Rome's foreigners' quarter, I clambered exhausted back
across Fabricius' Bridge to the familiar sights and sounds of central
Rome. The vitality under hardship and the determined battle with
xenophobia endured by these hardy foreigners weighed on my mind.
Rome's overseas immigrants were undoubtedly attracted westwards
by the 'bright lights' of the imperial capital and by the allure of new
money, but the demand for cheap labour that has thrown open the
gates of modern Europe was far less insistent 2,000 years ago. Then
slaves could be bought like modern fast food in the Forum. For the
city's foreign citizens, much of their life would have been played out
in a social limbo, a state of simultaneous belonging and social
ostracism. For the new immigrant bent on forging an easier life for his
family, the everyday battle against prejudice was an investment for his
children's futures.

Back on the broad tree-lined Lungotevere Pierleoni that snakes
around the River Tiber, I made my way to the exact spot where the
Triumph bestowed on the emperor Vespasian and his son Titus started
out. But all I could see were elegant eighteenth-century apartment
blocks, paint-chipped palaces, coffee shops and urchins kicking a
half-deflated ball across the narrow lanes. Searching out the ruins of
the Circus Flaminius, from where the Triumph was dispatched
into the heart of the city to the acclamation of thousands, is a
pointless exercise.

The Circus may have possessed a structural element, but it was
predominantly an open space ringed by funerary monuments and
temples. Although a considerable amount of the arena still stood in
the twelfth century, by the sixteenth century the Mattei Palace and

urban sprawl had consumed it. Only the memory of the ropemak-
ers who plied their trade from dark medieval arcades on the north
side of the Circus's shops lives on today in the names of the Via dei
Funari and the sixteenth-century church of Santa Caterina dei
Funari.

After the physical exertion of tramping around Trastevere, one of
the most remarkable realisations of my quest for the Temple treasure
of Jerusalem became apparent. Although I was aware that Rome's
present-day Great Synagogue stood, out of respect for the city's Jewish
ancestry, on the banks of the Tiber within the ancient foreigners'
quarter, as I looked around I realised that it was built on the precise
spot of the Circus Flaminius.

This surprising revelation was full of profound implications and
symbolic overtones. The four walls of the synagogue, the former
Circus, marked the scene of Judaism's greatest humiliation, the beginning of the end – the starting point of the Triumph that culminated
in the 'imprisonment' of the Temple treasure from Jerusalem and the
decapitation of the leader of the Jewish revolt. In a further twist, this
synagogue's topography precisely echoes Ostia's ancient synagogue.
Both were 'exiled' to the edge of town, right next to the River Tiber
and its cosmopolitan world.

The modern 'temple' is a 46-metre-high monument spanning an
area of 3,373 square metres and was built between 1901 and 1904 in
an eclectic style that mixes Roman, Greek and Assyrian-Babylonian
elements with the intention of blending in sympathetically with
the indigenous city architecture – a modern example of sensitive
acculturation.

In a twist of fate unappreciated by the Jews of present-day Rome
whom I met, modern Judaism has literally supplanted the memory of
Rome's subjugation 2,000 years ago by refounding itself in the Circus
Flaminius. The religious ritual of the Jewish community has rooted
itself in the profane soil and purified the past. Alongside the archaeological strata going back to the time of the arena's foundation in 220
BC is a second superimposed level, invisible to the eye and only felt:
the emotional. Perhaps more than anywhere else on earth, Rome's
Great Synagogue stands as a symbol of endurance against the odds,
against warfare and genocide. This building thus fulfils many of

Judaism's dreams and aspirations for a Third Temple in Jerusalem. Not in their worst nightmares could Vespasian and Titus have imagined that their conquest of Israel would have unfolded with such historical circularity, with the vanquished becoming the conquerors and a 2,000-year-old wrong being righted.

When this realisation dawned, a surge of invigorating thoughts and questions swept through my mind. During my search for the Temple treasure I had had the good fortune to visit Rome on several occasions, always coming back to the Great Synagogue in search of answers. The spot is endlessly intriguing. On a former visit in May 2004, lost in reflection, my face must have mirrored my turbulent feelings because it was then that I was almost arrested.

At the front of the synagogue, this part of the Field of Mars was under siege by hundreds of people, just as it would have been in AD 71. A ferocious security operation was under way. Scores of Jews in their Sunday best patiently queued to pass through the first of two security cordons, while television cameras surveyed the scene. What the dickens was going on? Rome's *carabinieri*, out in droves, proved unimpressed by my impassioned request for entry and swatted me away like the unwanted foreigner I was. Ducking along side streets I decided upon an oblique attack from the flanks, assuming the lost tourist persona. Unfortunately, the Israeli security guards monitoring entry to the synagogue were quick to pounce, charmlessly repelling my advances. My photography of the synagogue was apparently a security risk; I was invited either to have my camera confiscated and be introduced to the *carabinieri* or to scram. Finally, I played the Jewish card, explaining in Hebrew my lifelong desire to explore Rome's Jewish ghetto. The guards relented and I surged through the crowd − a popped cork − into the narrow lanes of the medieval ghetto.

Before my luck changed I ducked into the Taverna del Ghetto on the Via del Portico d'Ottavia, and ordered *carciofi alla Giudia*, a traditional 2,000-year-old Romano-Jewish dish comprising a whole artichoke, complete with stem, fried upside down once in hot oil, cooled and then fried again in sizzling olive oil. Piperno, the oldest Jewish restaurant in Rome, describes this delicacy as 'tender as a blade of grass, artistic as a chrysanthemum, colourful as a Roman sunset'. This culinary treat arrived looking more like a porcupine dipped in wood varnish. The artichoke's taste is quite rudimentary, lightly fried with a hint of garlic, rather like today's outrageously expensive designer potato crisps.

Eating inside the Roman brick walls of the Taverna del Ghetto, now plastered over and sponge-daubed with yellow paint, past and present fused like nowhere else in the Eternal City. Though this is no longer a ghetto, because the city's 27,000 Roman Jews – among a total population of 3.5 million Romans – are happily integrated into the fabric of society, the overwhelming tapestry of history and pain lives on in this special place.

My research in London had been intensive and systematic, but nothing had suggested that so much of the atmosphere and architecture extant on the day of the Triumph could be resurrected. This was no mere aura or whisper of memory: I had stumbled across a 2,000-year-old bridge of continuity linking the words of Josephus with the standing archaeology.

Leaving the restaurant, I tried inconspicuously to make my way back towards the synagogue as the media scrum intensified. The waiters in the Taverna del Ghetto had explained that my trip to the Great Synagogue coincided with the centenary celebrations of its foundation. Hence the security and television coverage to welcome Israel's religious and political leaders, two archbishops representing the Pope, and Prime Minister Berlusconi.

My ham-fisted attempts to avoid officialdom were doomed to fail. But edging my way east down the Via del Portico d'Ottavia, past the phalanx of machine-gun-toting *carabinieri*, I was confronted by the last thing I had expected to see: part of the first monumental Roman arched gateway through which the imperial Triumphs passed, the Porticus of Octavia itself, still standing. Originally this covered *porticus* had been a dominant landmark, elegantly marching 50 metres eastwards and 140 metres north towards Balbus' Roman theatre. The full range and visual impact, of course, is lost today because only the gateway survives, having been adapted in the eighth century AD into the atrium of a church, today surviving as the Church of Sant' Angelo in Pescheria ('In the Fish Market').

The double-sided columnar porch is monumental, impressively crafted of Corinthian columns of Italian marble from Luna and Greek Pentelic marble architraves offset against thousands of red clay bricks. When you walk between the double gateway, sculpted dolphins and tridents overhead remind the viewer of Rome's naval prowess. Though impressive enough today, the gateway was an artistic wonder in Roman times. Once the Porticus of Octavia (sister of the emperor Augustus) had replaced that of Metellus around 27–25 BC, Augustus tacked on schools, meeting rooms and a library housing a stunning display of Greek statuary and paintings. Pride of place was given to a bronze composition by Lysippus of Alexander the Great on horseback alongside his twenty-five cavalry companions who died in the battle of Granicus in 334 BC. Not surprisingly, this statue group was not an original Roman commission, but part of the spoils of war seized by Metellus from a sanctuary at Dion in northern Greece.

Absorbed by the moment, and the fascination of coming across such an important part of the Triumphal experience, I jumped abruptly when an austere voice behind me interrupted my reflections as I scribbled.

'Journalists not possible. What do you write?' proclaimed an armed policeman in shining uniform and sternly pressed black woollen trousers with dandyesque red piping.

After explaining that I was a tourist keeping a diary for my own amusement, two *carabinieri* frogmarched me beyond the security cordon – an extreme reaction in the circumstances, but yet another example of the fear of those factions which threaten religious toleration. Rather than incensed, I was entirely sympathetic to the policemen's harsh tactics. After all, the preservation of Prime Minister Berlusconi and the Pope's personal representatives, Cardinal Camillo Ruini (Papal Vicar of Rome) and Cardinal Walter Kasper (Head of the Vatican's Commission for Religious Relations), depended on the keen eye of the security forces.

Back in London I pieced together what happened inside the Great Synagogue on 23 May 2004. Inside the Jewish Temple the Cardinal had delivered a speech written by the Pope, declaring 'Behold, how good and pleasant it is when brothers dwell in unity!' – a reference to

Psalms 133.1. In his speech delivered *in absentia*, Pope John Paul II
called the Great Synagogue of Rome

> a symbol and a reminder of the millennial presence in this city of the
> people of the Covenant of Sinai. For more than 2,000 years your
> community has been an integral part of life in the city; it can boast of
> being the most ancient Jewish Community in Western Europe and of
> having played an important role in spreading Judaism on this
> Continent . . .
>
> You have been citizens of this City of Rome for more than 2,000
> years, even before Peter the fisherman and Paul in chains came here sus-
> tained from within by the breath of the Spirit. Not only the Sacred
> Scriptures, in which to a large extent we share, not only the liturgy but
> also very ancient art forms witness to the Church's deep bond with the
> Synagogue; this is because of that spiritual heritage which without being
> divided or rejected has been made known to believers in Christ and con-
> stitutes an inseparable bond between us and you, the people of the Torah
> of Moses, the good olive tree on to which a new branch was grafted.

Even though all rational citizens of the world can only applaud such
sentiments of religious friendship, the fanatical reaction of some factions reinforces the muscle-flexing of Rome's police that day. For
reaching out to foster inter-faith harmony and co-existence, some
Catholics denounced John Paul II as the 'anti-pope'.

Outside the security cordon a middle-aged woman dressed in
ghetto black scowled down at me with a mix of pity and pedagogic
impatience. She stood on the top step of the Jewish bookshop,
Menorah – Libreria Ebraica. Rather than engage in conversation, and
keen to conceal my embarrassment at being ejected, I pointed to a
poster showing a photo of the menorah from the Temple in Jerusalem
being carried along the streets of Rome in AD 71, as depicted on the
Arch of Titus at the high point of the Forum.

'Any idea where I can find that?' I asked, playing the light-hearted
joker.

'Everyone knows where it is,' sneered the shopkeeper. 'All the
Jewish community believes that the menorah fell into the Tiber and
was recovered by the Christians who took it to the Vatican where it
remains to this day.'

27

The Triumphal Way

ONCE I HAD tracked down the Circus Flaminius and discovered its geographical symbolism, and then stumbled across the Porticus of Octavia more by luck than judgement, the rest of the Triumphal route started to fall into place. Just as Josephus asserted, the procession did indeed pass 'through the theatres, that they might be more easily seen by the multitude' – specifically the Circus Flaminius followed by the Theatre of Marcellus and, lastly, the theatrical wonder of the age, the Circus Maximus.

Marcellus' theatre had served as a place of entertainment since the reign of Julius Caesar. Named after M. Claudius Marcellus by Augustus, in honour of his deceased nephew, this stadium was the most important of Rome's three contemporary entertainment facilities and, with its two superimposed arcades of travertine stone fronted by semi-circular columns, this structure became the model for contemporary theatres throughout the western Empire, including the Colosseum. Where spectators had watched the staged hunt of 600 African beasts in the inaugural festivities of 13 BC, a capacity crowd of 20,500 would have watched the passage of the Temple treasures of Jerusalem in the Triumph of AD 71 between the theatre and the Temples of Apollo and Bellona. The heavily pitted and eroded Roman road surface still survives, leading down towards the Via del Teatro di Marcello.

Here the gods of war within the Field of Mars were especially vigilant. The crowded presence of so many powerful monuments dedicated to warfare would have magnified the sense of might expressed by thousands of soldiers parading in polished breastplates, jangling swords and shields recalling the sound of steel on a battlefield. First, the triumphal soldiers would have acknowledged the Temple of

Bellona, a warrior mother-goddess who personified the battle-frenzy that underscored their victories in Israel.

Alongside, three white marble Corinthian columns from the Temple of Apollo Medicus Sosianus still stand today, their capitals supporting a frieze of laurel branches strung between bulls' skulls and candelabra with tripod bases. Appropriately, the temple once displayed sculpted battle scenes and even a triumphal procession, in which captives were tied back to back. Meanwhile, Greek statues of Apollo and the Muses, made by the master craftsmen Praxiteles, Philiskos of Rhodes and Timarchides, smiled down approvingly from the temple's arcades.

In passing the Temple of Apollo Medicus (the Healer), Rome deliberately began the process of forgiving itself for its actions on the killing fields of Palestine so that man and the military machine might distance themselves from the horrors of war and the scars of the battlefield. It was probably at this point that a huge bonfire would have been lit and on to it thrown the *spolia opima*, general enemy armour captured by Rome. These spoils could not be kept as souvenirs of victory because they were loaded with destructive enemy power, a danger if brought within the city walls.

Now the Triumph escaped the suburbs to be buffeted by the unwholesome smells of the Forum Holitorium, the Vegetable Market. Where the city usually bought its cabbages and onions, Vespasian and Titus once again made respectful offerings at the triple temple complex dedicated to Spes, Janus and Juno Sospita to assimilate these gods' personal attributes – Hope, Beginnings and Saviour. With so much blood on their hands they needed the blessing of as many willing gods as they could harness. The monumental foundations and façades of these buildings still grace the hybrid architecture of the twelfth-century church of San Nicola in Carcere. The church has literally boxed over the temples.

———— ◆ ————

If we could have frozen the action at this precise spot on that fateful day of AD 71, what would the people of Rome – from the city poor to the senatorial elite – have been thinking and feeling? Here the Triumphal parade escaped the humidity of the bottle-necked temples and theatres of the Field of Mars and prepared to surmount the dip in the road at the modern junction of the Via del Teatro di Marcello and the Vicus Jugarius that hugs the edge of the Capitoline Hill. This place was immensely potent in the ritual of the day because here the arcades of the Triumphal Way created a physical barrier between the Field of Mars and the Forum, between war and civilisation.

To the modern eye the jubilant atmosphere would have resembled the homecoming parade of a sports team that had just won the Olympics, adrenalin-inflated and on top of the world. But the Roman Triumph was far more than just a celebration for the victors and a holiday for the populace. The dozens of floats re-enacting battles from the victory, and showing scenes of strange cultures in far-flung lands, mixed with the sounds of trumpet and cymbal and the sweet smell of eastern spices released from silver censers, lent a distinct flavour of the circus and carnival. In the triumphal pageant Romans also learnt about the prowess of their armies and generals, about the nature of foreign peoples and the art, architecture, flora and fauna of the newly conquered lands. The event was a mix of entertainment and education, the *National Geographic* played out in street theatre.

The excitement of the spectacle jumps off the pages of Josephus who, in his description of Rome in AD 71, gives the most remarkable and detailed account of a Roman Triumph to survive from antiquity:

> Now it is impossible to describe the multitude of the shows as they deserve, and the magnificence of them all; such indeed as a man could not easily think of as performed either by the labour of workmen, or the variety of riches, or the rarities of nature; for almost all such curiosities as the most happy of men ever get by piecemeal were here heaped one upon another, and those both admirable and costly in their nature . . . for there was here to be seen a mighty quantity of silver and gold and ivory, contrived into all sorts of things, and did not appear as carried along in pompous show only, but, as a man may say, running along like a river.
>
> Some parts were composed of the rarest purple hangings, and so carried along; and others accurately represented to the life what was embroidered by the arts of the Babylonians. There were also precious stones that were transparent, some set in crowns of gold, and some in other ouches, as the workmen pleased . . . The images of the gods were

also carried, being as well wonderful for their largeness, as made very artificially, and with great skill of the workmen; nor were any of these images of any other than very costly materials; and many species of animals were brought, every one in their own natural ornaments.

The men also who brought every one of these shows were great multitudes, and adorned with purple garments, all over interwoven with gold; those that were chosen for carrying these pompous shows, having also about them such magnificent ornaments as were both extraordinary and surprising. Besides these, one might see even the great number of the captives was not unadorned, while the variety that was in their garments, and their fine texture, concealed from the sight the deformity of their bodies.

But what afforded the greatest surprise of all was the structure of the pageants that were borne along; for indeed he that met them could not but be afraid that the bearers would not be able firmly enough to support them, such was their magnitude; for many of them were so made, that they were on three or even four storeys, one above another. The magnificence also of their structure afforded one both pleasure and surprise; for upon many of them were laid carpets of gold. There was also wrought gold and ivory fastened about them all; and many resemblances of the war, and those in several ways, and variety of contrivances, affording a most lively portraiture of itself; for there was to be seen a happy country laid waste, and entire squadrons of enemies slain; while some of them ran away, and some were carried into captivity; with walls of great altitude and magnitude overthrown, and ruined by machines; with the strongest fortifications taken, and the walls of most populous cities upon the tops of hills seized on, and an army pouring itself within the walls; as also every place full of slaughter, and supplications of the enemies, when they were no longer able to lift up their hands in way of opposition.

Fire also sent upon temples was here represented, and houses overthrown and falling upon their owners: rivers also, after they came out of a large and melancholy desert, ran down, not into a land cultivated, nor as drink for men, or for cattle, but through a land still on fire upon every side; for the Jews related that such a thing they had undergone during this war. Now the workmanship of these representations was so magnificent and lively in the construction of the things that it exhibited what had been done to such as did not see it, as if they had been there really present. On the top of every one of these pageants was placed the commander of the city that was taken, and the manner wherein he was taken. (*JW* 7.132–47)

Josephus describes a lavish show that was a combination of entertainment, imperial self-glorification, and a moving image to validate the investment of millions of *sestertii* spent subjugating troublemakers in a far-off province. To the citizens of Rome the awesome spectacle of the Triumph would have had the sensory impact of the publicity staged by the armed forces of America and the United Kingdom during the First Gulf War. Like the scenes of precision smart-bombing in Iraq beamed through televisions into millions of Western living rooms, the Triumph acted as political propaganda to explain and justify the cause.

But the Triumph was much more than this; it was also a crucial magico-religious ceremony that goes beyond the rationality of the modern mind. Pomp, spectacle and largesse were all well and good, but in the final analysis the ceremony of the Triumph was an important rite of passage for Rome as a whole, thickly steeped in symbolic gesture.

The ritual of the procession took a standardised route following a meticulously planned format. First of all came white oxen destined for sacrifice to Jupiter (these beasts held the same connotations of purity and liberation that the white dove has today in Western consciousness). Next followed lictors in red war dress carrying *fasces*, the double-headed axes and traditional emblems of power from pre-Roman times (later adopted as a symbol by Mussolini's Fascists). Magistrates and the Senate then proceeded ahead of the emperor, whose two-wheeled chariot was drawn by four white horses, perhaps symbolising the four points of the compass controlled by the empire. Chained prisoners walked with bowed heads directly in front of the chariot. Finally, soldiers wearing laurel wreaths and singing coarse songs brought up the rear.

These tunes were odd. Rather than celebrate the good deeds of their commanders, the soldiers chose to deride them in the satirical style of rugby songs. Similarly, the motley crowd supposedly out in celebration would hurl insults at the passing emperor. How can the Triumph's contradictory combination of veneration and derision be explained?

If Roman society wished to play god, then it had to set in motion a complicated web of apotropaeic measures to counter the potential fury of the divine pantheon. For on the very day of a Roman

Triumph the victorious commander-in-chief was given the highest honour bestowed on a mortal by being elevated to the status of the supreme god, Jupiter. In the context of the Roman ritual, the term 'triumph' was originally not used as a noun but as an exclamation. As Vespasian and Titus drove their chariots along the streets of Rome the call of *triumpe* was not a cheer of victory, but an invocation of the god within the mortal to 'reveal yourself'.

Superstition was rampant within Roman society, which, at the drop of a hat, would consult the gods and animal entrails for advice on the most beneficial course of action, from the mundane to the monumental. In conferring the title of a god on a triumphant commander, Rome was aware that it ran the risk of unlocking the fury of its deities. Hence, the lewd marching songs and public insults. But even this was not enough protection for the commander-in-chief, so several further layers of religious armour were created to protect the *triumphator* from the envy of the gods.

Chests swelling amidst the adoration of the people, Vespasian and Titus would have been clothed in purple tunics and togas – family heirlooms reserved for state occasions. In their right hands each carried a laurel branch that imparted the power of plant life and regeneration (for the same reason that flower petals are strewn in front of a newly-wed couple today). Their left hands gripped ivory sceptres surmounted by an eagle, the ultimate symbol of Roman domination. Around their necks were placed a gold *bulla* to deflect the evil eye. Both the emperor and his son would also have been painted red for purposes that are not entirely clear, but possibly to imitate blood, perhaps to incite fear (in the manner of war paint) or to imitate the brilliance of the sun. Certainly statues of Jupiter, the ultimate Roman god, were painted red in antiquity, so this symbolic act mirrored the physiology of the supreme divinity.

Beneath the triumphal chariot – also decorated with laurel branches – hung a massive erect bronze phallus fastened with bells, whose purpose was again to instill strength in the riders and to counteract any ill-feeling of the gods. The giant phallus, a source of great humour to the modern mind, served as a kind of imperial lightning conductor against unwanted thunderbolts from the sky. The final piece of god-proof armour-plating was the heavy gold oak leaf crown, the *corona Etrusca*, held suspended by a state slave above the head of the *triumphator*. Both Vespasian and Titus may also have worn iron leg chains as expressions of humility, as the slave whispered into the victor's ears, 'Look behind you and remember that you are a man.' In other words a god for a day but, nevertheless, nothing more than a mere mortal elevated thus by the people of Rome. The gods were watching eagle-eyed and ready to pounce.

The spot where we have frozen the Triumph (at the junction between the Campus Martius and the Capitoline Hill, where the Via del Teatro di Marcello and the Vicus Jugarius meet today) was by far the most sensitive point of the procession. Not because of what Vespasian and Titus or the artistic directors of the pageant were doing, but because of the sacred landscape. For here most probably stood the mighty *Porta Triumphalis*, the Triumphal Gate that was only ever opened on the occasion of the Triumph.

The Gate was reached by a covered arcade, some of whose columns and arches can still be traced at the foot of the leafy Capitoline Hill, whose slopes would have offered a breathtaking view of the parade. From there the audience could enjoy the wide panorama of the River Tiber with the foreigners' quarter in the distance, the five temples just passed and the Theatre of Marcellus. The *porta*, however, was strangely not a true gate at all, but a free-standing structure that was not incorporated into a city wall. So why do ancient writers emphasise the importance of being able both to open and close the gate during the ceremony when, on any other day, you could simply walk around it to pass between city and riverside?

The brilliant mind of Sir James Frazer pondered precisely this enigma in his epic book, *The Golden Bough*, and concluded that rites of passage such as the Roman Triumph were intended to free people from certain taints or hostile spirits. For Frazer, the *Porta Triumphalis* was almost certainly a barrier meant to protect Rome against the pursuit of the spirits of the slain. By passing through the arch, and immediately locking its doors, any taboo could be lifted. The Triumphal Gate was thus a physical barrier between Rome and the angry ghosts of the Jews of Israel. Purification was extremely important for Rome to minimise war-born post-traumatic stress disorder, a point clarified by the Roman writer Festus: 'Laurel-wreathed soldiers followed the triumphal chariot, in order to enter the city as if purged of blood-guilt.'

However, the symbolism of this structure was even more complicated. Parallels can be drawn between the Triumph's rite of passage and a peculiar privilege bestowed on the winner of major athletic games in ancient Greece, who was allowed to enter his native town through a gap in the town wall knocked open especially for the occasion. Immediately after entry, the hole would be bricked up. Despite its ancient lineage, this rite was still practised and adapted by Rome for post-war rituals, and both the emperors Trajan and Nero are known to have assumed the honour. This eccentric behaviour was far more than a mark of respect; to ancient societies such rites of entry made it impossible for the bearer of good luck to disappear again.

Whether or not the victor swiftly left town through another gate was immaterial because symbolism equated to reality. The Triumphal Gate, an isolated structure set outside the city walls, may sound like nothing less than a pious fraud to us, but its powers were very real to Rome. Entry and closure until the celebration of the next Triumph guaranteed the ongoing blessing of good fortune upon the city by locking within it the bearer's newly acquired power. It was with the intent of not wasting a single drop of this energy that generals were compelled by the Senate to stay outside the sacred city boundary (typically around the Temples of Bellona or Apollo in the Field of Mars) until the Triumph started.

28

A Day at the Circus Maximus

WITH ABUSE RAINING down on Vespasian and Titus from the Capitoline Hill, the surreal sense of the Triumph was compounded by the event's extreme antiquity, dating back into the mists of Etruscan times and beyond into obscurity. For Etruria was the cradle of the Triumph. The resounding cry of *triumpe* that has bestowed its name on the event is a pre-Greek term disseminated to Rome by way of Etruria. The *insignia triumphalia*, both the gold laurel crown and royal robes, were all concepts borrowed from the Etruscan kings. The Triumph's ancient legacy greatly magnified the spectacle's sense of tradition and the sacred.

On the days when I walked the route taken by the Temple treasure of Jerusalem during the Triumph of AD 71, the passage beyond the Vicus Jugarius always left me uncomfortably numb. Immediately after exiting a landscape dedicated to bloodshed and war – the Field of Mars – Rome was purged of the estimated 1.1 million people Josephus alleges were killed in Judaea. In an instant the solemn ceremonial air fell away, forgotten, and the carnival began.

Today the road leading up the Vicus Jugarius to the south-western entrance of the Forum and the Precinct of the Harmonious Gods is lush with birds merrily chirping from coniferous trees, their own well-appointed avian theatre-stands. Taking a rest on the steps of the Church of Santa Maria della Consolazione, built between 1583 and 1606 and polished to a shine by a million dedicated feet, vivid images of the historical Triumph flashed across my mind. I found that I could not share Rome's ferocious celebrations. Consolazione? The irony fell as thick as the rain now lashing the afternoon sky. What consolation would the Jews of Israel, pantomime figures of amusement, have felt dragged in front of the gleaming chariot of the emperor Vespasian?

The Triumphal Gate was their personal Bridge of Sighs. Death or enslavement, at best, would be their prize.

Elegantly dressed Italians sauntered to church through the Piazza della Consolazione, located towards the end of one route of the ancient Triumphal Way, and a cacophony of joyous bells competed with the deep drum of thunder over the Palatine. The atmosphere was bleak. Rome's rocky foundations peered out from uninhabited parts of the Capitoline Hill, and I gazed at where it met the Forum and its ponderous, black-cobbled linear streets. Here the law of nature ended and the cruel civilisation of Roman rule began.

Shrouded in peals of lightning and rain, I took in the view of the short stretch leading from the Triumphal Gate to the Forum and immediately doubted whether Vespasian would have chosen this corner-cutting option. Josephus emphatically described the route as leading through the 'theatres' (in the plural), and certainly meant the Circus Flaminius and the Theatre of Marcellus. In view of the modest length and scarcity of monuments leading up the Vicus Jugarius, I was now convinced Josephus also alluded to the greatest entertainment facility of pre-Flavian Rome – the Circus Maximus. Why was I so sure?

First of all, this route makes sense geographically. Rather than creaking up narrow streets towards the south-western flank of the Forum, by continuing in a straight line parallel to the River Tiber the Triumphal snake would have escaped the narrow roads to emerge into the wide Forum Boarium, Rome's Cattle Market. The Triumph was thus structured to be a process of revelation, initially glimpsed in short sections by the dense crowd, but after the Field of Mars appreciated in its full glory. Along the way, various Roman temples offered an appropriately religious backdrop to the most spectacular act: procession down the Circus Maximus itself, opposite the Palatine Hill and the imperial palace. By taking this route the Triumph would have pursued Rome's logical topography and completed a perfect circular itinerary without ever turning back on itself or compromising its dramatic impact.

A further signpost of unequivocal proof are the remains of a second Arch of Titus built within the Circus Maximus itself in AD 80–81. Today it is completely destroyed, so the enticing question of whether it too depicted scenes of the triumphal subjugation of the

Jews – a fair bet – remains a tantalising enigma. Although the arch was levelled in the fifteenth century, a record of the bold wording once written up large on the Circus arch's façade is preserved:

> The Senate and People of Rome . . . to the Emperor Titus Caesar, son of Vespasian . . . tribunician power for the tenth time (AD 81), their princeps . . . because following his father's advice and policy, and under his auspices, he conquered the Jewish people and captured the city of Jerusalem, which by all kings, generals, or peoples before his time had assailed in vain or left unassailed.

Even though Titus' claim was yet again a flagrant piece of Flavian propaganda – both Pompey the Great in 63 BC and Sossius, Roman governor of Syria, in 37 BC had subdued parts of Palestine – the emperor clearly plastered this piece of self-glorification on the Circus arch as a memorial to the precise route of the Triumph of AD 71. But what did the Circus Maximus contribute to the magic of the day?

Despite the storm overhead, I was determined to pursue the question. Springing down the steps of the Piazza della Consolazione, I skirted the walls of palaces and Renaissance town houses to find the driest path back to the modern crossroads leading up to the Via del Foro Olitario, Fabricius' Bridge and the Tiber, and right back to the Theatre of Marcellus.

Cutting left down the Via Luigi Petroselli, I moved swiftly past the Comune di Roma, a great lump of Fascist architecture. Posters demanded 'Non Stop Per Cuba! Bush Vergogna' (Shame on George Bush for Sanctions Against Cuba), and two-tone faces of a black and white woman on a poster sponsored by the Ministry of Equal Opportunities invited victims of racial discrimination to call a toll-free telephone number. Beneath my feet the city's manholes, commissioned by Benito Mussolini, were emblazoned with the letters SPQR – *Senatus Populusque Romanus* (The Senate and People of Rome). The abbreviation once proudly carried into war on top of legionary standards would have been stamped on every piece of military kit carried in the Triumph of AD 71. What once struck fear in the empire's enemies now remains the urban legacy of a twentieth-century Fascist dictator. Like the SPQR manholes, Mussolini's reputation ended up in the sewers of history.

In the later first century AD, this part of town, the Ripa district, was thick with wharves and warehouses. Here the Triumph ran the gauntlet of the rougher elements of society, marching past the Temple of Portunus dedicated to the god of harbours and the circular Temple of Vesta of the sacred fire, who celebrated victory and successful commercial enterprise. Before heading uphill through the Via dei Cerchi, a giant eagle guarding the entrance to the old pasta factory on the Piazza Bocca della Verità (Square of the Mouth of Truth) watched my progress with beady eyes.

Today the Circus Maximus is little more than a pleasant park. Good folk lose themselves in books under shady trees (when it's not pouring with rain) and dogs chase sticks across the long shadows cast by the grass incline where the Circus seating was once installed. Joggers pound the ground where immaculately polished horse chariots once raced. Oblivious, tramps sleep off the night's hangover on beds of newspapers.

To the north-west the Circus flanks the back of the Piazza Bocca della Verità, which coincidentally houses the long-winded Laboratorio e Raccolta di Scene Attrezzi e Costumi del Teatro dell'Opera, where sets for the latest opera productions are brought to life. Past and present fuse in a common interest in the theatrical. On the southern side of the Circus Maximus a bronze statue of Giuseppe Mazzini (1805–72), the first politician to unite a fragmented Italy into a single country, and one of the patron saints of the Italian *Risorgimento* (Resurgence) movement, straddles a vast marble base sculpted with monumental scenes of soldiers on horseback trampling the enemy underfoot in a fight for independence. The area today is nothing like the scene in AD 71, when the Temple treasure entered the lions' den to 250,000 deafening cheers reverberating across the stands.

The Circus Maximus is by far the oldest and largest of ancient Rome's great places of entertainment: founded by the Etruscan king Tarquin the Elder (616–578 BC) in the Vallis Murcia, it was dedicated initially to horse racing during the Consualia festivities held in honour of Consus, the god of counsel and protector of harvests – a serious issue in the pre-pesticide age.

At the time, this part of rural Rome was characterised by a brook flowing down a valley and was home to a primitive harvest cult. Once a year, farmers would race one another on mules crowned with flowers. Over the course of 500 years the Circus would evolve dramatically to attract cults of the sun and moon, highly appropriate for harvest celebrations. By 493 BC, a Temple of Ceres, Liber and Libera – fertility and cultivation deities – arose close to the modern monument of Giuseppe Mazzini.

The Circus through which the Temple spoils of Jerusalem were paraded in AD 71 owed its anatomy largely to Julius Caesar, the Jews' champion, who confirmed its canonical shape – with two long sides terminating at a semi-circular end – for his own Triumph of 46 BC. Caesar's three-storey Circus measured 621 metres long and 118 metres wide, with stands rising 28 metres above the racetrack. Colonnades swept along its edges; boisterous shops abutted the outside of the stands.

Entering the Circus from the north-west, the treasures of Jerusalem and captive Jews were frogmarched through the arena, lambs to the slaughter. The sheer size of the Circus and the cacophony of the raucous mob would have been terrifying. Never before could these provincials have seen such artistic brilliance: along the central *spina* (barrier) were ranged a statue of Magna Mater (the ultimate Mother Goddess) mounted on a rampant lion alongside a palm tree; bridges covered with sculptures of animals and athletes; a statue of Victory with her chest puffed out; sculpted dolphins playing amidst flowing water. High on their palatial crow's nest on the Palatine Hill, on a podium jutting out over the centre of the Circus, the imperial family cheered on Vespasian and Titus.

Although the Circus Maximus was designed largely with chariot races in mind, a host of other entertainments could be enjoyed here from leopard, bear and elephant hunts to the ultimate seven-day spectacle of the Ludi Saeculares festivities of AD 204, when the emperor Septimius Severus had a massive wooden ship theatrically wrecked and its cargo of 700 animals of seven species released into the arena. Coins minted for this event aptly captured the *zeitgeist* with the legend 'What Happy Times'.

The Circus was indeed devoted to promoting an inclusive feeling of goodwill among Rome's hierarchy of citizens, from the imperial family watching on the Palatine to the populace rubbing shoulders in the unsegregated arena. This unusual freedom of seating earned the

Circus a reputation as a popular pick-up place. And if you weren't lucky, you could always buy sex. As Ammianus Marcellinus would complain in his history of the period AD 353–78, the plebs

> spend all their life with wine and dice, in low haunts, pleasures, and the games. Their temple, their dwelling, their assembly, and the height of all their hopes is the Circus Maximus . . . [They] often swear by their hoary hair and wrinkles that the state cannot exist if in the coming race the charioteer whom each favours is not the first to rush forth from the barriers, and fails to round the turning-point closely with his ill-omened horses. (*Res Gestae* 28.4.29–30)

Ammianus Marcellinus was right. The Circus Maximus was the people's palace, a theatre of dreams where they could watch a live form of reality television, with a crowd capacity over three times greater than the stadiums today of Manchester United or the New York Giants. Chariot racing was ancient Rome's football, a fanatical mass religion. Here, you could bet on high drama and bloodshed. For months on end, neighbours would duel verbally over fences about forthcoming races and talk trash down the bar. Real animosity divided the various teams, predominantly the Blues, Greens, Reds and Whites.

The social status of the drivers gave the Circus mass appeal. Whilst the African and Spanish chariot horses were well-reared thoroughbreds, the ancient equivalent of the Formula 1 racing car, the charioteers were *infames* of low standing, slaves or freedmen who were wholly dispensable. Yet fortunes could be won on the race track: the satirist Juvenal moaned that a charioteer could earn a hundred times the fee of a lawyer, while Martial begrudged the fifteen bags of gold Scorpus won in a single hour. The David Beckham of his age, however, was surely the second-century AD Portuguese immigrant, Gaius Appuleius Diocles, who earned over 25 million sesterces in 4,257 races (about £14 million), winning 1,462 times over a twenty-four-year career. Scorpus and Diocles gave the masses dreams of economic mobility and celebrity, an escape from the gutter. Betting at the Circus was Rome's National Lottery.

Into this scene – with its thousands of faces, stench of horse dung, prostitutes consorting with customers while the sun shone overhead: a scene observed in its totality from the royal box on the Palatine – I would like to think that the noise dwindled to an amazed murmur with the arrival of the Temple treasure. Of all the spectacles enjoyed that day, this was the crowning moment of acclaim for the emperor Vespasian and Titus. Again we are indebted to the meticulous mind of Josephus for capturing this moment:

> Moreover, there followed those pageants a great number of ships; and for the other spoils, they were carried in great plenty. But for those that were taken in the temple of Jerusalem, they made the greatest figure of them all; that is, the golden table, of the weight of many talents; the candlestick also, that was made of gold . . . the small branches were produced out of it to a great length, having the likeness of a trident in their position, and had every one a socket made of brass for a lamp at the tops of them. These lamps were in number seven, and represented the dignity of the number seven among the Jews; and the last of all the spoils was carried the Laws of the Jews.
>
> After these spoils passed by a great many men, carrying the images of Victory, whose structure was entirely either of ivory or of gold. After which Vespasian marched in the first place, and Titus followed him; Domitian also rode along with them, and made a glorious appearance, and rode on a horse that was worthy of admiration. (*JW* 7.148–52)

After soaking up the adulation of the crowd in the Circus Maximus, the Triumph turned left on to the modern Via di San Gregorio and passed the pink rose bushes flourishing today where, according to Roman tradition, Romulus and Remus were reared. Opposite the Palatine Hill the Church of San Gregorio Magno, named after Pope Gregory the Great (AD 590–604), stands on the spot where classical antiquity ended and the medieval age was born. From here St Augustine set off to convert England to Christianity. The aqueduct supplying the imperial palace on the Palatine is today severed by a fast-flowing thoroughfare speeding up to the Colosseum.

In AD 71, the Colosseum, however, was nothing more than a blueprint on an architect's desk, even though its funding – looted Jewish gold – was now secure. Once proclaimed emperor, Vespasian would have spared no time recutting the 35-metre-high gilded bronze Colossus of Nero commissioned from Zenodorus. Where the emperor playing god once looked down his monstrously huge nose at the citizens of Rome to the right of the Sacred Way, Vespasian refashioned the statue into the sun-god Helios. Under the Flavians the sun would shine on Rome every day. The memory of Nero, the perpetual showman who ransacked the provinces of its finest art for personal pleasure and left the treasury deeply in debt, was officially damned by decree of the Senate in an act of *damnatio memoriae*.

For scale of town planning and monumental architecture, the Roman Forum remains breathtakingly impressive. But as I approached the last leg of the Triumphal Way my heart wasn't in the chase any more. The sixth sense of death and jostling crowds baying for Jewish blood was all too oppressive.

Soaked to its core by the storm overhead, the Forum was deserted. At the summit of the Sacred Way the Triumph reached the high point of the Forum and gazed down on the most powerful and elaborate urban artery of the civilised world. On this very plateau in AD 80–81, Titus would immortalise the Triumph with the best known of his three arches. Artistic reliefs would replicate the all-conquering royal commander and later emperor parading by chariot across this very spot, and capture the Temple treasure being carted in triumph on wooden stretchers through this great arch – the golden Table, the pair of silver trumpets and the seven-branched candelabrum.

Under heavy skies I continued the pilgrimage down the Sacred Way. Its original black-cobbled path was now flooded, and a stream of water ran through my boots. So much for Rome's legendary hydrology. The narrow lane of the Via Sacra would have strung out the Triumph at this point, slowing its progress, which no doubt suited the patient and packed Forum. The Porticus (covered walkway) of Gaius and Lucius (the grandsons of the emperor Augustus) would have welcomed the head of the snake. Though one of the most magnificent buildings of the Roman world, today only its meagre foundations stand above ground. The fear of the Jewish captives would have mounted as they gazed at statues of barbarians crafted from Numidian yellow marble and Phrygian purple foreshadowing the Jews' pending life of slavery. The Land of Israel can never have felt further away.

I passed the Senate and the Orator's Platform, the *rostra*, where Vespasian and Titus received the blessing of Rome on the morning of the great day. By now the emperor and his son would have symbolically nailed the most important *spolia opima* to a mighty oak tree within the city gates. Although most military spoils had to be burned well outside the city precinct in the Field of Mars, the personal weapons of the enemy general were believed to retain magical powers. An impressive public trophy and a symbol of conquest, the spoils also emitted beneficial energy for the possessor, in this case the city of Rome.

A hushed silence now fell over the Forum as the final ritual approached, again reported at length by our chief witness, Josephus:

> Now the last part of this pompous show was at the Temple of Jupiter Capitolinus, whither when they were come, they stood still; for it was the Romans' ancient custom to stay, till somebody brought the news that the general of the enemy was slain. This general was Simon, the son of Gioras, who had then been led in this triumph among the captives; a rope had also been put upon his head, and he had been drawn into a proper place on the forum, and had within been tormented by those that drew him along, and the law of the Romans required that malefactors condemned to die should be slain there.
>
> Accordingly, when it was related that there was an end to him, and all the people had sent up a shout for joy, they then began to offer those sacrifices which they had consecrated, in the prayers used in such solemnities; which when they had finished, they went away to the palace. And for some of these spectators the emperor entertained them at their own feast; and for all the rest there were noble preparations made for their feasting at home; for this was a festival day to the city of Rome, as celebrated for the victory obtained by their army over their enemies, for the end that was now put to their civil miseries, and for the commencement of their hopes of future prosperity and happiness. (*JW* 7.153–7)

The Mamertine Prison, that 'proper place' where Simon was killed, still exists opposite the peaceful square dominated by the Church of Saints Luke and Martina, where pigeons perching on the top steps washed themselves in puddles of rainwater. The prison is a foul place through which spring water continuously dripped in antiquity. In 40 BC the Roman writer Sallust described this cell as 'a place called the *Tullianum* . . . about 12 feet deep, closed all round by strong walls and a stone vault. Its aspect is repugnant and fearsome from its neglect, darkness and stench.' Go there if you must.

Exhausted, I decided against entering Rome's subterranean death hole, today in the basement of the chapel of San Giuseppe dei Falegnami; instead, I imagined what the Jewish leader's last earthly sight might have been. Desperately looking over his shoulder as he was pushed into this evil hole, Simon ben Giora's gaze would have wandered across the Precinct of the Harmonious Gods and the *Umbilicus Urbis*, the Navel of the City and carefully guarded gateway to the underworld. Was this followed by the spectacle of a deep blue sky calling him heavenward?

For the sake of completeness I tracked down the Temple of Jupiter Optimus Maximus Capitolinus up the Clivus Capitolinus, or rather its foundations hidden beneath scaffolding currently used to restore the exterior of the Palazzo dei Conservatori. There, Vespasian and Titus awaited the screams of delight announcing the death of Simon the Jew. Over time Rome would fall, and the Temple of Jupiter be replaced by a centre of musical excellence, the Conservatory. And the roar of the bloodthirsty crowd would be drowned out by the dulcet tones of piano keys – the sound of angels imposed over the echoes of death.

29

A Temple for Peace

WITH THE HEAD of the Jewish uprising decapitated, and the Triumph confined to collective memory as one of Rome's most glorious days, Vespasian planned a more enduring legacy of his Judaean conquest.

What the emperor had in mind was something not just functional, but a visually stunning memorial that, for generations to come, would endure as a physical symbol of Rome's global power – military, political, economic and cultural. The Temple of Peace, *Templum Pacis*, was designed to be that symbol, an eternal reminder of the death and destruction wreaked by the Jewish Revolt, and also, crucially, a monument to Vespasian's brilliance in forging universal peace between Rome and the peoples brought within its borders. Thus Josephus informs us that:

> The triumphal ceremonies being concluded and the empire of the Romans established on the firmest foundation, Vespasian decided to erect a temple of Peace. This was very speedily completed and in a style surpassing all human conception. For, besides having prodigious resources of wealth on which to draw he also embellished it with ancient masterpieces of painting and sculpture; indeed, into that shrine were accumulated and stored all objects for the sight of which men had once wandered over the whole world, eager to see them individually while they lay in various countries. Here, too, he laid up the vessels of gold from the temple of the Jews, on which he prided himself. (*JW* 7.158–61)

So the Temple treasure of Jerusalem, symbol of the spiritual heart of Judaism seized in the bloodiest of circumstances, ended up 'imprisoned' in yet another temple across the seas. The tranquil-sounding name of its new place of rest should not deceive us into assuming that Rome retained any respect for the holy utensils' religious significance. Rather, the heart of Judaism had been torn out of a living body and was conspicuously displayed as the centrepiece of a public museum. The image of the Temple of Peace was both rhetorical and paradoxical. Although Vespasian represented the temple complex as a memorial to the domestic peace he forged after the civil wars that followed the death of Nero and the repression of the Jewish rebellion, to Judaism it symbolised public humiliation. The monument was a continual thorn in the flesh of Rome's Jewish population, a constant reminder of its perceived inferiority.

But what did this Temple of Peace look like and how long did the Temple treasure remain there? To digest these difficult questions I stepped aside for a break in the Angelino ai Fori pizzeria, whose prime location at the very top of the Via dei Fori Imperiali, the modern road that bisects the ancient Forum, offers panoramic views of the Eternal City 2,000 years ago.

Behind me rose the theatrical stage of the Colosseum, where every stone seat concealed a thousand tales. Directly in front, Trajan's Column recorded in picturebook relief the exploits of the emperor Trajan's conquest over the Germanic tribes. To my right stood the first-floor portico where, according to tradition, Nero wept as he watched his beloved Rome burn in the great fire of June AD 64.

Today we take architectural marvels in our urban jungles for granted and hardly blink at yet another Norman Foster creation rising in the middle of London or the erection of the world's highest skyscraper in Kuala Lumpur. But imagine trying to break the design mould, as Rome did, in the absence of three-dimensional computer modelling programmes? Ancient engineers had no computers, cranes or bulldozers to rely on, only manpower and human sweat. An estimated 15 per cent of Rome's adult population toiled in the building industry, manhandling some 5.5 million cubic metres of marble quarried over the course of 400 years for the Eternal City.

Wearily, I put down my dusty maps and the reams of ancient records that would help me pinpoint the modern location of the Temple of Peace. Through the window I watched local drivers startling tourists as they attempted to cross roads and weaving mischievously around islands of petrified people. My guidebook usefully confirmed that 'there can only be two sorts of pedestrian in Rome: the quick and the dead'.

I slowly pored over my maps, only to realise that I was eating within the very walls of the Temple of Peace. Or rather, had the temple survived I would be sitting in its eastern corner. According to my research, Vespasian commissioned the Temple of Peace in AD 71 on a vacant plot of land north-east of the Forum of Nerva, formerly used as the Republican cattle market, and celebrated its dedication four years later. So Josephus wasn't quite accurate about it being built in so short a time that was 'beyond all human expectations'. It was quick, but not that quick. The term 'temple' is also inappropriate because the *Pacis Opera*, as ancient texts initially called it, was a large precinct incorporating a suite of monuments and functions. Modern literature usually calls the complex the Forum of Peace.

The area certainly comprised a large assembly point similar to a forum, and was not just a triumphal monument standing in splendid isolation. The temple was square in shape – a typical forum design – measuring some 108 metres along both sides, with a large altar recessed inside a semi-circular exedra. The entire complex was surrounded by a lavish enclosed walkway supported by huge marble columns reaching 18 metres into the sky. The massive size of the temple, some ten times larger than Augustus' great Altar of Peace, was a deliberate architectural expression of Vespasian's power. Size counted for everything in Rome, especially to the Flavian dynasty, which needed to plaster over its lack of imperial qualifications. The finished edifice was considered by Pliny the Elder one of the three most beautiful buildings ever to grace Rome, alongside the Basilica Paulli and the Forum of Augustus.

Annexed to the temple were two intriguing structures, the *Bibliotheca Pacis* (Library of Peace) and a later addition, the Hall of the Marble Plan. Naturally, as the self-styled centre of the civilised world, Rome took its libraries very seriously, but not in the modern sense. Certainly logs of imperial accounts, military events and taxation were systematically maintained alongside scrolls of literature and plays. But the earliest libraries were assembled as spoils of war. According to Plutarch, Lucullus' public library derived from the booty he had obtained during military campaigns in Asia Minor:

He collected many well-written books, and his use of them was more commendable than their acquisition. He opened his libraries to everyone, and the colonnades and lounges around them were accessible without restriction to the Greeks, who would come there, as if to a reception hall of the Muses, and pass whole days together, happily staying away from their own duties.

By the time the emperor Augustus died in AD 14, Rome boasted three great libraries: Pollio's library next to the Forum, another at the Porticus of Octavia, and Augustus' library connected with the Temple of Apollo on the Palatine Hill. Over time libraries even appeared inside Roman bathhouses to increase the recreational experience. We all like to read the paper in the bath. However, we should not be misled. These institutions were not designed just as centres of learning for educated bookworms, but were excellent excuses for the ostentatious display of the owner's wealth.

The name of the *Bibliotheca Pacis* is thus misleading because, although it would have held papyrus manuscripts, its main purpose was the conspicuous display of Vespasian's artistic masterpieces. Alongside the Temple treasure, Pliny records how Vespasian returned to the public many of the artistic masterpieces originating in Greece and Asia Minor that Nero, his predecessor, had privately hoarded for personal gratification in his golden palace, the *Domus Aurea*, including antique Greek statues such as the Galati group from Pergamon, the Ganymede of Leochares, and masterpieces by Pheidias and Polykleitos, as well as an anonymous Venus, goddess of love.

The largest recorded example of a statue crafted from Ethiopian *basanites*, a rock described by Pliny as of the same colour and hardness as iron, also graced the Temple of Peace. This personification of the Nile in human form was surrounded by sixteen of the river-god's children playing merrily, denoting the number of cubits reached by the river in flood at its highest desirable level for watering agricultural fields. The masterpiece was thus an expression of perfect harmony and prosperity. Alongside hung vast paintings, including Nicomacus' Scylla, and Ialysus, the mythical founder of Rhodes, immortalised by Protogenes of Caunus holding a palm tree. In other words, this 'Library' of Peace was a very public and deliberate display of its patron's wealth, taste and munificence.

But where were the spoils and these other masterworks actually displayed? By a generous twist of fate, substantial evidence exists for the anatomy of the Temple of Peace: a whole wall of it. The last structure to grace the temple, the Hall of the Marble Plan, was a brilliant example of cutting-edge art and design. This room was custom-built to accommodate the *Forma Urbis Romae*, or what is known more familiarly today as the Severan Marble Plan, a giant-sized map of ancient Rome displayed vertically on the south-eastern wall of the Temple of Peace. The layout of the Eternal City between the River Tiber to the north and beyond the Colosseum to the south was incised between AD 203 and 211 at a scale of 1:240 on large rectangular slabs of white marble imported from quarries on the island of Proconnesus in modern Turkey's Sea of Marmara.

The map was enormous, measuring about 18 by 13 metres, and covered one entire wall of the Temple of Peace. Roman citizen or foreigner, the observer would never have seen anything like it in the civilised world. To a backdrop of some of that world's most important art – much of it antique and most of it looted – Rome's rulers illustrated the very city that was responsible for its world domination. The Severan Marble Plan was a flagrant form of self-publicity and imperial pride rather than an information point for lost tourists.

By virtue of early Christianity's respect for classical antiquity, the original Roman wall on to which the Plan was fixed still stands as the outer wall of the Church of Saints Cosmas and Damian, built by Pope Felix in AD 527, complete with a network of holes that once held pegs bolted to the backs of the slabs of Proconnesian marble. The map itself disappeared in the course of the early fifth-century Gothic invasions, to be cut up and reused in new building projects across the city; other fragments were thrown into limekilns, melting into historical obscurity.

Nevertheless, 1,186 fragments have cropped up in excavations across Rome since 1562. Even though the surviving 'document' only equates to 10–15 per cent of the original map, these fragments remain the single most important form of surviving evidence for reconstructing the ancient Roman ground plan of every architectural feature in the city.

By sheer luck, several surviving marbles show the Temple of Peace, allowing its square shape with an eastern main hall to be reconstructed. Ongoing excavations around the edges of the Via dei Fori Imperiali are also exposing key features, allowing Italian archaeologists to confirm that the monument was a vast square surrounded on three sides by an arcade built with pink Egyptian Aswan granite columns. An 18-metre-high outer wall slanted inwards to create an internal arcaded walkway.

The monumental entrance leading into two rectangular halls, fronted by gigantic Aswan granite columns and multicoloured marble revetment, was situated to the north-west, facing on to the Forum of Nerva. Long presumed destroyed by later development, especially Renaissance shops, in 2005 the Soprintendenza Archeologica di Roma found the Temple of Peace's original spectacular floor surface beneath three metres of smashed pottery and piles of horse bones. The fieldwork uncovered ritual libation basins adjacent to a raised *cella* reached by steps, and on it the 1.5-metre-wide rectangular plinth where the statue of the divine being maintained law and order. The marble floor is a fitting architectural wonder, combining exotic imperial purple granite from Egypt's Mons Porphyrites with Libyan peachy *giallo antico*. Circular foundations for six colossal 1.8-metre-wide columns stand in their original positions.

One remaining riddle in the Temple of Peace's design has long perplexed archaeologists: the purpose of twenty-four interconnected rectangular slots visible on the Severan Marble Plan. The new excavations have finally resolved this enigma by interpreting them as garden water features. Six long walls measuring 1.5 metres in height proved to be brick installations with marble veneer and channels used for water drainage. The tank podiums are thought to have held exotic plants, probably the highly prized Gallic rose.

The main area of the Temple of Peace thus seems to have been dedicated to a serene garden filled with fragrant flowers, peaceful flowing water and rolling gardens – a perfect backdrop for the artistic masterpieces that Vespasian positioned inside the temple. It was here, amidst a memorial to one of Rome's finest hours, that the great Temple treasure of Jerusalem would be gazed at in wonder for more than 350 years.

Vandal Carthage

30

Jewish Gold, Barbarian Loot

SOMETHING STRANGE HOVERED in the air. The city of Tunis was gasping for breath amidst dense smog. Ghostly outlines of cars weaved in and out of traffic; people and buildings were swallowed by a vile, thick pea soup of pollution and swirling Saharan sand boiled to a sticky 80 per cent humidity. Whatever Tunisians claim to pour into their petrol tanks, it surely isn't lead-free fuel. With manic policemen waving their hands and blowing whistles in a vain attempt to control the lawless traffic from red- and white-striped patrol booths – looking for all the world as if they were orchestrating a Punch and Judy show – I couldn't help but wonder whether I'd landed in the aftermath of some kind of chemical meltdown.

The surreal feeling was exacerbated by the blurred image of an oversized Super Mouse waving from the side of a street. Was I dreaming? My taxi driver laughed and explained in lyrical French laced with a local Arabic patois that this cartoon figure is the national symbol of government initiatives to protect the environment. The politicians may be seriously tackling local pollution, but when the mighty Sahara stirs and takes to the skies like a biblical swarm of locusts, nature beats civilisation with a stick every time. I would lose count of the number of Tunisians I met with a permanent frog in their throat, endlessly clearing grains of sand from their mouths.

Arriving in Tunisia in early October 2005, and observing this proud ancient country on an off-day, suited the purpose of my visit. I was chasing Armageddon. Over the weeks the smog would lift to reveal glorious azure skies and sun-kissed beaches confirming why this most democratic of North African countries is such a popular package holiday destination.

Ancient Tunisia, or rather its capital Carthage, was where the final death knell of classical antiquity sounded. For 200 years after Vespasian's epic Triumph of AD 71, Rome wallowed in its magnificent superiority, successfully commanding a labyrinthine globalised empire. Of all the satellite provinces great and small, far and wide, Tunisia dazzled most brightly within the imperial crown. A guide to the economic glory of Rome written in the mid-fourth century AD, the *Expositio Totius Mundi et Gentium*, described the region as 'rich in all things. It is adorned with all goods, grains as well as beasts, and almost all alone it supplies to all peoples the oil they needed.'

North Africa was certainly agriculturally blessed, but Tunisia was without doubt Rome's breadbasket *par excellence*. Not only did its wealthy estates and endless wheatfields, vine trellises and olive groves yield by far the largest taxes for the imperial treasury, but its corn and oil were staple forms of welfare doled out to Rome's city poor on a daily basis. The imperial government needed Tunisia desperately. She was irreplaceable.

However, in AD 429 Rome's love affair with its favourite province was brutally shattered – the barbarians were on the move. In May of that year a wave of 80,000 migrants, including soldiers, children and slaves, sailed across the Straits of Gibraltar and swept east along the North African coast. Although this motley crew were drawn from various barbarian tribes – among them Goths, Alans and even Hispano-Romans – the protagonists of pain were an east Germanic tribe whose bloody world view conjures up dark images to this day: the Vandals.

For generations, the Vandals in their frozen Germanic heartland had listened to endless tales about the luxuries of the lands to the south. Across the icy Danube they grew envious of the spoilt Roman soldiers manning the frontier, enjoying pork processed on imperial farms and wine imported from exotic shores. Towards the end of the fourth century AD, Rome was rocked by internal civil war, which punctured the vulnerable imperial infrastructure. The time was ripe for the Vandals to introduce themselves to their neighbours. In *The Fall of Rome and the End of Civilization*, Dr Bryan Ward-Perkins of Oxford University explains that 'The new arrival had not been invited, and he brought with him a large family; they ignored the bread and butter, and headed straight for the cake stand.'

After absorbing waves of exhausting Gothic raids, and with the empire itself now divided between the West and an eastern capital at Constantinople, the empire's resources were emaciated. Rome despaired as the barbarians, 'pressed by hunger', according to the Byzantine court historian Procopius, helped themselves to the best cakes in the land. Vast tracts of North Africa were conceded to the *rex Vandalorum et Alanorum*, as Rome knew the Vandals, by a treaty of AD 435. Four years later the barbarians seized the ultimate trophy, Carthage, the second greatest city of antiquity after Rome and, by AD 477, controlled an enormous swathe of the Mediterranean including the Balearic Islands, Sardinia, Corsica and parts of Sicily. The Roman Empire had relied on Tunisia for food and sustenance for so long that it had no alternative but to swallow its pride and trade with the new masters of Africa. It was the only way to maintain a way of life to which it had grown accustomed over 400 years.

Less than a generation after leaving behind their life as barbarians the Vandals had shed their animal furs, taken over the empire's old aristocratic estates and were mimicking the *dolce vita*. For decades they had watched the masters of decadence and oppression – and waited. Now they wasted little time in replicating Rome's extravagant ways. Only one final objective remained, to seize the cakeshop itself – Rome.

──────◆─◆──────

My taxi sped across the endless flatlands of suburban Tunis, a blend of 1970s France and Middle Eastern immaterialism. Few people were at large. Unfinished, low-rise housing drifted endlessly across the sandy soils. Most of it sat empty, like a makeshift refugee camp, awaiting more dinars for completion. Much of the typically single-storey housing seemed ill at ease in the landscape, as unwelcome as the Vandals. This was not the result of poor city planning, but because the flat terrain is not *terra firma* at all but the ancient seabed, long silted up.

A few kilometres east of Tunis the flatlands were interrupted by a lush, wooded hill straddling the sea of suburbia. Its summit is dominated by an enormous cathedral that proclaims the site to be the acropolis of ancient Carthage. The Cathedral of St Louis was built in 1890 and dedicated to King Louis IX who, in 1270, died of the plague while besieging Carthage in an attempt to convert the Muslim king to Christianity. An ignoble end and a grand memorial have sliced away at the heart of this once great city.

We drove past this imposing island of civilisation amidst sea and sand, and the mighty power of the place struck home. From here the Vandals planned the sack of Rome; from its military port the fleet sailed directly to the Eternal City in AD 455. Opinion is divided as to why the barbarians ravaged Rome: was this act driven by greed, expansionist policies or a will for retribution? The historian Procopius offers a pretty elementary explanation: 'And Gaiseric, for no other reason than that he suspected that much money would come to him, set sail for Italy with a great fleet. And going up to Rome, since no one stood in his way, he took possession of the palace' (*Wars* 3.5.1).

To delve a little deeper, it is clear that Rome was simply too large a prize for the Vandals to ignore, especially since petty palace intrigue virtually handed the city to Gaiseric on a plate. The roots of the sack of the Eternal City involved a cruel love triangle and the wantonness of the emperor Valentinian III, who was infatuated with a woman described by Procopius as 'discreet in her ways and exceedingly famous for her beauty', even if history has failed to preserve her name. The only obstacle stopping Valentinian from seducing her was the woman's inconvenient marriage to Petronius Maximus, an aristocratic Roman senator.

After scheming for some time, the lustful Valentinian invited Maximus to the palace and a gentle game of draughts. On winning, the emperor light-heartedly accused the senator of never making good his debts, and forced the senator's ring from his hand as a temporary pledge of payment. Valentinian now had his weapon, and duped Maximus' wife by sending her the ring. Assuming her husband had summoned her, she sped to the palace where the emperor had his way with the object of his desire.

Racked with rage and guilt, Maximus relentlessly plotted against Valentinian, finally killing him and seizing the throne in AD 455. With his own wife now dead, Maximus sealed the ring of fate by forcibly marrying Valentinian's wife, the empress Eudoxia. With nothing left to lose, Eudoxia responded by writing to the Vandal king, Gaiseric, entreating him to come to Rome and avenge the death of the emperor. The Vandal king needed no second invitation to seize this opportunity with both hands. Eudoxia has gone down in history as the empress who personally handed the barbarians the keys to Rome. No surprise, then, that ancient writers such as Theophanes Confessor immortalised her in his *Chronographia* as an immoral witch who 'cohabited with other women in demonic fashion and continually conversed even with those who practised magic'.

The Vandals had an ambivalent attitude to Roman culture. On the one hand they torched, raped, and pillaged property. On the other, they mimicked aristocratic Roman lifestyles, minting imitation coins and retaining traditional forms of architecture. With no indigenous ideology to promote, the barbarians seized a ready-made culture as their own.

So with time-honoured Roman flair, the Vandals set Italy alight as they marched on Rome in AD 455. Only a few years ago, between 1999 and 2001, Rubens D'Oriano and Edoardo Riccardi uncovered a fleet of ancient ships in the port of Olbia in north-east Sardinia. Construction work for a modern subterranean tunnel had exposed a 380-metre stretch of the Roman foreshore and an incredible cluster of at least eleven merchant vessels, all in a line in the precise positions where they were torched in Vandal raids. This spectacle is the most graphic image of barbarian destruction to survive from the mid-fifth century AD.

History otherwise glosses over the ignoble fall of Rome under the barbarian axe. But there can be no escaping the true objectives of the city's sack: first, it aimed to create chaos at the heart of the imperial political structure; secondly, it was intended to fill the Vandal coffers. To this end Procopius of Caesarea recorded how King Gaiseric's troops plundered the Temple of Jupiter Capitolinus, where nearly four centuries earlier the emperor Vespasian and his son Titus celebrated the end of the Triumph in honour of the subjugation of the First Jewish Revolt. Now, Gaiseric tore down the gilt bronze roof which had cost Vespasian's second son, Domitian, 12,000 talents – the present-day equivalent of over £2.4 million.

The official Byzantine court historian goes on to give a convincing overview of the massive scale of looting that took place over fourteen days from 15 to 29 June, AD 455:

Now while Maximus [the emperor] was trying to flee, the Romans threw stones at him and killed him, and they cut off his head and each of his other members and divided them among themselves. But Gaiseric took Eudoxia captive, together with Eudocia and Placidia, the children of herself and Valentinian, and placing an exceedingly great amount of gold and other imperial treasure in his ships sailed to Carthage, having spared neither bronze nor anything else whatsoever in the palace. (*Wars* 3.4.2–3)

This passage has long intrigued me. So few words, such great implications. Reading between the lines, did the Temple treasure of Jerusalem possibly accompany these shipments back to Carthage? We left the treasure on public display in the Temple of Peace, opened in the heart of imperial Rome at its peak in AD 75. But just how long did it survive there? Was it still in existence to be hauled to Carthage in AD 455?

It is a source of great regret that very little of the physical infrastructure of this temple survives to answer this key question. As I write, Italian archaeologists are currently unravelling these secrets in the Roman Forum. Yet, other than the odd column, floor and wall foundation, the Temple of Peace has been largely despoiled by the superimposition of Renaissance shops over its walls. So we are forced to return to the written word.

What we do know from the historian Cassius Dio is that the temple was apparently destroyed by fire just before the death of the emperor Commodus around AD 191:

many eagles of ill omen soared across the Capitol and, moreover, uttered screams that boded no peace, and an owl hooted there; and a fire that began at night in a dwelling leaped to the Temple of Pax [Peace] and spread to the storehouses of Egyptian and Arabian wares, whence the flames, borne aloft, entered the palace and consumed very extensive portions of it, so that nearly all the State records were destroyed. (*Epitome* 73.24.1–2)

Whatever the extent of the damage – evidently exaggerated by the historian's fertile imagination – the temple must subsequently have been restored, probably under the emperor Severus, because Ammianus Marcellinus mentions the Forum of Peace as one of the sights of the city that most impressed the emperor Constantius II, the Roman emperor of the east, during his first ever visit in AD 357.

The district was still intact in AD 408, when Rome was rocked by seismic disturbances for seven successive days. However, by the time Procopius of Caesarea wrote his history of the barbarian wars, the Temple of Peace had been destroyed by lightning. Crucially, however, some original works of art were still displayed in its vicinity, including bronze statues of a bull and a calf crafted by Myron.

By the fifth century AD, Rome's glory days were over. Masterly paintings were peeling off palace walls and temples were abandoned to the ravages of time. Yet as the Eternal City strove to keep up appearances, her ideology lived on. If the years of global domination were a thing of the past, the Eternal City still traded on those past splendours, and it is likely that the Temple treasures of Jerusalem remained in or around the Temple of Peace into the mid-fifth century. The sack of Rome in AD 455, however, was the beginning of the end. Her El Dorado, Tunisia, was lost to the Vandals and now the barbarian king had seized the trappings of royalty from the Eternal City as a new birthright. As Victor of Vita confirmed, 'At that time he took into captivity the wealth of many kings, as well as people.'

Did this wealth include the Temple treasure? The reply must be a resounding yes. Not only do historical circumstances point to this conclusion, but one of the greatest historians of Late Antiquity, Theophanes Confessor (c. 760–817), confirms the theory. This grand seigneur was no mere bookworm, but a man of high culture. Though a Christian monk, Theophanes loved sport and enjoyed taking the waters in the fashionable spas of Constantinople and Bithynia, where he lived and wrote. His 1,200-page *Chronographia*, an epic history of the period AD 284–813, is the most ambitious and systematic account of the ancient past ever written by a Byzantine historiographer. His words carry serious weight.

Theophanes is very clear about the fate of the Temple treasure. After accepting Eudoxia's cry for help, Gaiseric,

> with no one to stop him, entered Rome on the third day after the murder of Maximus, and taking all the money and the ornaments of the city, he loaded them on his ships, among them the solid gold and bejewelled treasures of the Church and the Jewish vessels which

31

Felix Carthago

THE TRANSFER OF Jerusalem's Temple treasure to Carthage in AD 455 completed the tribal Vandals' dream of acquiring all the perks of the Roman good life – lock, stock and barrel. Roman loot would drive hunger and poverty from their door. Nevertheless, the question remained: how did the relocation of the treasure fit the sociological and psychological profile of the Vandals? Was the treasure simply a money chest or were they aware of its religious and symbolic power? The barbarians had to confront the same dilemma as Vespasian almost four centuries earlier: to melt down the symbols of Jewish faith or show them off as signs of their superiority.

Vandal Carthage is the ugly stepsister of ancient history. The period is completely misunderstood for one very good reason: no one is interested in suspending for one moment the popular pre-conception that these barbarians were anything other than evil enemies of culture. That the Vandals perpetrated heinous forms of torture on the Catholics of North Africa and had no regard for Roman property is clearly chronicled. Yet this is only one side of a very complex argument stacked heavily in favour of the Romans. For it was both a Byzantine court historian, Procopius of Caesarea, employed by the emperor Justinian, and a Romanised Catholic native to Libya, Victor of Vita, who recorded the Vandals' misdemeanours.

Other than a few Vandal poets such as Dracontius, whose verse reflects his personal demons, and Florentinus' bloated homage to King Thrasamund, no record explains events factually from the barbarian perspective. So how can we be certain of the truth? Should we condemn the Vandals outright as assassins of civilisation?

If one accepts the written word at face value, then the Vandals are condemned out of hand. Typical is the bleak judgement of Victor of Vita writing in his *History of the Vandal Persecution*:

> Finding a province which was at peace and enjoying quiet, the whole land beautiful and flowering on all sides, they set to work on it with their wicked forces, laying it waste by devastation and bringing everything to ruin with fire and murders. They did not even spare the fruit-bearing orchards, in case people who had hidden in the caves of mountains or steep places or any remote areas would be able to eat the foods produced by them after they had passed. So it was that no place remained safe from being contaminated by them. (*HVP* 1.3)

These lines echoed in my ears as I drove to my hotel in the Gammarth district of north-east Tunis in October 2005. Today the country is well disposed to outsiders, and the colossal sculpture of an out-stretched hand at the centre of a fountain in front of my hotel seemed a perfect reflection of Tunisia's singular welcome amidst countries renowned for Islamic fundamentalism. Despite the allure of a pool flanked by palm trees, and the sky's strange hue of inky blue, I was not going to linger. If the true character of the Vandals could be gauged anywhere, then the ancient port was that place. Society's attitude to economics typically exposes the true behaviour and politics of a civilisation.

Ripped off by a taxi driver for the second time within an hour, I set off on foot from the edge of Carthage's Byrsa Hill, the heart of the ancient metropolis. The scale of development engulfing the site surprised me; no wonder UNESCO felt compelled to draft in crack teams of international archaeologists in the 1970s to try and preserve something of its fast eroding antiquities.

The Byrsa district of Carthage is a million miles from Tunis' drab suburbia. Dark red and purple bougainvillea drooped over fences and crept around palm trees, on which sparrows merrily hopped and chirped. Here white villas adorned with blue doors and railings roll down the hill towards the Antonine Roman baths and the sea. Freshly polished Mercedes cars are parked outside pristine villas, the updated counterparts of Roman Carthage, when the houses of the rich and famous, replete with landscaped gardens and elaborate mosaics, were blessed by the same sea breeze.

Even the street names recall past splendours. I passed down Rue Hannon, named in honour of the pioneering Phoenician sailor who was the first man to circumnavigate Africa, and turned on to Rue Baal Hammon, a reminder of the chief male god of the Phoenicians. Large drops of rain started to splatter the promenade and I quickened my walk in search of the ancient port. How much of this prosperous district survived the arrival of the Vandals, I wondered, as the rain turned into a storm. Roman writers condemned the Germanic barbarians for flattening the theatre, the Odeon and the Via Caelestis, a two-mile-long grand avenue – Carthage's very own Rodeo Drive – adorned with mosaics, columns and pagan temples flowing down to the Mediterranean. Did this typify Carthage as a whole or were the Vandals just trying to make a statement, to show who were the new bosses in town?

With 200,000 citizens, Carthage was the second largest city of classical antiquity after Rome. On previous trips to Tunisia I had walked in awe across the enormous La Malga Roman water cisterns, a series of fifteen semi-circular installations at the foot of Carthage's Byrsa Hill. The cisterns are still intact today, so the Vandal administration clearly maintained key parts of the urban infrastructure.

I also knew that the barbarians developed shipyards at Misuas in Carthage and that King Thrasamund (AD 496–523) commissioned elaborate villas and baths at Alianae near the capital, said to rival the infamous imperial mansions of Baiae in Campanian Italy. Poetry even flourished under the Vandals, even if the illiterate King Gunthamund threw the poet Dracontius into the palace gaol in offence at his lines.

One of the main reasons why Vandal Carthage has earned its reputation as the ugly stepsister of classical antiquity is due to the absence of archaeological remains in the form of coins or inscriptions attributable to the period of Vandal occupation. It is said that, like the camera, archaeology never lies. But how you read excavation results is relative. Even if the Vandals did build major new villas and public monuments, they could be invisible.

Unlike the Romans, the barbarian masters weren't interested in blowing their own trumpets by plastering marble inscriptions on walls unashamedly advertising how much money they had invested in public monuments. Add to that the problem of coins – or, rather, the lack of them. For the first forty years of their rule, the Vandals didn't mint any coinage and so failed to leave any calling cards showing where they lived, played and died. For instance, only eight graves across the whole of North Africa have been identified as unequivocally Germanic, which is unreal given that the 80,000 migrants who crossed into Morocco in AD 429 must have swollen to over 100,000 by AD 500.

When archaeologists dig up Roman coins of AD 500 they have tended to assume that the building exposed belonged to a local Roman Libyan, who happened to be living under the Vandal yoke. Even after AD 477, the quantity of barbarian coins minted was low and primarily an unconvincing attempt to promote their political sophistication. For everyday commercial transactions the newcomers were happy to rely on coins minted elsewhere across the Roman world. The Vandals, we are told, were far too busy raping nuns and enjoying the high life.

To cloud the picture even more, the archaeological remains of Late Roman Carthage are a mess. Rather than dealing with regular decay, we have to contend with the ruins of ruins. Not only is the super-structure of most buildings long gone, but even the foundations have been rudely stripped bare for recycling, a reality confirmed in 1899 by Ernest von Hesse-Wartegg's *Tunis. The Land and the People*, in which he described the modern city:

[there were] many houses in which the colonnades were marble monoliths with splendid capitals, evidently taken from that great quarry which lies in the immediate neighbourhood, where the building stones are ready cut, and beautifully ornamented, and where there is no dearth of them – Carthage. The ancient town was such a fruitful field for the Tunisians that in every second house are found Roman stones with inscriptions or sculptures, parts of columns or cap-itals. If Tunis were destroyed her ruins would be the ruins of Carthage!

For these reasons the Vandals have never received a fair press. One of my reasons for visiting the ancient port was to do just that, to assess whether their attitude towards the Temple treasure of Jerusalem would have been based on pure greed or a degree of respect. In other words, did ignorant barbarians melt down the treasure or did they preserve these centuries-old symbols of divinity?

As a marine archaeologist I had studied the greatest port of antiquity for over a decade and had even lectured about it at an international conference in Oxford. Yet visiting the site was an altogether different experience, which I had been eagerly anticipating for months. Soaked to the skin by the early autumnal downpour, I was nevertheless tense with excitement as I rounded a corner to the sea and walked down Rue de l'Amirauté. And there she was: the Circular Harbour built by the most famous merchants the world has ever known.

Once a Phoenician military port, the local topography retained the ancient circular shape of the harbour. Despite the storm, the circular Admiralty Island was surrounded by a sheet of flat, glassy water. To the east stretched the silted commercial Rectangular Harbour on the lee side of the Rue des Suffêtes, Rue Plutarque and Rue Hannibal. The environment was surreal. My mind had conjured up images of daily toil and bustle as sailors from all parts of the Mediterranean jostled and argued in foreign tongues, enveloped by a hundred different smells. All forms of industry were confined by law to the commercial district, the outskirts of the city, which would have been thick with smoke from pottery and glass kilns and infused with the stink of fish being boiled down into sauces for packing into stacks of red clay amphora jars propped up against warehouse walls.

Today, however, the ancient port district is dolled up. Where storehouses stood and well-heeled Romans once bartered over the prices of cargoes of olive oil, palatial villas grace the shore – amongst the most stunning of any Mediterranean country. The babbling tongues of antiquity are today replaced by chirping crickets. Later, I would revisit the port under blinding blue skies to find newly-weds sitting on seawalls, hands intertwined. Old men relaxed in the shadows, gently singing; a few urchins splashed around in the port's becalmed circular channel, apparently without a care in the world. Who is happier, I pondered, the wealthy family man with a luxury villa full of worldly goods or the carefree kid with one pair of sneakers and no mortgage or financial responsibilities?

With major and minor questions pressing, I strolled towards the centre of the port, Admiralty Island, and passed the immense Institut National des Sciences et Technologies de la Mer. Peering through its gates, the skeleton of a giant squid overlying a fountain greeted me from the Institute's forecourt. At this point it seemed best to suspend all judgement and let the surreal sights of past and present wash over me.

Long before Rome and her renowned technological brilliance came on the scene, the Carthaginians designed the most ground-breaking port facility of all antiquity, a gigantic civil engineering project whose concept endures today in yachting marinas all over the world. In the third or second century BC, the Phoenicians scooped 300,000 cubic metres of soil from the Salammbo lagoon to create space for two basins jointly covering about 13 hectares, a circular military port and a rectangular commercial harbour.

In military port was the showpiece of the scheme, an elegant circular water channel capable of accommodating 140 warships. At its heart stood Admiralty Island, across which another fifty ships could be dry-docked. The Carthaginians built to last, and although Rome notoriously razed Carthage to the ground in 146 BC after a prolonged war with Hannibal, the entire port complex was left intact. Rome fully appreciated the potential wealth of Tunisia, which could only be tapped through a major port. Once again economics drove foreign policy.

In the late second century AD, Admiralty Island was entirely rebuilt. An octagonal temple now dominated a colonnaded enclosure and the old quays were renovated. By the third century the military function of the Circular Harbour was well and truly forgotten. After assessing the untapped agricultural and industrial potential of Tunisia, Rome's entrepreneurial interests were satisfied by a rambling commercial district – saltery, dyeworks and metal workshops – that arose around the ships. Sometime between the third and fifth century AD, the heart of the island was converted into a series of small offices, each probably manned by different shipping officials and private merchant companies.

The rain lifted and I set about exploring Admiralty Island. Fishermen nodded towards me as I examined the ancient dry-docks and observed the sad erosion at the edges of the Circular Harbour. For such a major archaeological site, the port is badly neglected. The walls of a small octagonal temple are exposed to the elements and the wounds of various other archaeological trenches lie open for all to see.

The island's soils are thick with pottery, commercial waste abandoned by the ton in antiquity. Enough rims of African Red Slip semi-luxury bowls were scattered at my feet to make it certain that the port continued to be exploited by the Vandals. The harbours were also still standing in AD 533, when Belisarius, general of an invading Byzantine force dispatched from Constantinople, entered a sheltered basin called Mandracium. So why did the barbarians keep the harbours but allegedly torch so much of the rest of Carthage?

As rough as the barbarians' reputation was, its leaders were no fools. There was no point in expending so much effort and bloodshed in securing North Africa if they couldn't enjoy its natural bounty. And enjoy its wealth they certainly did. Dazzling multi-coloured mosaic floors continued to be commissioned in the Vandal period, but perhaps the most telling sign of high standards of living was the massive amount of pottery imported during this period. Where their Roman predecessors largely preferred home-grown foods, the Vandals took their new liberty to extremes by importing vast quantities of exotic consumables from across the entire Mediterranean. In many places where amphora dumps have been studied, the barbarians shipped in three times more luxuries than their predecessors.

Far from being uninterested in cooking, the nouveau riche Vandals loved ostentation. And why not? They could afford the expense. By the time Rome was sacked, they controlled all of coastal North Africa, as well as Sardinia, Sicily, Corsica, Ibiza, Majorca and Menorca. Gaiseric was quick to hoover up as much portable wealth as he could, a policy confirmed by Victor of Vita in his description of the Vandals' seizure of Carthage on 19 October, AD 439:

> After these wild and frenzied acts of wickedness Geiseric gained and entered Carthage, that great city, and reduced to slavery its old class of free men, freeborn and noble; for his captives included not a few of the senators of the city. He thereupon published a decree that each person was to bring forward whatever gold, silver, gems and items of costly clothing he had, and so in a short time the greedy man was able, by means of this device, to carry away property which had been handed down from fathers and grandfathers. (*HVP* 1.12)

The Vandal administration was now free to divide the greatest agricultural estates amongst the king's family. This was what the invasion of North Africa was really about. Forget cakes; the barbarians had their hands around the neck of the golden goose.

The barbarians now possessed a commodity so important that the Late Roman government was compelled to swallow its pride and sign what contemporaries described as 'an endless' peace treaty. This treaty forced on the emperor Zeno (AD 474–91) would endure until AD 532. What was this most precious of products that humbled the Roman Empire?

Oil. Or more accurately olive oil; billions of tons of the stuff. After wheat, olive oil was the second most important cog in the machine that sustained daily life in antiquity: not just a basic form of subsistence into which every culture of antiquity dipped its bread – like modern butter – but also a vital product for personal cleansing, lighting, and a base for medicines, skin oils, perfumes and cosmetics. The olive was king in classical antiquity. Its oils provided one-third of the caloric intake of the daily diet and was consumed in staggering quantities: about 20 litres per person annually across the entire Mediterranean, a demand of about one million metric tons each year. Command this crop and you held the economic purse-strings of the empire. Olive oil was to antiquity what Middle Eastern crude oil is to the West today. In occupying Tunisia, the Vandals were behaving not unlike George W. Bush in his policy towards Iraq.

The epicentre of this trade was the Sahel, the coastal hinterland of Sousse in Tunisia, where an estimated 10 million olive trees marched across the sides of foothills yielding 40,000 tons of olive oil each year. Add to this up to two million trees flourishing inland at Sbeïtla, Kasserine and Fériana and you had a gold rush on your hands. Now the Vandals were driving the gravy train. No wonder the barbarians issued coins in the late fifth century declaring FELIX CARTHAGO (Happy Carthage) alongside Lady Carthage raising shafts of freshly cultivated wheat. She had good reason to be smug.

Hardly a surprise, then, that the Vandals spared Salammbo's ports. As the centre of the oil industry, all major deals were brokered right where I was sitting on the edge of one of the Circular Harbour's dry-docks. The picture was coming together. The barbarians clearly had a long-term goal in invading Tunisia. Strange to think that this great port was sustained on the back of a viscous form of grease.

My mental time-travelling was abruptly shattered. A fisherman approached with a mischievous sneer, unwrapping something precious from folds of wrinkled newspaper. No beating about the bush: 'You like coins? Come, sit. Take a cigarette and I show you my coins. You like old oil-lamps, marble heads . . .?' I made a quick getaway. For me the past has always been about knowledge, not possession.

32

Heresy and Holocaust

I F THE VANDALS were selective about the property they chose to demolish in Carthage, depending on what message they wished to hammer home, their attitude to the Early Christian Church was systematic and cold-blooded. Before heading up to Byrsa Hill to test an idea about where the barbarians stored the Temple treasure of Jerusalem from AD 455 to 533, I had one last stop to make. The *Aedes Memoriae* was a monumental Christian rotunda probably dedicated to the cross of Christ, a piece of which was put on public display for the adoration of passing pilgrims. This elegant structure dominating the villa quarter of Carthage suffered the wrath of the Vandals in AD 439, and I was keen to compare the physical damage with the written word.

The Neptune Restaurant just beyond the ancient port seemed an opportune place to dismiss economics and mull over the barbarian holocaust in Catholic North Africa. I dipped slices of baguette into freshly pressed Tunisian olive oil and appreciated the purity of the local produce that had made the city so famous in antiquity. No bitterness or aftertaste; in fact the oil tasted more like a thick fruit juice. Plates of fried fish with lemon, and a salad of cucumber, carrot and radish soon followed – basic yet honest, and full of flavour. The Mediterranean Sea quietly licked the submerged walls of the dilapidated Byzantine city wall; Punic houses on the foreshore reminded me that Phoenician architecture with its meticulously laid masonry and elegant forecourts could be even more impressive than Roman designs.

Refreshed, I ducked passed the Antonine Baths, amongst the largest public washing facilities of the ancient world, and walked west up the Avenue 7 Novembre. A quick detour into the deserted grounds of the Roman theatre confirmed that the Vandals did indeed smash this structure to smithereens. Now reconstructed for Tunisian music extravaganzas, only three minor sections retain the original Roman stonework.

With their religious intolerance and penchant for pandemonium, the Vandals set the scene for the emergence of Islam and its rigid doctrines in seventh-century North Africa. At the end of the nineteenth century, Ernest Hesse-Wartegg, visiting Tunis, still felt obliged to remark how

> the customs of the Middle Ages and religious intolerance are the commanders who rule over an army as obstinate as it is orthodox . . . At the gate of the fortress the Islam keeps watch and rejects every innovation, and every change of what has existed for centuries, with the conscientiousness of a Prussian custom-house officer. Emancipation of women, the press, machinery, free trade, social entertainments, theatre, sport, dinners, evening parties – all stand outside this gate.

How times change. As a French colony up to 1956, fanaticism was flushed away and Tunisia was exposed to Western customs. Today the country is a constitutional republic and a bulwark of democracy between the chaos and instability of Algeria and the dictatorship of Gaddafi's Libya. Islam is, of course, thriving, but avoids the frenzy found in other eastern countries. The Tunisians are proud, traditional, god- fearing stock, but they do not ram their beliefs down your throat. It feels safe to walk the streets late at night.

Rue Tanit, the street dedicated to the goddess of child sacrifice, emerged. I crossed the street, mulling over the character of Victor of Vita, author of the *History of the Vandal Persecution*. This is a no-holds-barred tale of blood and thunder, a record of facts that makes Quentin Tarantino's fictional *From Dusk till Dawn* seem like child's play. But did this brutal vendetta against the Early Christian Church ever really happen? Was Victor reflecting fact when he mournfully recorded: 'Then that river of eloquence, which flowed richly over all the fields of the church, dried up in the midst of its courses, and the pleasant sweetness, so sweetly provided, was turned to bitter absinth' (*HVP* 1.11).

The degree of the Vandals' religious observance is a matter of great uncertainty. Their mother religion, Arianism, may simply have been a convenient weapon with which to beat up the local Catholics. In the end, however, it would induce the collapse of the Vandal occupation of North Africa.

By the time the treasures of the Second Temple of Jerusalem were on a ship bound for Carthage in AD 455, the Church had already been fighting Arianism for 200 years. Arius was a deacon of Libyan descent who lived between AD 250 and 336, and was the cat who put the question of the fundamental truth about the nature of Christ firmly amongst the pigeons, initiating a row that persists today. In 321, Arius, and his views based on earlier Gnostic philosophy, were condemned at Alexandria by a synod of a hundred Egyptian and Libyan bishops. Excommunicated, he fled to Palestine. Although his books would later be burnt, his approach would divide the Church for ever.

In the simplest terms of a very complicated debate, Catholics worshipped Christ as the true Son, a God in his own right, inseparable from the Father. However, Arianism questioned this relationship because the technical terms of the doctrine were never fully defined: Greek words like essence (*ousia*), substance (*hypostasis*) and nature (*physis*) bore a variety of meanings. Hence, the opportunity for misinterpretation. Arians could not accept that God could have spawned a physical Son, and thus denied any notion of the Son as of equivalent essence, nature or substance to God. Christ was not consubstantial with the Father or equal in dignity, or co-eternal, or existing within the real sphere of Deity.

Victor was a priest who lived through the Arian atrocities perpetrated by the Vandals before becoming bishop of Vita in the province of Byzacena, modern southern Tunisia. As a man of the cloth who saw his fellow clergy subjected to harrowing tortures, he deplored the Vandals. He opens his history with a simple overview: 'In particular, they gave vent to their wicked ferocity with great strength against the churches and basilicas of the saints, cemeteries and monasteries, so that they burnt houses of prayer with fires greater than those they used against the cities and all the towns' (*HVP* 1.4).

If you were one of the lucky members of the clergy, the barbarians simply stripped your clothes and exiled you from your church, naked, without a possession to your name. Many of the atrocities of King Gaiseric's reign were bully-boy tactics straight out of an SS manual. A favourite ploy was to force open the mouths of bishops and priests with poles and stakes, and pour dirt into their jaws to extort confessions from them about the hiding places of ecclesiastical funds. Victor of Vita added that the Vandals 'tortured others by twisting cords around their foreheads and shins until they snapped'.

A yet worse atrocity was the Vandal policy of burning bishops' bodies with 'plates of glowing iron', as befell Pampinianus and Mansuetus. By the time Gaiseric died in January AD 477, only three of the original 164 bishops active in Tunisia at the time of the barbarian invasion were still preaching.

The start of the reign of Huneric, the son of Gaiseric, enjoyed a return to religious tolerance. General assemblies of Catholics were once again permitted, Eugenius was ordained bishop of Carthage in AD 480/81, and almsgiving resumed. Vandals were even spotted frequenting Catholic churches. But this was a false dawn, a calm before an even more ferocious storm.

Huneric's mood swiftly darkened when the Arian bishop Cyrila accused the king of unacceptable moderation and of failing to enforce the mother religion. Writes Victor of Vita, Huneric then 'turned all the missiles of his rage towards a persecution of the Catholic Church'. The first step was to stop Vandals entering Catholic churches. A very special torture was reserved for such apostates from Arianism: 'they were straightaway to thrust tooth-edged stakes at that person's head and gather all their hair in them. Pulling tightly, they took off all the skin from a person's head, as well as the hair. Some people, when this happened, immediately lost their eyes, while others died just from the pain' (*HVP* 2.9).

The anti-Catholic holocaust swiftly intensified, with conversion to Arianism being forced on all palace officials or Romans in public employment. Those who refused to turn had their tongues cut off. Catholics were now barred from even eating with Vandals. The heretic government also ended the hereditary ownership of church lands, seizing bishops' possessions as their own by riding their horses into churches and forcing out the clergy. Churches were closed down throughout Africa and their rich estates gifted to Arian bishops. In total, Huneric exiled 4,966 bishops, priests and other members of the Catholic Church to the desert. Prayer books were burnt by the thousands.

Elsewhere, the Vandals had licence to enjoy themselves in other dastardly ways. Consecrated virgins were sexually violated and tortured 'by hanging them in a cruel way and tying heavy weights to their feet; they applied glowing plates of iron to their backs, bellies, breasts and sides.' At the central Tunisian city of Thuburbo Majus, a nobleman called Servus endured an equally degrading fate:

> After receiving countless blows from rods he was frequently lifted up by machines with pulleys and, as he hung, taken throughout the city for the whole day. Now he was lifted on high, but when the ropes were released again he fell quickly and tumbled down with the full weight of his body on the pebbles of the streets, coming down upon the stones like a stone. (*HVP* 3.25)

Huneric's reign of terror lasted for seven years and ten months. 'His death', wrote Victor of Vita, 'was in accordance with his merits, for as he rotted and the worms multiplied it seemed not so much a body as parts of his body which were buried.' The king had proved a shameful assassin.

<hr />

Nowhere can the heretical intentions of the Vandals be resuscitated so vividly as at the *Aedes Memoriae* monument in Carthage. The trouble was that none of the locals had a clue as to its whereabouts. Nor had the tour guides, nor the policeman standing at the junction of Avenue Habib Bourguiba and Avenue 7 Novembre watching the traffic approaching the presidential palace, even though a wonderful modern map crafted of mosaic cubes occupying an entire wall directly behind him marked its general position.

Dropping into the Roman theatre to see the handiwork of barbarian vandalism with my own eyes, neither the security man nor the old timer who had peddled local crafts to tourists for years knew what I was talking about. Fortunately, as I was about to head away up Byrsa Hill I spotted a pile of marble columns abandoned on the edge of a high wall adjacent to the Roman theatre. As I bounded up the hill, the majestic walls of the rotunda came into view.

I found myself amidst deserted ruins, a witness to hideous ancient crimes. My sense of unwelcome was heightened by the heavy security presence ringing the President's Palace, whose gleaming marble façade and soaring towers dwarfed the rotunda. I had a sixth sense that something appalling once happened here, a crime that mankind would prefer to sweep beneath the carpet of time. The guards' boredom seemed to be targeted in my direction. Palace photography was strictly forbidden and physically enforced. I would need to move fast and subtly.

What Victor of Vita calls the *Memoria* (Memorial) was the site of the final major stand between North Africa's bishops and the heretics of Arius. Sometime between AD 478 and 484, King Huneric ordered the region's men of God to congregate at this spot, where a declaration was read out offering liberty to preach to those bishops who promised to support the king's son, Hilderic, and not to complain about the Vandal king to the Byzantine emperor (with whom the barbarians held a fragile peace treaty). Many of the bishops refused, reiterating that 'At all times we say, have said and shall say: we are Christians, we are bishops, we hold the one, true apostolic faith!'

Holding to Catholicism to the very last, these obstinate bishops were taken into custody and banished to a life of hard labour in the king's shipyards in Corsica. Next the Vandals sprang their final trap. Those who had sworn allegiance were abruptly accused of betraying the Gospels, and were banished to live as slaves in the fields of Vandal estates. Never again would they hold a prayer book, ordain or baptise.

The ruins of the Memoria, where North Africa's bishops made their last stand, are an impressive sight. Swallows dive-bombed around my head and encircled the outer walls of the rotunda as a puppy howled across the street. Amongst the thickets overgrowing the dignified walls rising 10 metres above ground, crickets the size of my hand hopped across the field of martyrs.

Enough of the original plan of the Memoria survives to give a clear sense of its original glory. Its mosaics and marble veneer may have been destroyed, and reduced to rubble across the derelict site, but the scale and feel of the structure survive. Animal bone, ancient wine jars, quarter sides of Late Roman ceramic dishes, and purple, yellow and grey marble litter the ruins – an archaeologist's dream.

I would have liked to stay longer and examine the apsidal structure annexed to the Memoria – surely a contemporary early Christian church – but I had overstayed my welcome. The President's guards were

33

Keeping the Faith

THE VANDALS' PERSECUTION of Catholic North Africa turned out to be their downfall. From his palatial perch overlooking the Bosphorus, the emperor Justinian's outrage increased with every fresh report of Arian atrocities. Yet his hands were technically tied by the peace treaty signed by his royal predecessors.

Moreover, Justinian's advisers were strongly opposed to war. The Vandals had settled on the other side of the world: the distance presented a logistical nightmare. It would take 140 days for a Byzantine army to reach Carthage and launch a strike. More pressing was the perilous condition of the imperial coffers, running dry through a combination of Justinian's free-and-easy spending and prolonged skirmishes with the Persians hammering at the empire's eastern borders. Throughout the fifth century AD, and as late as AD 562, the Byzantine state grudgingly handed over kings' ransoms to buy the peace: 11,000 lbs of gold in AD 532 and 30,000 gold coins annually for a fifty-five-year peace agreed in 561. Gold was getting scarce. The imperial troops were exhausted.

The empire had already attempted once before to invade Vandal Africa with disastrous consequences. In AD 468, Leo ordered an all-out attack, dispatching a fleet of over 1,000 ships against King Gaiseric, characterised by Procopius as 'a cunning fellow and base at heart and well versed in undertaking revolutionary enterprises and in laying hold upon the money of others'. The forces met off Cape Bon, 50 kilometres north-east of Carthage, where the Vandals sent an unmanned, burning ghost fleet against the Byzantines. Opportune winds propelled the barbarians' phantom ships against the forces of the empire, sinking the entire Byzantine fleet. One day I should like to run an expedition to find this ships' graveyard amid the eerie depths off North Africa.

Justinian, however, was not easily dissuaded. The hungry ambitions of the Vandal king Gelimer posed a clear threat to peace. Here was a volatile man who had usurped the kingship from his cousin Hilderic, and imprisoned both the king and his sons Euagees and Hoamer, whom he also blinded for good measure. How could you trade with a man who was happy to commit dynastic murder to gain the throne? In a final ultimatum, Justinian sent his envoys to Gelimer, accusing him of acting in an unholy manner and demanding safe passage for Hilderic and his sons to Constantinople. Gelimer's reply bluntly told Justinian to mind his own business.

Belisarius, General of the East, was immediately summoned and ordered to prepare for battle. The Byzantine invasion of Libya was represented by the Byzantine court as a holy war. The turning point for Justinian came, it was said, when God visited a bishop in a dream and rebuked Justinian for his caution: Christianity had to be protected from the heretics of Libya. Forget what you may have been taught at school or read in later years about Richard the Lionheart and the eleventh- and twelfth-century Crusades. The invasion of AD 533 was, in fact, the First Crusade of history, the earliest holy war between Christian and infidel. Once in Tunisia, Procopius – who personally accompanied Belisarius to Carthage as chief court historian – tells us that on one occasion the tips of the Byzantine spears were said to have 'lighted with a bright fire and the points of them seemed to be burning most vigorously', a sure sign of divine blessing.

Fearful of the barbarians' reputation and their access to the vast riches and resources of North Africa, Justinian almost certainly overestimated the perceived military threat. In reality, the Vandal force of AD 533, having grown fat off the land, lacked the primitive hunger of a hundred years earlier. Luxury had made them soft, just as it had rendered Rome susceptible to a fall in AD 455.

The cultural sea change that overtook the Vandals is aptly reported by Procopius:

> For all the nations which we know, that of the Vandals is the most luxurious . . . For the Vandals, since the time when they gained possession of Libya, used to indulge in baths, all of them, every day,

and enjoyed a table abounding in all things, the sweetest and best that the earth and sea produce. And they wore gold very generally, and clothed themselves in the Medic garments, which now they call 'seric' [silk], and passed their time, thus dressed, in theatres and hippodromes and in other pleasurable pursuits, and above all else in hunting. And they had dancers and mimes and all other things to hear and see which are of a musical nature or otherwise merit attention among men. And the most of them dwelt in parks, which were well supplied with water and trees; and they had a great number of banquets, and all manner of sexual pleasures were in great vogue among them. (*Wars* 4.6.6–9)

A mammoth military machine was assembled in Constantinople comprising 10,000 foot soldiers and 5,000 horsemen. Some 500 ships manned by 30,000 Egyptian and Ionian fighting sailors were recalled from across the eastern empire, as well as 92 *dromones* – sleek and swift warships ('runners') – and 2,000 sailors. This battle of the seas was to witness a new and deadly weapon explode on to the Mediterranean: the *dromones* were equipped with flame throwers that spat Greek fire from their bows.

Granted the blessing of absolute power by Justinian, Belisarius, originally a native of Germania, was an all-action hero whose life reads like a modern soap opera. The general was equipped with a brilliant strategic mind, endless courage and, as events would unfold, both good fortune in his military career and terrible reversals in his personal life. As Procopius recorded, in North Africa Belisarius earned 'such fame as no one of the men of his time ever won nor indeed any of the men of olden times'.

While taking on provisions in Sicily, Belisarius received an immediate stroke of good luck: the Vandal king Gelimer, it materialised, was away from court, staying near Hermione in Byzacium, four days inland from Carthage. The coast was clear for a full-scale assault, aided by favourable winds that blew the Byzantine fleet past Gozo and Malta far out to sea. Belisarius deliberately gave Carthage a wide berth to land at Caputvada, Shoal's Head, in Libya, five days east of the Tunisian capital. If Carthage was ever attacked, the Vandals would be expecting to spy a fleet approaching from the west, not sneaking up unawares from the unprotected eastern flank.

General Belisarius was as much concerned with the battle for the hearts and minds of the local population as with military success. In Libya he was quick to let it be known that the casual stealing of farmer's produce would result in corporal punishment. The holy war had to be accompanied by just behaviour:

> For I have disembarked you upon this land basing my confidence on this alone, that the Libyans, being Romans from of old, are unfaithful and hostile to the Vandals . . . this is the time in which above all others moderation is able to save, but lawlessness leads to death. For if you give heed to these things, you will find God propitious, the Libyan people well-disposed, and the race of the Vandals open to your attack. (*Wars* 3.16.3–8)

Belisarius was proving a born leader of men. Later, after capturing the all-important public post used to ferry political dispatches by horse, rather than killing the chief courier, the general gave him a pledge of loyalty and a letter from Justinian reading: 'Do you, therefore, join forces with us and help us in freeing yourselves from so wicked a tyranny, in order that you may be able to enjoy both peace and freedom.' The point was crystal clear: acquiesce, save your souls, enjoy prosperity. Only once did the general have to resort to a brute show of force when the local Romanised Libyans sold information about Byzantine strategy to the Vandals. Belisarius responded by impaling a Carthaginian called Laurus on a hill in front of Carthage on the charge of treason. An 'irresistible fear' gripped the capital – problem solved.

Once the Byzantines had killed Gelimer's brother, any Vandal military masterplan went out of the window; the Vandal army's discipline crumbled, and Belisarius was able to march on Carthage unhindered. In the Circular Port of Mandracium the Carthaginians lifted the iron chains guarding the entrance to the harbour mouth from enemy ships and waved in the Byzantine fleet. The Vandals had proved to be parasitical leeches, sucking the life out of Tunisia. Marching up towards Byrsa Hill, Belisarius must have been overcome by the sight of hundreds of locals cheering the arrival of Byzantium and a return to Roman values. As evening fell on Tunisia's Byzantine independence day, the general was amazed by the

highlight of Vespasian's Triumph was its passage through theatres such as the Theatre of
Marcellus. Sacrifices would have been offered at the Temple of Apollo Medicus Sosianus,
marked by three columns, where enemy armour was burnt to destroy its power

The arcades of the Porta Triumphalis, Rome, was only opened for Triumphs. By closing the
gate immediately afterwards, the power of the Roman conqueror was locked inside the city

A second relief on the Arch of Titus shows Titus parading along the Triumphal Way in AD 71. The goddess Roma accompanies him and a winged Victory holds a wreath over the commander's head

In AD 75, Vespasian publicly displayed the Temple treasure of Jerusalem in his new Temple of Peace, Rome, whose marble floor still survives

Reconstruction of Vespasian's Temple of Peace precinct

In AD 455, the Vandals looted Rome and relocated Jerusalem's Temple treasure to the palace in their capital, Carthage, in modern Tunisia, which afforded majestic views of the great port

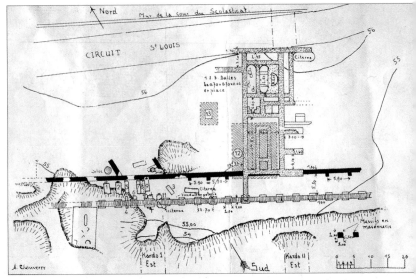

A plan by Father P. Lapeyre of Punic tombs (left) and the rectangular palatial structure exposed at Carthage in 1933 (at right-angles), marking the spot of the Vandal palace, where the Temple treasure of Jerusalem was displayed from AD 455 to 533

The Vandal palace on Byrsa Hill, Carthage (right), looking south towards pier supports for a massive terrace and beyond down to the port

In AD 534, the Byzantine emperor Justinian granted General Belisarius, in honour of his victory over the Vandals, a Roman style Triumph in Constantinople's Hippodrome, where the Temple treasure of Jerusalem was paraded

The Hippodrome was also a museum of antique artwork, including a bronze Serpent Column originally dedicated at the Temple of Apollo at Delphi, Greece, in 479 BC

Left: Theodosius' Column in the centre of Constantinople's Hippodrome

Below: The base of Theodosius' Column in Constantinople's Hippodrome. The emperor Valentinian II hands out a laurel wreath to a sporting victor from the royal box, the *Kathisma*. Below, the crowd watch a chariot race. Although sculpted in AD 390, the scene captures the atmosphere of the Triumph of AD 534

The ruins of the Church of St Polyeuktos – built in AD 527 using the biblical royal cubit of King Solomon's Temple – where the Temple treasure was housed while in Constantinople

Sculpted vine leaf and grape motifs in the Church of St Polyeuktos recalled the decoration of King Solomon's Temple in Jerusalem

The Monastery of St Theodosius in the West Bank whose superior, Modestus, spirited the Temple treasure away from the Church of the Holy Sepulchre around AD 614 into the wilderness to escape the clutches of Persian invaders and their Jewish allies

Disturbed soil and the entrance to an underground cave in the grounds of the Monastery of St Theodosius. The Temple treasure of Jerusalem probably ended up concealed in just such a place

welcome: 'For the Carthaginians opened the gates and burned lights everywhere and the city was brilliant with the illumination that whole night, and those of the Vandals who had been left behind were sitting as suppliants in the sanctuaries' (*Wars* 3.20.1).

But did the light of the golden menorah from the Temple of Jerusalem still sparkle amidst the Vandal treasuries on Carthage hill?

34

In a Vandal Palace

SITTING CROSS-LEGGED ON the summit of Byrsa Hill, dominated by a library dedicated by the emperor Augustus, I too watched the brilliant lights twinkle across Carthage – or rather across the bay of Tunis. These, though, were generated by electricity rather than olive oil and wick. The kaleidoscope of Tunis past and present played out in front of me in the few minutes it took for the orbiting sun to set. Imams in dire need of singing lessons hollered from minaret towers, completely ignored by children playing football next to the Roman amphitheatre.

From the acropolis of Carthage the ancient port set amidst a fertile lagoon of calm water and palm trees faded into the shadows. Wherever you may be in the Mediterranean, there is something magical about watching a city unwind after a stressful day. Flickering lights sprinkle beauty across highways and suburbs as families come together to share stories of daily anguish and joy. Urban landscapes ugly by day assume a bewitching mystique at night.

This was both a highly peaceful and a satisfying moment for me. I came to Tunisia in October 2005 with few expectations: to examine the ancient ports and the way the Vandals operated religiously, politically and economically; to work out just how much of Carthage was destroyed or retained under Vandal rule; and to try and locate the Memoria, where so many fifth-century Christians were duped into slavery by the barbarians. In truth, however, these were secondary interests. My main goal was to rediscover an ancient building exposed in 1933 that looked suspiciously regal to me.

After three days on Byrsa Hill I had exposed a startling piece of evidence that left me quietly jubilant. Now I knew where the Temple treasure of Jerusalem had been housed for a hundred years of Vandal occupation. With sweat drying across my brow in the early evening breeze, I smiled in recollection at the discovery. The pieces of the Temple treasure jigsaw were falling into place.

My reading of Procopius and other lesser sources made it clear that the major palace of Vandal rule lay on Carthage's Byrsa Hill. As the capital of all North Africa, and hence the Vandal world, this would have been the showcase where King Gaiseric and his descendants stored their extraordinary treasures. After warning his army against looting and harming the civilians, Procopius reported that in September 533 General Belisarius 'went up to the palace and seated himself on Gelimer's throne'. At the same hour and on the same spot where I was resting on Byrsa Hill, the Byzantine army dined in the Vandal palace:

> And it happened that the lunch made for Gelimer on the preceding day was in readiness. And we feasted on that very food and the domestics of Gelimer served it and poured the wine and waited upon us in every way. And it was possible to see Fortune in her glory and making a display of the fact that all things are hers and nothing is the private possession of any man. (*Wars* 3.21.6–8)

Other than on Byrsa Hill, the heart of the ancient city of Carthage elevated 56 metres above the plains of Tunis, there is nowhere within a 10-kilometre radius of the port where it is geographically possible to 'go up' to a palace. This expression restricts the location of the Vandal royal seat to Byrsa. Earlier in England I had spent weeks poring over all published accounts of excavations conducted across Carthage since the early twentieth century. I had rapidly become fed up with the Phoenicians on finding that almost all fieldwork pre-dating the 1970s was geared towards exposing the deepest city deposits attributed to the legendary Queen Dido and her Punic descendants. In fact almost all early explorers were glorified trophy hunters in search of Phoenician tombs and rich grave goods. The Roman and later remains stratified closer to the modern ground level were largely ignored and only uncovered because they lay in the way of excavations cut beneath them into the Phoenician 'basement'.

To make matters worse, the Late Antique levels that intrigued me and dated from the mid-fourth to seventh centuries AD, spanning the Later Roman, Vandal and Early Byzantine empires, didn't seem to exist.

Where Rome has always been subject to intense scrutiny as the root of classical and contemporary culture, Late Antiquity has traditionally been dubbed the Dark Ages. Only from the 1980s onwards have scholars come to appreciate just how many forms of Roman institutions and administrative systems, from city councils to theatres, still flourished across the Mediterranean as late as the seventh century AD. The Byzantine Empire that evolved in Constantinople from the early fourth century AD took no more than its name from its earliest colony, Byzantium. In truth, it was no less than the New Rome, the Eternal City transposed to the Bosphorus.

Immersed one evening in Oxford's Sackler Library in a sea of plans of Punic tombs, I had stumbled across a 'treasure map' – or, more precisely, a plan of Punic tombs excavated by Father Lapeyre in 1933. The drawing looked quite abstract since above the Phoenician levels the explorer didn't really know what he was dealing with. Thankfully, Lapeyre didn't destroy the ruins he uncovered as he shifted tons of soil to descend 10 metres below the modern ground level to his beloved eighth-to-third-century BC tombs. This was probably due more to luck than to cultural enlightenment: the two 'Roman' structures he uncovered were so monumental that it would have been too much bother to get rid of them. And Lapeyre, like most of his contemporaries, was interested in swift results.

What caught my eye and set my heart pounding was a massive rectangular slab of architecture running perpendicular to Lapeyre's tombs. Although his plan didn't make complete architectural sense, its overall form reminded me of a palace recently excavated at Butrint in Albania by a close colleague, Professor Richard Hodges of the Institute of World Archaeology at the University of East Anglia. The mystery structure in Carthage terminated to the north with a separate wing characterised by a tripartite room. Towards the late third century AD the Roman dining experience in elite villas and palaces was revolutionised. Villa owners introduced the *stibadium*, a semi-circular dining couch set around a semi-circular marble table. The rigid Roman rectangular dining experience was replaced by a new style offering a more relaxed, egalitarian atmosphere. The cosy alcove with its smoothed curves was far less formal than the Roman form, which was designed for spectacle alone. Sitting on a semi-circular couch neither host nor guest was head of the table

Initially, the *stibadium* was built at the end of the dining room, furthest away from the entrance door. At some point in the fourth century AD, however, the scheme witnessed a logical development: the creation of a three-winged triconchal room, whose curved inside walls snugly accommodated the semi-circular dining tables at which one sat cross-legged and low down, as at a traditional Chinese meal. The plan of the 'Roman' structure exposed by Lapeyre looked like a template for this elite form of Late Antique dining space. Could it be the Vandal palace? On grounds of style, I was optimistic, but an obstacle was a coin of the emperor Constans I found in the building's foundations, the only published piece of dating. Constans ruled from AD 337 to 350, so this coin was far too early for a Vandal presence between AD 439 and 533.

I had turned up at Carthage a little green behind the ears, equipped with only Lapeyre's plan and a photocopy of a 1930s photograph showing the general area of his excavation. I figured that if I could track down the two distant buildings in the photo I might be able at least to find the spot where the 'palace' was excavated, and get a feel for the place where the Temple treasure of Jerusalem once resided during its remarkable history. No modern maps or travel books even mention this building. Was this because modern archaeologists have failed to fathom its function or was it because the structure had been bulldozed? I simply had no idea and little grounds for optimism. Other than the photograph from the early 1930s, images of this building were suspiciously absent. Lapeyre's find was an enigma that John Ormsby's *Autumn Rambles in North Africa* (1864) left me with little hope of finding intact:

> From the top of a heap of rubbish [the traveller] may trace the features of a rusty hill-side, a strip of thirsty plain relieved by a patch or two of Arab cultivation, a broken line of low-lying shore, and this is all the memento of Carthage he can carry away on the leaf of his pocket-book . . . Better for Rome's great rival to lie dead and buried in that rubbish-strewn plain, than to live on as a frowsy Moorish city.

The heart of ancient Carthage, Byrsa Hill, is something of a time warp. Not because of the ruins themselves, familiar friends to me, but because the site museum and description plaques are retro-1970s. In a museological sense, Carthage is a little jaded and frayed around the edges. To the non-specialist, the mass of ancient walls can be nothing but confusing.

Two maps carved on to stone display plinths on Byrsa Hill are all the help you get to navigate the ruins, and I was immediately dispirited to see that neither labelled any palace. Nevertheless, I started to roam around the ruined esplanade – three times the size of Augustus' Forum in Rome and twelve times larger than any other public space in Roman North Africa – from the outside inwards in ever decreasing circles. My neck soon ached from continuously staring between the skyline and my 'treasure map' and photo. After scrambling around the northern perimeter of the hill with no luck for thirty minutes, I made my way south. Standing amidst piles of Roman pottery and apsidal walls, the penny dropped. In typically academic manner I had got lost amidst the detail rather than stepping back to appreciate the overall plan. The top left corner of my photo showed a semi-circular tower annexed to a monumental building. From the south it immediately became obvious that this was the huge Cathedral of St Louis that has dominated the hill since 1890. This feature allowed me to cross-reference a small one-storey building with a crenellated roof, and from these bearings I soon had Lapeyre in my sights.

To my delight I suddenly realised I was standing on top of the 'palace', which had survived the decades after its excavation intact. I quietly thanked the Tunisians for this insight, even though no one really knew the nature of the beast straddling the south-eastern hillside. I had not anticipated the sheer scale of the building, whose massive foundations plummeted some 8 metres down.

I spent three long days under the relentless rays of the sun studying this monument, scrutinising the stone architecture, the building's geography, and cross-referencing the site with ancient historical texts. Lapeyre's mystery building turned out to be quite majestic – both an eyesore and a wonder. So much of the building's outer stone veneer, and everything above ground level, has long gone. All that survives are the deep, dungeon-like foundations of the structure, ugly rubble cemented with crude plaster in the typical Late Antique style. This was no elegant Roman building crafted according to strict Vitruvian principles. These walls were never meant to be seen, let alone undressed by a critical scientific eye.

The 'palace' measures 12 metres wide and 33 metres in length. An extension over the earlier-dated southern ruins extended the complex by a further 9 metres. The main wing is a rectangular edifice with a raised apse to the north originally covered with shining grey marble. This was without doubt the site of the original *stibadium*, where the high and mighty feasted. A puzzling feature of the same wing is a massive central rectangular foundation, 9 metres long and 5 metres wide, which veers deep down into the ground. The question of what kind of installation needed such massive footings perplexed me. Was this the Vandal palace's dungeon, which Procopius describes as a room filled with darkness, which the Carthaginians called Ancon and into which anyone with whom the tyrant was angry was summarily cast?

Dark it was, true, but far too small, I concluded. However, I did recall that the barbarian soul was softened in North Africa by flowing water. During his march to Carthage, Belisarius' army passed Grasse, 65 kilometres east of the capital, which was renowned as 'a palace of the ruler of the Vandals and a park the most beautiful of all we know. For it is excellently watered by springs and has a great wealth of woods. And all the trees are full of fruit' (*Wars* 3.17.9–10). Landscaping was crucial to Vandal aesthetics and I was certain that the rectangular feature at the heart of the Carthage palace was the foundations of a fountain. The soft sound of flowing water would have been a perfect feature for aristocratic meetings and feasting. Moreover, I had a sneaking suspicion that the palace was also surrounded by flowing water or at least a landscaped park.

The structure's southern wall was built over a monumental rubble pier, one of a series of two sets of seventeen parallel piers that march along the southern flank of the palace in an east–west direction. The piers once supported a *cryptoporticus*, a network of covered passageways that underlay extensive terraces and parkland. Almost nothing has been published about this immense feat of engineering, which runs for at least 80 metres before dropping off the end of Byrsa Hill. Personally, I had never seen a feat of architecture like it, not even in Rome.

North of the main rectangular hall of the building lies a separate room, an audience chamber with triconchal wings, exactly like the palace of Butrint and other high-status Late Antique buildings. The floor levels are confused today, but the raised *stibadium* base can still be seen beneath vegetation before being swallowed by a modern road. Adjacent sits a second apse.

Architecturally, the layout of Lapeyre's mystery building works perfectly as a palatial structure. Further, it occupies the dominant view of Carthage's ports, the ultimate geography of power: visitors to the palace would have been awestruck by the unhindered vista down to the port – master of all it surveyed – just as the jaws of merchants sailing into harbour would have dropped at the majestic view of a marble palace gleaming against Carthage's skyline. If an emperor or king was going to build a palace anywhere in the capital, the exact space occupied by the triconchal structure was that spot.

I would have happily closed the case if it were not for two problems. First, the problem of dating and the coin of Constans I; secondly, however I juggled the evidence, the edifice seemed simply too small for a palace. Was I wrong after all, simply building subjective castles in the air?

The dilemma of chronology was not so grave since Lapeyre, in his eagerness to get to the Punic levels, simply dug the palace out like a dog ferreting for a bone. No pottery, coins or any other finds survive from inside the building. Further, I knew that we could discount the limited evidence offered by a single coin, especially since the fourth to early fifth centuries were decades of extreme inflation. This meant that copper coins were largely worthless, and only bags holding tens of thousands were worth anything at all. Hoards of copper and bronze *nummi* were thus left to rot in the soil by the sackload. A scarcity of metal also ensured that early fourth-century coins remained in circulation for over one hundred years.

So there was every reason to believe that the coin of Constans I found close to the palace's foundations may have been around for a very long time before being lost. Even if it did correctly date the foundations of the palace, this was no serious problem because the Vandals would simply have assumed control of a pre-existing Late Roman imperial *palatium* before adding the audience chamber to the north.

But what of the palace's relatively modest size, surely in no way grand enough for imperial use? Not so, however, if this structure was merely one part of a larger edifice whose sprawling wings are today buried to the north or were destroyed in antiquity and recycled into later buildings in Tunis. Personally, this is my preferred interpretation but one that need not be exclusive. Back in London I eagerly met up with Professor Hodges, director of excavations at the UNESCO World Heritage Site of Butrint in Albania and its triconch palace of comparable date. Richard is a world expert on Late Antiquity and his take on my 'palace' was worth its weight in gold. I was also very keen to hear about the new mosaics and headless marble statue his team had just dug up in their forum. Butrint has become a byword for meticulous excavation and publication.

As ever, Richard turned up in my offices at *Minerva* magazine brimming with ideas and exciting schemes. We discussed his triconch palace and, very cautiously, I took him through my plans of Carthage's equivalent and a sequence of photos. I was fully expecting my theory to be shot down on the basis of the 'size matters' equation. After all, what survives in Carthage – the second largest city of antiquity – is even smaller than at Butrint, a relatively minor provincial capital.

However, I ended up tingling with satisfaction when Professor Hodges bestowed his blessing on my idea, pointing out that the walls of his palace were 'tiddly' compared to the 'colossal' foundations on Byrsa Hill. Then the bombshell: the Carthage palace may seem small but it was designed to go up not out, perhaps to as many as three storeys high.

Of course; this made perfect sense. Byrsa was honeycombed with endless ancient buildings of Phoenician, Punic and Roman date. By Late Antiquity there was little room left to breathe other than upwards. The Vandal palace, seat of the Temple treasure of Jerusalem, was the skyscraper of its day.

And then Professor Hodges dropped his second bombshell: with its water features and narrow hall, the structure reminded him of Early Islamic palaces in Spain, such as the Alhambra. Such buildings combine the oriental with the classical and must have been inspired by North African architecture. Could the Vandal palace of Carthage have been a prototype of Umayyad and Abbasid elite buildings, he mused? Numerous leads to follow, but for now my quest for the final resting place of Jerusalem's Temple treasure in Tunisia was over.

Well, not quite.

* * *

It was from the mighty port of Carthage that Gaiseric's expeditionary force against Rome sailed in AD 455; the victorious army returned by exactly the same route, only this time laden with the emperor's wife, children and 'an exceedingly great amount of gold and other imperial treasure in his ships'. Geographically, historically, architecturally and archaeologically, the palatial structure on Byrsa Hill was the only place where the Vandals could have housed their finest treasures. Just like Vespasian and Titus almost 400 years earlier, Gaiseric would have divided the spoils into those to be converted into liquid capital and those worthy of being kept as crown jewels. Of humble origins, the Vandals had no dynastic claim to power. In such circumstances, the barbarians would have been eager to assume the Roman trappings of civilisation. The Jewish treasure symbolised the heart of that mentality: empowerment through the possession of the crown jewels of vanquished civilisations.

However, when Belisarius entered Gelimer's palace in AD 533, no treasure was to be found. All that remained were some eastern merchants locked away in the dungeons. Providently, the Vandal king had removed the state treasures out of Byzantine reach. The main battle for North Africa took place not at Carthage but at Tricamarum, 30 kilometres from the Vandal capital. Gelimer had fled west, buying the loyalty of armed farmers with gold. The king had assembled his troops, along with mercenary Moors, on the plain of Bulla Regia close to the border with modern Algeria.

Some 800 Vandals and 50 Romans died in the battle of Tricamarum, which also revealed Gelimer to be a total coward. As soon as the Byzantine army advanced, the Vandal king leaped on his horse without saying a word and fled down the road to Numidia. In the heat of battle the barbarians had no time to break camp before following suit, and it was at Tricamarum that the Byzantine army got its hands on a mountain of gold:

248

And they found in this camp a quantity of wealth such as has never been found, at least in one place. For the Vandals had plundered the Roman domain for a long time and had transferred great amounts of money to Libya, and since their land was an especially good one, flourishing abundantly with the most useful crops, it came about that the revenue collected from the commodities produced there was not paid out to any other country in the purchase of a food supply, but those who possessed the land always kept for themselves the income from it for the ninety-nine years during which the Vandals ruled Libya. And from this it resulted that their wealth, amounting to an extraordinary sum, returned once more on that day into the hands of the Romans. (*Wars* 4.3.25–8)

Even though Procopius' account confirms that the Vandal treasure contained riches looted from Roman lands, the Temple treasure was unlikely to have been part of this windfall. For the most important barbarian treasures had already been spirited away.

King Gelimer had bolted westwards. At Hippo Regius he headed inland, climbing the precipitous Papua Mountains in order to hide amidst his Moorish tribal allies – much as Osama bin Laden disappeared in Afghanistan in 2003, vanishing amidst the impenetrable mountains bordering Pakistan.

General Belisarius sent John the Armenian in hot pursuit of Gelimer, aided by a crack force of 200 commandos charged with capturing the Vandal king dead or alive. Meanwhile, a surprise awaited Belisarius' main army at Hippo Regius. Today this ancient town sits on the coast of eastern Algeria and typifies the source of North Africa's prosperity in antiquity. As well as being a major harbour, some eight ancient roads converged on Hippo.

Iron and marble were mined nearby, and the mid-eleventh-century Arab historian El Bekri described the local agricultural resources as 'very rich in fruits and cereals. To the west of the city is a stream which waters the gardens and makes that locality a pleasure-ground. Meat, milk, fish and honey are found there in great abundance.' Hippo Regius was also a main exporter of the wheat tax shipped annually by the hundreds of tons to Rome. For this reason Hippo was the first city to be besieged by Gaiseric in AD 430; ironically, it would also be the last city controlled by a Vandal king before the Vandal state collapsed.

Along the town's plain two hills rise some 60 metres above the hinterland, a bastion of early Christianity. One of the consequences of
the Arian Vandals' suppression of Catholicism was the emergence
of the cult of the martyr in North Africa. In Late Antiquity, martyr-
dom – now the province of other extremists – was the preferred fate
of many Christians obliged to live under the Arian yoke. It was here
at Hippo, among his congregation, that St Augustine chose to die.
After the reconquest of Africa, the seven city churches would include
ecclesiastical structures memorialising the evil decades of Arianism:
the Basilica of Eight Martyrs and Chapel of Twenty Martyrs.

Against a backdrop of bath-houses, gleaming statues, a theatre and
lavish mansions like the Villa of the Labyrinth – their floors adorned
with spectacular mosaics depicting masks, singers and wild animals –
a huge wooden ship rocking in the harbour of Hippo Regius cut an
isolated and forlorn sight in December 533. On its deck stood a scribe
called Boniface, a native of Libya entrusted with the state secrets of
the Vandal court. This man held the ultimate key to the Temple
treasure of Jerusalem. Thus, according to Procopius:

> At the beginning of this war Gelimer had put this Boniface on a very
> swift-sailing ship, and placing all the royal treasure in it commanded him
> to anchor in the harbour of Hippo Regius, and if he should see that
> the situation was not favourable to their side, he was to sail with all
> speed to Spain with the money, and get to Theudis, the leader of the
> Visigoths, where he was expecting to find safety for himself also, should
> the fortune of the war prove adverse for the Vandals. (*Wars* 4.4.34)

As soon as the battle of Tricamarum had begun, Boniface duly
planned his escape.

> But an opposing wind brought him back, much against his will, into
> the harbour of Hippo Regius. And since he heard that the enemy were
> somewhere near, he entreated the sailors with many promises to row
> with all their might for some other continent or island. But they were
> unable to do so, since a very severe storm had fallen upon them and
> the waves of the sea were rising to a great height. (*Wars* 4.4.35–6)

The scribe's plans were scuppered. Terrified of the Byzantine forces
approaching the port, he resorted to seeking sanctuary in the town's
church. In typical humanitarian fashion, Belisarius freed Boniface with

an enormous handout plundered from this floating money chest. From Hippo it was a short sail back to Carthage from where, under the long shadow of the palace on Byrsa Hill, the greatest treasures of the Vandals, including the Temple treasure of Jerusalem, finally made their way across another sea to Constantinople, capital of the Byzantine Empire.

Constantinople – New Rome

35

Treasures Recycled

'WELCOME TO HELL' announced the banner unfurled outside Istanbul airport, an intimidating greeting awaiting the Swiss national football team's crucial game against Turkey on a mid-November evening in 2005. Already two goals down from the away leg, the Turks were rapaciously exploiting their home advantage. The affable Swiss were bombarded with eggs and cartons of milk on entering Galatasaray's stadium, while local fans drew their thumbs under their chins, maliciously promising to cut the players' throats should they win.

Next day the Turkish capital was in mourning. The national team gave away a penalty inside the first thirty seconds and went on to lose to European minnows, Switzerland, on aggregate and drop out of the 2006 Fifa World Cup. A calamity.

Istanbul was fast freezing up, physically and emotionally. Icy winds blew across the Sea of Marmara, whipping round mosque domes and hundreds of merry ships bobbing at anchor in the Golden Horn, the greatest natural harbour in the world. V-shaped arcs of storks flew south to escape winter.

I was moving in the opposite direction, having just left the sunny shores of Tunisia. Winter was fast closing in and so was the end of my quest. But Constantinople, the Late Roman city built by the first Christian emperor, Constantine I (AD 311–37), held further secrets somewhere beneath its domes and kebab shops. The capital of the Later Roman Empire was the last place where the Temple treasure of Jerusalem appeared in public before dropping out of the pages of history.

By AD 534, Justinian I (AD 527–65), the most colourful ruler of Late Antiquity, had been on the throne for eight years. Not only was I certain that the menorah, trumpets and Table of the Divine Presence passed into his personal possession, but I also had a theory – based on the discovery of some extraordinary Byzantine sculpture and poetry – about where he may have stored them: the Church of St Polyeuktos.

The return to town of the Byzantine Empire's new golden boy, General Belisarius, was met with great fanfare. North Africa and its rich olive groves were once again Roman, and Justinian's court historian, Procopius, reveals the emperor's eagerness to mark this great event for posterity:

> Belisarius, upon reaching Byzantium with Gelimer and the Vandals, was counted worthy to receive such honours, as in former times were assigned to those generals of the Romans who had won the greatest and most noteworthy victories. And a period of about 600 years had now passed since anyone had attained these honours, except, indeed, Titus and Trajan, and such other emperors as had led armies against some barbarian nation and had been victorious. For he displayed the spoils and slaves from the war in the midst of the city and led a procession which the Romans call a 'triumph', not, however, in the ancient manner, but going on foot from his own house to the hippodrome and then again from the barriers until he reached the place where the imperial throne is. (*Wars* 4.9.1–3)

Why resurrect a dead Roman custom? Why refer to Titus? The historian seems deliberately to emphasise the historical link between the Triumph of AD 71, the Temple treasure and the loot captured from the floating treasure chest at Hippo Regius in AD 533. The streets of Istanbul held unsolved secrets and the Hippodrome was the core of the mystery. If I could find it, I was confident of penetrating the mind of a dead emperor to ascertain the Temple treasure's fate under Justinian.

Outside my hotel, the morning light illuminated a poor Ukrainian ghetto filled with cold, industrious souls, their faces a collage of Russian and oriental features. Istanbul has always been a melting pot of cultures, a land and sea bridge where East meets West. Legend has it that the city was originally founded around 660 BC by Byzas of Megara, who lent his name to the city of Byzantium.

Byzantium was a backwater until the reign of Constantine the Great. The first Christian emperor needed a virgin capital fit for Jesus. Polluted by its blood-stained pagan altars and pantheon of gods, Rome was impure. Constantinople was consecrated on 11 May, AD

330, and would remain the capital of a Late Roman and Byzantine Empire until the city fell to Sultan Mehmet II and the Ottomans on 29 May 1453.

Constantinople was not only a clean slate for Christianity, it was also the spyglass for all that passed between the eastern and western Mediterranean. Here, the city could keep a beady eye on sea-lanes and land routes bridging Europe and Asia, the Black Sea and the Mediterranean. The city's natural harbours were outstanding, blessed with perfect docking facilities along the Sea of Marmara and within the confluence of the Golden Horn and the Bosphorus. By AD 413, the city of emperor Theodosius II had virtually doubled in size to eight square miles, enclosing 250,000 citizens and monuments as impressive as any gracing Old Rome, including 14 churches, 14 palaces, 153 private baths and 4,388 major houses.

The Russian quarter is a concrete jungle of charmless boutiques peddling acrylic trousers and four-inch killer stilettos and boots adorned with myriad zips and straps. Up Ordu Caddesi Street I joined the daily grind of pedestrian traffic shuffling silently to work. The mass movement reminded me, briefly, of the 1960 film adaptation of H. G. Wells' *The Time Machine*, where the 'automated' Eloi assemble as one when called to temple. I was unsure whether to blame the surreal hush of this city in motion on the weather or the football.

My comrades and I passed Koska Helvacisi, a wonderland founded in 1907 and stocked with a dizzying eleven varieties of Turkish delight stuffed with walnuts, coconut, hazelnut and double pistachio. Later in Istanbul's Ottoman bazaars, I would see the same delights marketed as Turkish Viagra.

Unlike the streets of Rome – a living museum – Roman and Byzantine Constantinople rarely rears its head above the pavement. But opposite a dilapidated mosque, its façade blackened by pollution, and Istanbul University's pink cement Faculty of Aquatic Sciences, stands a jigsaw of marble architecture quarried on the island of Proconnesus in the nearby Sea of Marmara. The emperor Theodosius' Forum, built in the late fourth century AD, is today reduced to a couple of large podiums, forgotten bases from a triumphal archway. On top, the upper sections of elegant column shafts have been gnawed away by the ravages of time. Curiously, their overall form is classically

Roman, yet the decorative scheme is characteristically Byzantine. The carving is said to replicate peacock feather patterns, but looks more like the drip of giant tears.

Theodosius' Forum stood for over 150 years, and still attracted shoppers during the reign of the emperor Justinian, when the Temple treasure was in town. This marketplace was a major landmark along the Mese, the main arterial road that descended from the heart of Constantinople, the imperial palace and Church of St Sophia, west to the Golden Gate and on to Thrace and the Balkans. Today the ruins are dwarfed by the main road, Anatolian gold jewellery boutiques and kiosks offering freshly squeezed pomegranate juice. No one notices them.

Across the road in Beyazit Square the silent uphill trek of commuters continued. Street cleaners in glowing orange worksuits swept up late autumn leaves using old-fashioned witches' brooms and plastic pans cut out of oil cans. Constantinople would have approved: where Rome bought new and expensive, and discarded huge amounts of waste after a single use, the Early Byzantine Empire recycled everything from old stones to clay wine jars, whose broken shards were refashioned into floor tiles and crushed to form plaster temper.

Commuters quietly queuing for bread and *çay* (Turkish tea) shivered in the biting winter winds. On street kerbs old men polished shoes from glass bottles filled with red, black and brown dyes. A florist arranged wreaths on a cart, while a swarthy man grinned mischievously at me as he sharpened his long knife and lit rolls of charcoal to heat his kebab spit. Behind the smiling façade of Istanbul, however, is a more sinister world. Its backstreets offer an unhealthy array of rifles, pistols and daggers, and for 15 Turkish lira you can also pick up *Intifada*, the video game.

———◆———

After skirting the emperor Justinian's ecclesiastical masterpiece, the Church of St Sophia, I found myself down by the shore. I followed a cart laden with fresh fish past the Byzantine seawalls and uphill. This was the original route leading from Justinian's port to the Hippodrome – though the journey taken by General Belisarius and the Temple treasure in AD 534 would have been decked with glory, not sullied by the smell of tuna and cod. But the route was identical and would have taken less than thirty minutes to cover. The Triumph of AD 534 would have been far more subdued than that of AD 71. Constantinople had nothing like the population density of first-century Rome and Justinian was paranoid about his colleagues' potential power, so restricted Belisarius' 'triumph' to little more than a parade. Nevertheless, its symbolism was in many ways as important to Justinian as it had been to Vespasian.

Trucks bursting with fridges, televisions and microwaves precariously roped together rumbled down to the port, while I mulled over the comparisons and contrasts between Old and New Rome. Rome was a brilliantly progressive empire, always looking to the future, a trailblazer in art, architecture and politics. Thanks to endless television programmes and films, we all know what the Romans did for us. But who knows what legacy, if any, was transmitted down the generations by Byzantium?

Constantinople, however, was far from a pale imitation of its older brother, but like all subsequent Mediterranean civilisations its achievements are dwarfed by the scale of Rome's brilliance. The Eternal City didn't just think big, it thought colossal. Compared to her, anything that followed would always look second best. In many ways Constantinople was a bipolar place. In her preference for recycling old architecture into new monuments, New Rome was the original eco-friendly society. The Byzantine state enjoyed vast wealth and could have commissioned spanking new monuments if it wished (and frequently did). Recycling is not about prosperity, it is a question of ideology, and the Byzantine Empire, in its respect for the built environment and earth's natural resources, has never been given the credit it deserves for this progressive legacy.

However, Justinian was also a prodigious patron, enabling Constantinople to produce extraordinary art and architecture. It was he who popularised the dome, plucking the style from Roman bathhouses and temples like the Pantheon for his flagship churches at St Sophia in the capital and in cities as far apart as Jerusalem and Ravenna, former capital of the Late Roman Empire on the Adriatic coast. The stereotype of the dome as an Ottoman invention is myth. The gilded wall mosaics of Christ, the apostles and New Testament scenes, found at the Church of St Sophia and St Catherine's monastery in the Sinai, preserve the flavour of his lavish and innovative tastes. The alleys around Justinian's palace were lively artisanal centres, where great craftsmen worked ivory and jewellery, engraved precious gems and illuminated manuscripts. The emperor also introduced the highly lucrative and prestigious silkworm into Constantinople, converting the Baths of Zeuxippos alongside his palace into an imperial silk factory, where he could personally keep an eye on production.

Politically, modern Istanbul often feels like a tragi-comedy, a hangover of the ancient Byzantine paradox. Society is progressive, yet wrapped in traditional garb. Turkey dreams of joining the money-spinning European Union; the West remains suspicious of her identity and ambitions. Many members are clearly frightened at the prospect of 63 million Muslims joining the club. The Cradle of Civilisation is today trapped between East and West, geographically and socially. However, the country retains a healthy sense of humour in the matter of geopolitics. Contemporary cartoons portray Turkey's current position in terms of an Ottoman man sitting backwards on a donkey. The beast of burden moves slowly up a hill, but his master faces in the opposite direction. Turkey is frustrated: she tries to embrace the West, yet is seen as backward thinking.

The emergence of this conflicted condition can be blamed on Byzantine society. When he founded Constantinople, Constantine and his successors were besotted with Rome. Or rather, while simultaneously trying to escape her physical clutches, the new city needed to prove she was a worthy successor. Thus, New Rome – as she styled herself – also sat backwards on a donkey. Politically this was the Roman Empire rekindled. Constantinople mimicked Rome geographically, claiming she too straddled seven hills. Even though the Early Byzantine Empire technically started with the relocation of Roman power to Asia Minor, her citizens still referred to their way of life as *romanitas*.

Nowhere is this split personality better exemplified than in the Hippodrome, where Belisarius and the Triumph of AD 534 paid homage to the emperor and the people. The Hippodrome had been built around AD 200 by the emperor Septimius Severus at the same time as he renovated the Circus Maximus in Rome. What was initially a free-standing theatre of fun in the Roman period became the people's parliament in Constantinople. The Byzantine emperors needed a forum to control the populace, a convenient soap box from which to monitor the mob. The Hippodrome was that place, and how better to manipulate its political will than by sugaring the pill.

The Hippodrome was the all-seeing eye of an Orwellian Big Brother that had a serious ulterior motive. The state-sponsored chariot races whirling around the arena, and rivalry between supporters of the Blues and Greens teams, were entertainments that kept the population sweet, as were the daily dole rations distributed from here to the poor. However, the Hippodrome was also the epicentre of the religious and imperial ceremonies that shaped the annual calendar.

In reality, Constantinople's inferiority to Rome was obvious. So its emperors went to extraordinary lengths to justify its imperial right of succession. Not without reason was the eastern capital dubbed New Rome. First and foremost, Constantine created a physical barrier to control his people in the form of a mighty palace around the arena. Along with the city walls, which defended Constantinople from the enemy without, John Malalas in his sixth-century *Chronicle* tells us that the emperor's first major building programme had been to renovate the Hippodrome and establish a palace to protect the empire from the enemy within:

> He also completed the hippodrome and adorned it with bronze statues and with ornamentation of every kind, and built in it a *kathisma*, just like the one in Rome, for the emperor to watch the races. He also built a large and beautiful palace, especially on the pattern of the one in Rome, near the hippodrome, with the way up from the palace to the *kathisma* in the hippodrome by a staircase.

In other words, Constantine deliberately copied both the layout and function of Rome's Circus Maximus and Palatine palace, and boosted his imperial control by siting the royal box directly next to the Hippodrome. Palace and circus were thus one and the same, a physical artery bonding emperor, politics and people. Never before had such an intimate and coercive policy been enacted.

In AD 534, Justinian's city of 500,000 people was in no doubt that Constantinople, and more precisely the Hippodrome and the adjoining palace, was the centre of the civilised world. The new didn't just imitate the old, it supplanted it. And the dominant means of conveying this message were the artistic masterpieces, steeped in symbolism, for which the Early Byzantine emperors ransacked the Mediterranean.

The Hippodrome was in effect a museum where at least twenty-five famous antiquities plundered from the Mediterranean basin were permanently exhibited. Here statues of the greatest rulers of classical antiquity rubbed shoulders, from Alexander the Great to the Roman dictator Julius Caesar and the emperors Augustus and Diocletian, ransacked far and wide from Rome to Nicomedia in modern Turkey. The legendary founders of Rome and, hence, of the Byzantine Empire, Romulus and Remus, were prominently displayed. Each year their foundation festival, the Lupercalia, was re-enacted in the Hippodrome. All of these golden memories united the great rulers of antiquity with those of the present. This was reputation by association.

Although Constantinople was originally selected to be a new imperial capital partly as a central Mediterranean bridgehead from which to launch operations against the northern barbarians and the eastern threat from Persia, the city proved highly vulnerable. Once the barbarians had crossed the Danube in AD 378, no natural barrier existed to delay their menacing advance. To address this fear, the emperor Theodosius II created a deeper set of land walls in AD 413. Reflecting the mounting external threat, Anastasius (AD 491–518) eventually turned to an even more extreme defence in depth, building a 45-kilometre-long wall 65 kilometres west of Constantinople between the Black Sea and the Propontis. New Rome finally had its own Hadrian's Wall.

To protect the empire, palace and people from the frightening image of barbarians at the gates, the Hippodrome was peppered with *apotropaia*: statues of Zeus, hyenas and sphinxes, patron gods and talismans who warded off evil. This psychological shield with its veneer of imperial respectability was complemented by the greatest artistic wonders of the age, all assembled within the Hippodrome's walls. The Ass and Keeper originally displayed at Nikopolis in Greek

Epiros to commemorate Octavian's momentous victory over Mark Antony – paving his transformation into the first and greatest of Rome's emperors, Augustus – now told viewers that after his decisive defeat of Licinius at Chrysopolis, Constantine was Augustus' equal.

All of these masterpieces and their conscious messages were intermixed with statues more naturally associated with a hippodrome. The great charioteers, horse tamers and pugilists, the brothers Castor and Pollux, blessed the arena, as did Hercules, the epitome of strength and guile, fighting the Nemean lion and outwitting the Hesperides sisters for their golden apples. Hercules' successful completion of the Twelve Labours made him the perfect symbol of male virility and aspiration, and thus the presiding genius of athletics competitions.

The reused antiquities reflected Constantinople's respect for classical Greek and Roman values, but more crucially harnessed the past to validate the present and future. The accumulation of the greatest art under one roof linked to the palace, sent out a potent message: the centre of the civilised world had been transposed to New Rome. The Hippodrome became a microcosm of the universe, which the emperor controlled. Sound familiar? In some respects, Constantinople's Hippodrome was a mirror image of Vespasian's Temple of Peace in Rome. And how better to boost control of the past and mastery of the future than to house here the Temple treasure of Jerusalem. The masterpieces already on show illuminated the Byzantine Empire's earthly domination. Possession of the Jewish menorah, trumpets and Table would allow Early Christianity to claim dominance of the heavens too.

36

Hunting Hippodromes

I FOLLOWED BELISARIUS' footsteps of AD 534 along the Kennedy Caddesi highway, only today I was pursuing the wheels of a fishmonger's cart rather than a gold-plated chariot. Other than stunted sections of seawalls, I passed little Byzantine architecture. Would the Hippodrome reveal itself readily or had it been completely obliterated by modern development?

At Aksakal Sokagi Street I turned left up the steep slope of Istanbul's First Hill. Like the Palatine in Rome and Carthage's Byrsa Hill, this was the business end of ancient Constantinople, where the emperor and senate held court – the Houses of Parliament, Buckingham Palace and Wembley all rolled into one. I roamed quiet backstreets, startling chickens looking for a comfortable bed to lay an egg or two. Not ten minutes from the throbbing nerve centre of Istanbul, this district still feels like a sleepy peasant village.

I wound my way uphill passed Fedex and UPS depots superimposed over ancient warehouses. The window of a wooden shack above a secluded children's playground suddenly cracked open to expose a buxom elderly lady, her head wrapped in a tea towel. She beat a rug against the side of her flimsy hut and stared at me, bemused by this oddity prowling the backstreets of Istanbul. I smiled back, relieved we no longer live in Ottoman times when far worse refuse would have been thrown over me.

This distraction quickly faded as behind the shack my eyes focused on a wall of red Byzantine brick. Some 15 metres tall, it curved uphill for about 30 metres. The arched entrances blocked with brick were somehow reminiscent of an architectural spectacle in Rome: the entrances to the Colosseum. Liberate the arches and you had exactly the same concept. Quickly checking my location on a map, the penny dropped with a satisfying clunk: this was the monumental semi-circular southern entrance to the Hippodrome, the *sphendone*, its walls now incorporated into an earthen bank supporting the edge of the hill and Marmara University. Crushed marble and pottery gleaming on the ground reminded me of long forgotten splendours. The ghost of an Ottoman-period building, a cross-section of its domed roof and floor still plastered on to the Byzantine walls, made it clear how lucky any section of the Hippodrome is to survive.

The drains purred with rainwater escaping down to the sea and I hurried uphill, eager to discover what the Hippodrome looked like on the summit. Rounding the corner I was greeted by a series of yellow, pink and blue wooden peasant huts opening on to a broad park dominated by the Blue Mosque to the east. But still no sign at all of any Hippodrome superstructure.

Ottoman and modern Istanbul were alive and kicking, but Byzantium was obliterated. Turks dressed in baggy brown MC Hammer cotton trousers and matching suit jackets fed pigeons. The tones of an ice-cream van competed surreally with the traditional cries of imams calling people to prayer across the city. While nothing of the Hippodrome's walls still stands above ground, a modern road now replicates the original position of the charioteer's racetrack. I also spied the original central *spina* terrace intact, although now landscaped into a peaceful garden.

To the north, the Hippodrome's starting gates – the 'barriers' to which General Belisarius paraded in the Triumph of AD 534 – have been consumed by the tramlines of Divan Yolu, the main road running from the Russian Quarter and Theodosius' Forum into the heart of Istanbul. The domed roof and minarets of the Church of St Sophia swallow the panorama and dwarf a stump of masonry, all that remains of the *Milion*, a four-way arch from which the new Byzantine territories were mapped out. On the edge of the pavement a youngster sat at a table with a rabbit, carrot and a handwritten cardboard sign that invited you to part with some loose change and 'Let the Rabbit Tell Your Fortune'. I decided to give its wisdom a miss.

Unlike Rome's Circus Maximus, whose grassy banks still soar into the sky opposite the Palatine, Constantinople's Hippodrome is one-dimensional. A bird's-eye view would betray its 450-metre-long elliptical contours, but on the ground the original layout has vanished. The smell of sweat and the 50,000-strong cheering throng are hard to resurrect. The arena's saving graces are three original antiquities still standing at the south-western end of the central *spina* around which chariots once careered.

I walked down the flattened central terrace where bronze and marble statues of Hercules, an eagle, wolf, dragon and sphinxes once gleamed in the eastern sun. A flowerbed arranged in the shape of a crescent moon and five-pronged star, the flag of Turkey, adorns the original podium where a classical Greek statue of Helen of Troy was once on show. Today not one statue of Helen survives, but in the late twelfth century Niketas Choniates, chancellor of the Byzantine Empire, enjoyed a close encounter with this beauty, revealing in his *Historia* how

> she appeared as fresh as the morning dew, anointed with the moistness of erotic love on her garment, veil, diadem, and braid of hair. Her vesture was finer than spider webs . . . the diadem of gold and precious stones which bound the forehead was radiant . . . The lips were like flower cups . . . and the shapeliness of the rest of her body were such that they cannot be described in words and depicted for future generations.

Helen of Troy may have vanished, but three of the Hippodrome's surviving antiquities still hint at the arena's original style. Furthest south is a roughly built pillar of stone soaring 32 metres high. Once sheathed in bronze, its original function remains a mystery. Nearby is the Serpent Column, composed of the intertwined bodies of three bronze snakes and, according to local legend, with venom enclosed in its walls. Now only 5.5 metres tall, the column was originally surmounted by three snake heads supporting an enormous bronze victory bowl. These relics once formed the shaft of a trophy that was the centrepiece of the Temple of Apollo at Delphi, seat of the great Oracle, where it had been dedicated to the god by the Greek allies who had defeated the Persians at Plataea in 479 BC. This Greek masterpiece remained intact in the Hippodrome well into the medieval period. Only in April 1700 did the Serpent Column come to an ignoble end, when an exuberant member of the Polish Embassy sliced off the snake heads under the influence of raki, the next best thing to stealing police traffic cones.

The most complete ancient monument surviving within the Hippodrome, however, is Theodosius' Column. Once again, it was time to confront an old 'Roman' friend. Atop a sculpted base is Constantinople's token Egyptian obelisk, yet another nod to artistic tastes in Old Rome. Commissioned by the pharaoh Tuthmosis III (1504–1450 BC), it stood originally in Egypt's Temple of Amon at Deir el-Bahari opposite Thebes. Weighing 800 tons, and 27 metres tall, the skewer is covered with hieroglyphs commemorating the pharaoh's victory over Syria. The obelisk, however, broke during its sea voyage to New Rome, where a disgusted Constantine abandoned it by the shore. A few decades later, in AD 390, the emperor Theodosius recycled the monument. The surviving upper two-thirds of the obelisk were mounted on four bronze blocks and an exquisite marble sculpted base.

I was especially interested to examine this slab of marble during my trip to Istanbul because it depicted the faces of Theodosius and the royal family enjoying a day out at the Circus: the very scenes that Justinian and Belisarius would have experienced in the Triumph of AD 534. One side of the base brings to life the emperor receiving homage from barbarian captives; on another, his nephew, Valentinian II, ruler of the western Roman Empire, and his sons Honorius and Arcadius, hand out laurel wreaths to a sporting hero. The tightly packed crowd in the Hippodrome is also visible, as well as chariots tearing around the arena to a backdrop of dancing maidens and musicians (whose poor artistic perspective makes them look more like aliens).

Theodosius' Column holds a huge amount of information about the art and social customs of the age, not least a very un-Roman, cartoon-like cameo revealing the mechanical logistics of how the obelisk was erected. This was evidently a major operation and a big coup for Theodosius, though the kind of feat that happened in ancient Rome daily. The Roman emperors simply let monuments speak for themselves. I stared long and hard at the *kathisma*, the royal box sculpted on the base of Theodosius' Column as an arched chamber supported by columns and jutting out across the Hippodrome. Soldiers armed with spears and shields guarded the royal box.

After breathing in the bygone atmosphere of a day at the imperial races, I crossed the *spina* and entered the courtyard of the Blue

Mosque, which hovers over the exact position of the Byzantine palace and *kathisma*, the most powerful seat in the Byzantine Empire. Here emperors communicated with their people, entertained the masses and expressed their omnipotence. The concept reminded me of a more sophisticated version of medieval jousting. From the elevated mosque podium above the entrance stairs I replayed the magic of the Triumph of AD 534, as recorded for posterity by Procopius:

> And there was booty – first of all, whatever articles are wont to be set apart for the royal service – thrones of gold and carriages in which it is customary for a king's consort to ride, and much jewellery made of precious stones, and golden drinking cups, and all other things which are useful for the royal table. And there was also silver weighing many thousands of talents and all the royal treasure amounting to an exceedingly great sum (for Gaiseric had despoiled the Palatium in Rome . . .), and among these were the treasures of the Jews, which Titus, the son of Vespasian, together with certain others, had brought to Rome after the capture of Jerusalem. (*Wars* 4.9.4–6)

So, I had been right all along: the Jewish Temple treasure was recaptured from the floating treasure chest at the port city of Hippo Regius. Finally, the Vandal king, Gelimer, had been coaxed down from his hiding place amongst the Moors on Mount Papua. The final straw had been the failing health of his children, who had started discharging worms. Gelimer would eventually be exiled with his family to the province of Galatia in modern central Turkey, but for now was compelled to endure public humiliation and pay obeisance to Justinian. Procopius writes:

> And there were slaves in the triumph, among whom was Gelimer himself, wearing some sort of purple garment upon his shoulders, and all his family, and as many of the Vandals as were very tall and fair of body. And when Gelimer reached the hippodrome and saw the emperor sitting upon a lofty seat and the people standing on either side and realised as he looked about in what evil plight he was, he neither wept nor cried out, but ceased not saying over in the words of the Hebrew scripture, 'Vanity of vanities, all is vanity.' And when he came before the emperor's seat, they stripped off the purple garment, and compelled him to fall prone on the ground and do obeisance to the

Emperor Justinian. This also Belisarius did, as being a suppliant of the emperor along with him. (*Wars* 4.9.10–12)

Not much survives of Early Byzantine Constantinople, but enough texts and ruins remain to give us snapshots of the Triumph of AD 534. Theophanes Confessor would later confirm Procopius' report of the Temple treasure's presence there. The event may have been a heavily diluted version of Vespasian's spectacular Triumph of AD 71, but it was nonetheless a pivotal rite of passage. For a brief period of time Justinian was able to enjoy the sense of being a Roman lord of the entire Mediterranean. Little did he know that the end of classical antiquity was nigh, and that his reign would mark the curtain call of *romanitas*. The real Dark Ages were coming and time was running out for the Temple treasure of Jerusalem.

37

Imperial War Games

LIKE MODERN TURKEY, Constantinople lived for today but grounded its political institutions and social habits firmly in the past. Thus, the Hippodrome wasn't a museum in the modern sense but a museum of the mind, a place where emperors and citizens were subtly brainwashed into believing themselves the worthy successors of Rome with no reason to feel inferior. The recovery of the Temple treasure of Jerusalem was a coup for Justinian, a divine reminder from God that Christianity was the chosen successor to the Judaism of the Old Testament. The new world religion fully appreciated the legacy. For the first time since AD 70 Palestine was back in imperial favour, reinvented as the Holy Land. Pilgrimage to the biblical sites was encouraged, popular itineraries went on sale, and the concept of tourism was invented.

Some five centuries old, the Temple treasure of Jerusalem was a splendid showpiece for Justinian's city. Back in England I had pondered long and hard about the destiny of the Jewish booty when it arrived in Constantinople: where was it kept, was it publicly exhibited and how long did it remain in the capital?

The answer would have been straightforward if the reign of Justinian had been rational. So far Justinian has appeared to be a defender of the Catholic faith and a strong leader willing to take tough military decisions. However, the man was also a psychopath who could compete with Nero or Caligula for mental instability.

Justinian has gone down in history as a master builder who made King Herod look small fry. In Constantinople, he built St Sophia, the greatest church in Christendom, and filled the city with endless marbles and monuments. Across the empire he threw buckets of gold at entirely new cities like Justiniana Prima in modern Serbia, refortified old towns, constructed new ports and erected places of worship in a quest for immortality.

At least, that was the party political line of the time. The modern age views Justinian differently: as an insecure and selfish egomaniac who not only bankrupted the treasury, but also opened the gate to the grim reaper of classical antiquity, a world that had endured for over a thousand years. His reign was saturated with scandal from the moment he married a former prostitute. Theodora, the daughter of Acacius, a keeper of wild beasts in the amphitheatre of Constantinople, had an appalling reputation. In the sanctimonious words of Procopius, 'On the field of pleasure she was never defeated. Often she would go picnicking with ten young men or more, in the flower of their strength and virility, and dallied with them all, the whole night through . . . she flung wide three gates to the ambassadors of Cupid' (*Secret History* 9).

An embittered Procopius chronicled the life of Justinian and Theodora blow by sordid blow. The same courtier who had so faithfully recorded the great deeds of the Byzantine army against the Arian Vandals returned home to Constantinople angry and disillusioned. Of course, he could do little physically or politically to counter the emperor's erosion of imperial and family values. So, with feathered nib dipped in poisoned ink he composed his *Secret History*, a work that could never be aired during Justinian's lifetime without costing the historian his life. The chance survival of this work is a unique counterweight to Procopius' official histories and an amazing window into the social life of one of the greatest epochs of antiquity. Procopius clearly detested his paymaster and did not hold back the punches.

The truth about Justinian probably lies somewhere between the two extremes of the *Wars*' trumpet blowing and the *Secret History*'s venom. Certainly, Theodora calmed down after marriage, reinventing herself as an ancient Eva Perón. The ex-hooker turned empress founded the Convent of Repentance for reformed prostitutes and was renowned for sheltering large numbers of monks in her own palace. She also championed a successful campaign to end Monophysite Christian persecution. No doubt Procopius had good reason to denounce Justinian and his wife, but we must beware of accepting the full details of their scandalous life verbatim.

However, there is no smoke without fire and Justinian epitomised the fatal identity crisis that rocked the Early Byzantine Empire. First of all, in terms of succession he had no ancestral claim to the throne because his uncle, Justin I, was by birth an uneducated soldier in the palace guard, who started life as an Illyrian peasant. However he shuffled the pack, in the dead of night Justinian knew full well he was not of noble birth and was in many respects an impostor. This background undoubtedly explains his eccentric and unstable behaviour. Procopius accused Justinian and his lowborn wife Theodora of ruling like vampires, sucking the life out of the empire:

> For he was at once villainous and amenable; as people say colloquially, a moron . . . His nature was an unnatural mixture of folly and wickedness . . . deceitful, devious, false, hypocritical, two-faced, cruel, skilled in dissembling his thought . . . A faithless friend, he was a treacherous enemy, insane for murder and plunder, quarrelsome and revolutionary, easily led to anything evil, but never willing to listen to good counsel, quick to plan mischief and carry it out. (*Secret History* 8)

Justinian is characterised as ruling the empire through corruption, selling positions of power to the highest bidder and enforcing his will through a web of spies. He imposed his personal neuroses on the physical world around him, raiding the treasury coffers for his colossal building programme. Certainly, the war drums beating in Persia were a serious threat to western ways, but Justinian built fortifications as if they alone could protect him from his internal demons. The emperor lost no time in depleting the treasury's entire gold reserve.

What makes it hard to second-guess Justinian's behaviour is his unpredictability. General Belisarius, you might presume, would have become a great celebrity back in Constantinople. After all, he was afforded the honour of a Triumph. Not so. Justinian fancied that Belisarius harboured imperial ambitions and was a threat to the throne. He also accused him of hiding most of the loot seized from the Vandals. Whipped into a frenzy by Theodora, Justinian was riddled with jealousy at Belisarius' success.

So the battle-weary general, who had put his life on the line for the empire, ended up under house arrest, the ultimate humiliation. To make matters worse, Belisarius had to contend with his wife pursuing a string of public affairs that made him the talk of the town and butt of endless jokes. Procopius tells us that Belisarius was a broken man, certain he would be assassinated: 'Accompanied by this dread, he entered his home and sat down alone upon his couch. His spirit broken, he failed even to remember the time when he was a man; sweating, dizzy and trembling, he counted himself lost; devoured by slavish fears and mortal worry, he was completely emasculated' (*Secret History* 4).

If an emperor could crush an all-conquering hero like Belisarius, it was anyone's guess what he might have done with the Temple treasure of Jerusalem. Nevertheless, I had a theory, and to put it to the test I left central Istanbul for the suburban district of Saraçhane. There, in AD 526, craftsmen were putting the final touches to one of the greatest churches in Christendom, the Church of St Polyeuktos, a soldier martyred for his Christian faith at Melitene in eastern Turkey in AD 251 and perhaps best known from Pierre Corneille's play *Polyeucte* (1642) and an opera by Charles Gounod (1878).

Of the thousands of churches that sprang up across the Mediterranean between the fourth and seventh centuries, the Church of St Polyeuktos was unique. Its construction was sponsored entirely by one of the most formidable women of the Byzantine world, Princess Anicia Juliana (AD 462–528). Juliana was the wealthiest heiress of her age, a woman of high birth. Her mother was descended from the emperor Theodosius the Great and her father, Flavius Anicius Olybrius, traced his lineage back to notables who had fought Hannibal seven centuries earlier, and briefly served as emperor of the West. Juliana's own husband had even been offered the throne, but refused the honour.

The Church of St Polyeuktos was built inside three years, from AD 524 to 527, and lay along the processional route, the Mese, running from the Forum of Theodosius to the Hippodrome and palace complex. In 1960, bulldozers developing Istanbul's new city hall bit into the side of the church by chance. The structure was subsequently excavated over six years from 1964 by Professor Martin Harrison of Dumbarton Oaks Institute in Washington and Dr Nezih Firatli of the Istanbul Archaeological Museum.

By 1964, hundreds of ancient churches had been uncovered by eager archaeologists the length and breadth of the Mediterranean, but St Polyeuktos would make the entire world sit up and stare. The church measures just under 52 metres square and is arranged around the usual central nave and side aisles. Its brick barrel-vaulted passage-ways and crypt with marble floor — which no doubt once held the bones of Polyeuktos — proved remarkably well preserved.

If the church's layout was of standard plan, the originality and scale of its decoration were extraordinary. Over 10,000 pieces of marble came to light, imported from across the civilised world: red porphyry from Egypt, green porphyry from the Peloponnese, yellow *giallo antico* from Tunisia, green *verde antico* from Thessaly, black marble flecked with white from the Pyrenees, purplish marble streaked with grey and white from Bilecik in western Turkey and, of course, abundant local Proconnesian marble from the Sea of Marmara.

Offset against this marble rainbow was extremely elaborate inlay: serrated leaves of mother-of-pearl and strips of yellow glass coated with gold leaf. New styles of columns appeared for the first time, decorated with squares of amethyst framed by green glass triangles and gold strips, a futuristic departure from Roman ideals. If the precious stones made Princess Juliana's church gleam, the quality of the archi-tectural sculpture set new standards for ecclesiastical structures. With their wealth of experience, Professor Harrison and his team had never seen anything approaching the under-drilled lattice- and strap-work sculpture. Exuberant vegetation, especially vine leaves, had been cut so delicately that it was virtually detached from its background. Elsewhere, painted peacocks were rendered realistically in the round. Four types of 'basket' capitals, another Byzantine innovation, complemented a dazzling range of stylised plants and palmettes. For novelty, variety, abundance and technical quality, nothing like this had ever been seen before.

What made Princess Juliana tackle an innovative project that left all previous church design schemes in its wake? The church is believed to have once adjoined her palace, as yet undiscovered. Does this explain the glory of St Polyeuktos? What statement was Juliana trying to make?

These unanswered questions played on my mind as I cut through an arch of the aqueduct built by the emperor Valens in AD 375. Where fresh water once flowed into the heart of Constantinople, the aqueduct's arches now support the Bahçeli Kafeterya café and a host of fizzy drink refreshments. Trucks and taxis dart through the arch, hardly pausing to gauge its dangerously narrow hips. Today, the district between the Forum of Theodosius and the Church of St Polyeuktos houses the core of Istanbul University. Students rushed to class past the Blue King Disco and Bar and specialist music shops stocking exotic looking *uds*, eleven-stringed large-bodied instruments with short stems, similar to the European lute.

The key to St Polyeuktos is a vivid Greek poem discovered inside the church. The first forty-one lines were carved around stone grapevines and peacock sculptures extending along the church's nave before proceeding into the narthex and courtyard. The poem, recorded in full in the eleventh-century Palatine Anthology, praises Princess Juliana's royal descent and the miraculous quality of her new church. One section of the immortal dedication reads:

> What choir is sufficient to sing the work of Juliana, who, after Constantine – embellisher of his Rome, after the holy golden light of Theodosius . . . accomplished in few years a work worthy of her family, and more than worthy? She alone has conquered time and surpassed the wisdom of renowned Solomon, raising a temple to receive God, the richly wrought and graceful splendour of which the ages cannot celebrate.

Evidently the princess wanted to glorify her own achievements, but surely claiming to have 'surpassed the wisdom of renowned Solomon' was not just arrogant but blasphemous? Why would a God-fearing Christian claim such celebrity? The plot thickens even more when the unit of measurement by which the Church of St Polyeuktos was laid out enters the equation. Princess Juliana boldly and bizarrely rejected contemporary architectural standards. Not for her the Greek, Roman or Byzantine foot.

Instead, she resurrected an ancient measurement based not just on the biblical cubit but the royal cubit used by Solomon to build the First Temple of Jerusalem. This is a hugely important revelation; none of the thousands of Early Christian churches recorded as far afield as Israel and France dared follow in Solomon's footsteps. The cubit traditionally measured the length of a man's forearm, from his elbow to clenched fist, and was the principal unit of linear measurement in the Bible. Using the royal cubit of 0.518 metres, the Church of St Polyeuktos measured precisely 100 royal cubits (51.45 x 51.90 metres). A sanctuary that probably overlay the crypt measured 20 cubits square: the exact dimensions of the Holy of Holies in Solomon's Temple.

Given this biblical act of emulation, the church's decorative scheme no longer seems eccentric. Its rich vegetation simply mimics 1 Kings 6.29: 'Round all the walls of the house he carved figures of cherubim, palm-trees, and open flowers.' Only here winged cherubim were replaced by peacocks, symbol of Byzantine empresses and royalty.

The relevance of the Church of St Polyeuktos to the Temple treasure is obvious. Where would be more fitting to deposit the birthright of the 'Chosen People' than in a temple fit for God? Did St Polyeuktos fit the bill? This enigma was a key reason behind my trip to Istanbul. Certainly, the timing fitted. In AD 532, the greatest church in Constantinople, St Sophia, had burnt down. Justinian's new creation was commissioned from Anthemius of Tralles and Isidorus of Miletus, theoretical engineers who designed a 'wonderdome'. St Sophia, however, was only dedicated in 537. So for ten years St Polyeuktos was the largest and most sumptuous church in Constantinople.

Saraçhane today is a vibrant hub of local politics and higher education. Machine-gun-toting police saunter in front of the Town Hall, its exquisite gardens landscaped with fountains and water pools tiled with blue swirling mosaics. Busts of civic dignitaries like Hizir Bey Çelebi, the first mayor of Istanbul in 1453, keep a beady eye on modern wheeling and dealing.

Across the road, Sehzade Camii, the Mosque of the Prince, and its turban-topped Ottoman grave markers, weeps across the skyline in memory of its source and inspiration. Even the graceful genius of Sinan, chief architect of the Ottoman Empire, cannot hide the structure's sadness. The mosque was commissioned by Süleyman the Magnificent as a tribute to his eldest son, Prince Mehmet, who died of smallpox in 1543.

Unfortunately, nothing magnificent about the Church of St Polyeuktos survives today *in situ*. The ruins, in fact, are an embarrassing eyesore. A fortune has been spent on a delightful park adjacent to the church. Old men mull over the good times under shaded trees, as passing businessmen off to impress civil servants in the Town Hall present their shoes for a quick polish. Locals hawk tea next to the park's primeval 'Stonehenge' sculpture. Students and nurses stride towards the Medical Park Hospital, but no one bothers with the Byzantine ruins that stand in desperate need of surgery.

Today the sagging green-mesh wire fencing surrounding St Polyeuktos has been cut open to facilitate a new use for one of Istanbul's most important monuments. The church has been transformed into a municipal garbage dump and, worse still, a latrine overflowing with human excrement. Princess Juliana's golden walls are now rendered black from tramps' night fires. In the West, historians speak in hushed tones of this amazing church and what it has taught us about the Byzantine world. The reality was a deep disappointment to me. The church has died an unflattering death; both Polyeuktos and Princess Juliana must surely be turning in their graves. I couldn't help but wonder if the monument would have been better protected if an Ottoman ruler had stuck a minaret above its walls.

After walking to Saraçhane straight from the Hippodrome, I was also disappointed by the isolated location of the church. Surely Justinian wouldn't have allowed the Temple treasures to languish so far away from the seat of imperial power, geographically peripheral to his campaign for publicly unifying past and present? This may have been the most important church in town, but it was also way off the beaten track.

Another dilemma for me was Justinian's hatred of the Princess Juliana. Both royals knew that his claim to the throne was ancestrally bogus. Justin I, his uncle, had been a nobody promoted above his station. Juliana had expected the throne to pass to her own son, the younger Olybrius, after the death of the emperor Anastasius in 518, and with time her profound contempt for Justinian became increasingly public. Did more than four generations of blue blood count for nothing?

Juliana was the emperor Justinian's *bête noire*, the Church of St Polyeuktos a dynastic statement immortalising her family's noble lineage. When the emperor demanded a contribution from Juliana for the rebuilding of the Church of St Sophia, she cheerfully invited him to pop over to St Polyeuktos and help himself. On entering the church

Justinian discovered that the princess had hammered her entire wealth into golden plaques plating the divine roof. A house of Christian worship could not be ransacked, even by an emperor, and Justinian knew he had been outfoxed. No wonder when the Church of St Sophia was finally dedicated in 537 he declared, 'Solomon, I have vanquished thee.' In other words, his flashy new building outstripped Princess Juliana's.

The feisty aristocrat died in AD 528, and Justinian confiscated her church-palace after her son was implicated in a plot against the emperor and sent into exile. Under these circumstances would Justinian have housed the Temple treasure so far away from the seat of power? If not, was it put on public display or thrown into a deep dungeon?

Two possibilities remain. The Hippodrome museum was a likely candidate. Brilliant bronze and marble masterpieces certainly graced its central terrace, but none were royal treasures of such symbolic and monetary sensitivity. This left one last resort: Justinian's palace, which the emperor rebuilt from scratch after Constantinople went up in smoke during the Nika revolt of January AD 532. Over four days of rioting and anarchy – blamed on inter-factional fighting between Blues and Greens supporters, but really a political coup to oust Justinian's high officials – everything from the churches of St Sophia and St Irene to the Senate House and the great porticoes of the city was reduced to ashes. Justinian's new creation would stretch from the *kathisma* in the Hippodrome all the way down to the sea.

A convincing clue to the treasure's possible location in the palace lies in an obscure passage of Procopius. While painting a picture of Justinian's new building work, he described the Chalke (Bronze Gate), the palace's main entrance, where eight arches enclosed a miraculously adorned room:

> And the whole ceiling boasts of its pictures, not having been fixed with wax melted and applied to the surface, but set with tiny cubes of stone beautifully coloured in all hues, which represent human figures and all other kinds of subjects . . . On either side is war and battle, and many cities are being captured, some in Italy, some in Libya; and the Emperor Justinian is winning victories through his General Belisarius, and the General is returning to the Emperor, with his whole army intact, and he gives him spoils, both king and kingdoms and all things that are most

prized amongst men. In the centre stand the Emperor and Empress Theodora, both seeming to rejoice and to celebrate victories over both the King of the Vandals and the King of the Goths, who approach them as prisoners of war to be led into bondage. (*Buildings* I.10.15–17)

If only this ceiling mosaic survived. In reality, almost nothing of Justinian's great palace exists amongst the Ottoman ruins of Istanbul other than a few rooms of extremely fine mosaics. If it had, Procopius' allusions are sufficient to be sure that the scene would have included the presentation of the Temple treasure of Jerusalem to Justinian in the Hippodrome Triumph of AD 534. This would have been Constantinople's equivalent of Rome's Arch of Titus. Instead, the site of the Chalke Gate is today covered by parklands between the Blue Mosque and the Church of St Sophia.

I walked over the site of this forgotten legacy, but could not reconnect with the past. Istanbul had yielded all its secrets and it was time to jump on another plane. Before disappearing, though, I had one last date with destiny: I wanted to look through a window into the Byzantine world and at the same time collect my thoughts. Did the quest for the Temple treasure of Jerusalem draw to a close in central Istanbul?

Down by the shore, a few hundred metres east of Justinian's swallowed port, is a remarkably well-preserved section of the Byzantine palace, seawall and modern shacks married together, its owners' washing flying in the wind. The majestic ruins were deserted; I had them all to myself. Fallen leaves chased cars down the Kennedy Caddesi highway. Some 350 metres away the site of Justinian's private jetty is marked by a soaring white tower, an all-seeing eye overlooking the Sea of Marmara, its horizontal radar rotating monotonously. Next to the seawalls a Byzantine lighthouse reminded me, yet again, of modernity's debt to the past.

Exhausted from my travels, I sat on a wall and absorbed the scene confronting me. Eight arched windows with three of their windowsills still intact framed the best preserved surviving section of Justinian's palace. These delightfully situated royal apartments once accommodated the emperor and his wayward wife. Here they whispered sweet nothings and plotted how to exploit the empire for ever greater riches. The seat of their power is today an exquisite spectacle. Romantic red creeper drooped down the palace walls and swallows flitted from window to window. The red-bricked veneer looks more like a medieval castle than a Roman palace.

My reverie was soon shattered by a black and white sheepdog snarling down from the right-hand window. His warning bark reminded me that my journey was incomplete. I had one last stop to make. The treasure had not died in Istanbul at all. In describing the 'treasures of the Jews' presented to Justinian during Belisarius' Triumph of AD 534, Procopius emphatically reported an altogether different fate:

> And one of the Jews, seeing these things, approached one of those known to the emperor and said: 'These treasures I think it inexpedient to carry into the palace in Byzantium. Indeed, it is not possible for them to be elsewhere than in the place where Solomon, the king of the Jews, formerly placed them. For it is because of these that Gaiseric captured the palace of the Romans, and now the Roman army has captured the Vandals.' When this had been brought to the ears of the Emperor, he became afraid and quickly sent everything to the sanctuaries of the Christians in Jerusalem. (*Wars* 4.9.6–9)

Justinian was a split personality controlling a city of paradoxes. He was lord of the Mediterranean, yet at the same time scared of his own shadow. The emperor saw plots and conspiracies all around him. Deeply respectful of his classical inheritance, and familiar with the destructive power of the Jewish treasure, no doubt Justinian's paranoia prevented him from putting it in his own palace. So in all likelihood it did end up, after all, in the Church of St Polyeuktos, where the emperor was happy for it to wreak havoc on the House of Anicia Juliana. The subsequent transference of the Temple treasure back to the Holy Land was also precisely the kind of quixotic behaviour to be expected of Justinian. How ironic that the birthright ripped out of the heart of Jerusalem in AD 70 to travel the world should now end up where it started: back in Jerusalem.

The Holy Land

38

Sanctuary of the Christians

THE GUN-TOTING ISRAELI army girls can hardly have been out of their teens. Behind amicable smiles and blue military security uniforms we exchanged pleasantries, as they methodically ransacked Abou George's rusting car. The lights of Jerusalem twinkled down the road in the morning dew. Ahead sprawled the unappetising wasteland of the West Bank.

What would typically have taken Abou George, an Israeli Arab, several hours of pleading and negotiation, only took me three minutes. George would usually have been treated as guilty until proved innocent, tarred from birth with the taint of suspicion. By contrast, I was virtually waved through, a jovial westerner flashing a United Kingdom passport and conversing in pidgin Hebrew. What would the soldiers have thought if they knew the truth, that I was about to expose the secret of the Temple treasure – Israel's ultimate birthright – which I was convinced lay hidden almost under their noses, less than 20 kilometres from the Temple Mount?

The main road into Bethlehem's Manger Street, the traditional site of Jesus' birth, is today inaccessible. It wouldn't make any difference if you were a wise king, you would still not get through. An 8-metre-tall slab of concrete bars access: the head of what to many people is an evil 225-kilometre-long snake – Israel's Security Fence. Abou George took a detour, wiggling his car over potholes until he finally found a narrow gap in the concrete curtain.

Today Manger Street is part of a ghost town dreaming of its own resurrection. The security fence has dislocated its inhabitants from what tourists deem to be the civilised world, strangling Bethlehem's economy. You may as well put up a billboard saying 'Enter Here to be Blown Up', or so the television news falsely implies. The bored owner of Mitri's Souvenir Store sat outside his shop cursing his birth. The Golden Bakery emitted no smell of fresh pita bread; the birds had flown from the Paradise Hotel. Battered green and white Palestinian buses veered through town, startling a Japanese tour group clad in black T-shirts emblazoned with pink elephants and the legend 'God's Original Creatures', no doubt symbolising Ganesha, the Hindu elephant-deity, lord of success and destroyer of evils and obstacles. Bethlehem, gateway to the West Bank, enjoys no prosperity and lives on the edge of despair. Wise kings are in very short supply here.

We left the ghost town behind and headed into the wilderness of Judaea. The flattened summit of the artificial hill of Herodium, King Herod's palace and mausoleum, loomed into sight. A stench of sewage swamped the air; mangy donkeys sniffed out blades of grass by the dusty road. This no man's land is inhospitable and uncomfortable. I wasn't overjoyed to be here, but the truth was just around the corner. My destination was the Arab village of Ubeidiya and the Monastery of St Theodosius. Why was I here, playing a dangerous game in the West Bank, the heartland of Hamas, source of Israel's military antagonism and stumbling block for peace?

We left the Temple treasure with Justinian in sixth-century Constantinople. A Jewish courtier had just spooked the Byzantine emperor with a shocking revelation. Every civilisation possessing the treasure since AD 70 had crumbled: the Jews of Israel, Rome and finally the Vandals. Justinian, a great student of the enduring life-force of antiquity, dispatched the golden menorah, silver trumpets and Table of the Divine Presence back to the sanctuaries of the Christians in Jerusalem. The treasure had come home, but when and where?

The repatriation clearly took place before Justinian's death in AD 565, and can be further narrowed down to the date when Procopius of Caesarea, chronicler of Byzantium's wars with the barbarians, put down his pen in 554. The historian alleges that the emperor's action was a spontaneous decision made at the time of the Triumph of AD 534. Allowing for Procopius' sense of drama, perhaps chronologically compressing several historical events, the most logical conclusion dates the relocation of the Temple treasure between 535 and 554.

At this time the Holy Land was enjoying a golden age when emperors and aristocrats were pampering the biblical homeland.

Religious circumstances had transformed a sleepy Roman backwater into a gold mine. Between AD 330 and 640 hundreds of churches and monasteries emerged across Palestine, boosting the local economy and society at large. Nobody typified this building spree more than the empress Eudocia, who expended an extraordinary 20,480 lbs of gold (1.5 million gold coins) putting up churches in Palestine between AD 438 and 460, at a time when two gold coins sufficed to keep a person for a year. Dozens of ecclesiastical buildings sprang up in individual cities – at the latest count, over 255 churches and 50 monasteries.

Even though ancient texts gloss over the precise movements of the treasure in Byzantine Palestine, only one place would have been sufficiently holy to house them: Jerusalem's Church of the Holy Sepulchre. In AD 335, five years after founding Constantinople, Constantine the Great dedicated the Martyrium basilica at Golgotha, an Aramaic term meaning 'place of the skull'. What would later become world renowned as the Church of the Holy Sepulchre straddled the holiest place on earth to Christianity, the traditional location of Christ's crucifixion (Rock of Cavalry) and tomb (holy sepulchre).

The Church was appalled at the condition of the hallowed ground, which the Roman emperor Hadrian had polluted in AD 135 with a temple dedicated to Venus, goddess of love. Constantine tore down the temple's walls and healed its profaned soil with a Christian basilica, 58.5 metres long and 40.5 metres wide. A semi-circular annex supported by a circle of columns, the Anastasis, would later be added. The basilica was surrounded by double porticoes, and three gates faced the rising sun, opposite which was a dome crowned by twelve columns, symbolising the apostles, surmounted by silver bowls.

The fourth century witnessed a new global phenomenon that would persist into the modern era – tourism. Rather than a cultural extravaganza, the Byzantine Grand Tour was a religious pilgrimage to the holy sites described in the Bible. Books could be bought setting out itineraries, and safe hostels, *mansiones*, sprouted up every 25 kilometres across the empire. The Church of the Holy Sepulchre swiftly gained a reputation as the epicentre of Christian pilgrimage. Here was the physical spot where Jesus was said to have been crucified, and where his tomb was located. Even more spectacular, however, pilgrims could gaze at the True Cross of Christ, which went on display after Helena, the mother of Constantine the Great, found it rather conveniently lying between an inscription and two other crosses. Further attractions included the reed, sponge and lance from the Crucifixion story held in the Chamber of Relics.

The True Cross proved a huge sensation. Writing around AD 348, Cyril of Jerusalem confirmed that 'The holy wood of the cross, shown among us today . . . has already filled the entire world by means of those who in faith have been taking bits from it.' Wearing lockets containing fragments of the cross became the latest fashion. More often than not, zealous pilgrims, who had risked life and limb to get to Jerusalem, just couldn't resist biting off a bit of the relic when they were finally allowed to bow over it and kiss the gnarled wood.

In reality, the survival of an intact Roman cross in the soils of Jerusalem is virtually impossible. The ground is neither waterlogged nor arid enough to create a sufficiently anaerobic environment. But this didn't matter. Belief is a state of mind, and the relic certainly served a crucial missionary role. Ironically, the arrival of the far older and historically authentic Temple relics was not met with any fanfare. On the contrary, Christianity had taken over 300 years to break free from the shackles of Judaism and paganism and was not about to have its thunder stolen. The repatriation of the Jewish treasure to Jerusalem was a double-edged sword for the city's patriarchs, which reflected the very real muscle-flexing between Church and State. But the patriarchs adhered to Justinian's imperial prescription and quietly locked the Temple relics away in a deep recess of the Church of the Holy Sepulchre.

———•———

The West Bank's timeless landscape drifted past my window. Goatherds and their flocks idled by water cisterns, a vista frozen since biblical times. Across the fields terraced walls of stone built by Jewish farmers remain fossilised since the Roman era.

The Temple treasure of Jerusalem languished beneath the Church of the Holy Sepulchre for seventy years, as neglected as this panorama. With its special status as the Holy Land, the flagship of Early Christianity, Byzantine Palestine was initially insulated from the deep cracks starting to split the empire at large. But the end of classical antiquity was just over the horizon.

Justinian may have been a distinguished builder and resolute leader, who successfully reconquered Roman North Africa, but just like King Herod at the port of Caesarea and George W. Bush in New Orleans, he was powerless against Mother Nature. In mid-July AD 541 calamity struck the Byzantine Empire. Black rats boarded a ship at Pelusium in southern Sinai and headed for the harbour of Constantinople. The bubonic plague ravaged the city for four months, with 10,000 souls dropping like flies each day. The corpse administrators stopped counting when the dead numbered 230,000.

Once they had consumed the capital, the rats were on the move once more, jumping ship to export death as far and wide as Naples and Syria. In the great port cities, delirious merchants swore they saw headless Ethiopians sailing brass ships and maliciously spreading disease along the beaches. The contemporary historian and leader of the Monophysite Syriac Church, John of Ephesus, moaned that in Palestine 'All the inhabitants, like beautiful grapes, were trampled and squeezed dry without mercy.'

The Justinianic plague was a highly contagious evil of biblical proportions. If the vehicle of death was *Rattus rattus*, the bullet was the Nilotic flea, *Xenopsylla cheopis*, which could jump 40 centimetres off the ground and induced hallucinations, fever, severe diarrhoea and eventually bubonic swelling in the groin, armpits, ears and thighs. Weeping with pus, victims would end up in a deep coma and generally die after two to three days. The first great pandemic in history had a mortality rate of 78 per cent, wiping out one-third of the entire Mediterranean population. After the initial rage, like a forest fire the plague re-emerged every twelve years, eventually reaching Britain and Ireland in 664. Only in AD 750, after eighteen outbreaks, did the curse run out of steam.

The empire never had time to recover from this initial shock. Further hammer blows continued to rain down. From AD 547/8 a succession of disasters shook the east. Earthquakes hit the coastal metropolises of Tyre, Sidon, Beirut, Tripolis and Ptolemais (Acre) in Palestine with such violence that mountain tops fell into the sea. Tsunamis inundated maritime cities, and terrifying thunder and lightning criss-crossed the skies. In 556/7, a spear-shaped fire appeared in the heavens and in 610 a solar eclipse obscured the earth.

With the empire on its sickbed, the Sasanian Persians, who had been knocking at the gates of the east for decades, finally emerged. In AD 613, Persian forces under the command of Chosroes II, the self-styled King of Kings, crushed Damascus and swept south into Palestine, just as Rome had done almost five and a half centuries earlier. According to Procopius, his predecessor, Chosroes I, had dreamt of getting his hands on the treasures of Palestine since AD 542: 'And his purpose was to lead the army straight for Palestine, in order that he might plunder all their treasures and especially those of Jerusalem. For he had it from hearsay that this was an especially goodly land and peopled by wealthy inhabitants' (*Wars* 2.20.18–19).

Most of the province willingly bowed to the King of Kings, and as the coastal cities of Caesarea, Apollonia and Lod capitulated to his forces, a historical marvel occurred for the first and last time. The region's Jews, united in celebration at casting off the yoke of Christianity after 300 years, joined ranks with the Persian force and its 'Arab' confederates. For the first and last time in Middle Eastern history, Arab and Jew shared swords.

The Sasanian resolve hardened as Jerusalem approached. Following a twenty-day siege in April 614, the Holy City was sacked for three days. Those capable made a run for it. Widely respected holy men, such as John Moschus and Sophronius, fled by ship to Syria, while the thousands of monks minding their own business in the wilderness of Judaea sought refuge in Arabia. The Holy Land was abandoned to the invaders.

In Jerusalem, almost every ecclesiastical structure was ransacked or burnt down, its treasures looted. The Churches of Gethsemane and Eleona on the Mount of Olives were blitzed, as was the Church of St John the Baptist. The Persians ran through the streets like banshees, inflicting random destruction and decapitating priests. In the Convent of St Melania 400 nuns were raped. Tens of thousands of Christians were sacrificed for the cause and 66,000 skilled workmen enslaved to Persia.

Antiochus Strategos, a monk from the Monastery of St Sabas in Jerusalem, saw at first hand the bloodletting across the city in AD 614 and recalled the horrors in his *The Sack of Jerusalem*:

For the enemy entered in mighty wrath, gnashing their teeth in violent fury; like evil beasts they roared, bellowed like lions, hissed like ferocious serpents, and slew all whom they found. Like mad dogs they tore with their teeth the flesh of the faithful, and respected none at all . . . massacred them like animals, cut them in pieces, mowed sundry of them down like cabbages . . . Then their wrath fell upon priests and deacons: they slew them in their churches like dumb animals . . .

Some had their belly cloven asunder with the sword and their entrails gushing out, and others lay cut into pieces, limb by limb, like the carcasses in a butcher's shop . . . Some had fled into the Holy of Holies, where they lay cut up like grass . . . Others were clasping the horns of the altars; others the holy Cross, and the slain were heaped on them. Others had fled to the Baptistery and lay covered with wounds on the edge of the font. Others were massacred as they hid under the holy table, and were offered victims to Christ.

The invasion ceased as rapidly as it had started. Palestine was, in reality, no more than a launch pad for the ultimate goal, an assault on Egypt, now the richest province in the Byzantine Empire. The Sasanians returned home counting their booty and left their Jewish allies to mop up. After so many years of oppression and life as second-class citizens, the Jews reacted with grim ferocity. In Acre they set fire to a church, tortured the deacon and burned Christian books of prayer. At Tyre they systematically destroyed churches, but ended up losing a war of attrition: every time a church fell, the inhabitants of Tyre decapitated 100 fettered Jews and threw their heads over the ramparts. The pile of headless dead was said to have numbered 2,000 by the time the Jews capitulated. Even the Sasanian commanders eventually lost patience with the Jews' wrath, crucifying many and seizing their property. Once again, the children of the Old Testament were expelled from the gates of Jerusalem.

During these decades of chaos and confusion wrought by man and nature, what happened to the Temple treasure? The texts are silent on the matter. However, it was almost certainly spirited away. Pillage was clearly the name of the game, and the Sasanians deliberately targeted the True Cross of Christ as the most valuable icon of Christianity. The anonymous seventh-century *Khuzistan Chronicle* records that, in Jerusalem, General Shahrbaraz

breached all the walls and entered it, seizing the bishop and the city officials, torturing them [in order to get hold of] the wood of the Cross and the contents of the treasury . . . God left no place secret which they did not show the Persians; they also showed them the wood of the Cross which lay concealed in a vegetable garden. The [Persians] made a large number of chests and sent them along with many other objects and precious things to Khosro.

Some five and a half centuries earlier, the Romans had seized the menorah, trumpets and Table from Herod's Temple to leave no doubt about who was the new boss in town. The Sasanians were treading a predictable path in removing the True Cross to Ctesiphon in Iraq.

Arab sources speak volumes about the fate of the Cross, but include no reference to the Temple treasure, leading to the conclusion that it never reached Persia. I suspect the Sasanians and Jews cut a deal. The discovery of the True Cross was a struggle. The Persians had to torture numerous priests, and eventually even the Patriarch Zacharias, until it was discovered buried in a gold box in a garden. Did the Jews extract a tip-off through similar coercion? Certainly this would explain what they were doing violating the tomb of Christ:

The descendants of the crucifiers also approached the Persian commander and told him that all the gold and silver and the treasures of Jerusalem were placed beneath the tomb of Jesus. Their crafty design was to destroy the place of the burial. When he yielded to them they dug some three cubits around it, and discovered a casket with the inscription: 'This casket belongs to Joseph the Councillor' – the man who provided the tomb for the body of Jesus. (*Khuzistan Chronicle* 23)

The Jewish commanders failed to find the treasures of the Second Temple for one obvious reason. Just as the modern discovery of the ancient menorah would be met with rapture amongst fanatical Jews and evangelical Christians, a divine sign validating the immediate building of a Third Jewish Temple in Jerusalem, so in AD 614 the Christian community resolutely refused to furnish the Jews with any ammunition that would justify the building of a new Jewish city. But the treasure cannot simply have disappeared into thin air.

Amidst the cloud of death and retribution that devastated Jerusalem, the Patriarch Zacharias was taken hostage and dragged off to Persia. A remarkable man replaced him. Modestus is one of the forgotten protagonists of ancient history, a rare visionary in a time of great chaos. While the lights of classical antiquity – a Graeco-Roman world that had endured since the fifth century BC – were going out across the eastern Mediterranean, this man of God held aloft the beacon of Christianity.

On the eve of the Persian Invasion, Modestus was serving as *hegumen* (superior) of the Monastery of St Theodosius at Deir Dosi, today in the West Bank. By 614, Zacharias and Modestus already enjoyed a close working relationship based on mutual respect. When the threat to Jerusalem materialised, the patriarch quickly summoned the monk and, according to the chronicle of Antiochus Strategos, 'bade him go and muster men from the Greek troops which were in Jericho, to help them in their struggle'.

Once Zacharias was taken hostage, Modestus filled the breach, becoming locum tenens in his absence. After a truce was agreed between the Sasanian and Byzantine forces, the monk dedicated what would prove to be a brief life to burying the Christian dead and rebuilding the holy places of Palestine. He travelled to Lod, Tiberias, Tyre and Damascus raising funds to renovate the Church of the Holy Sepulchre, which reopened amidst jubilant scenes in AD 621. The monk successfully petitioned John the Almsgiver, Patriarch of Alexandria, to donate money, supplies and 1,000 Egyptian workmen to help rebuild and repair the churches.

From AD 628 to 635, Palestine was back under Byzantine control. The gleaming domes of the Church of the Ascension on the Mount of Olives and the Church of Holy Zion shone again under Mediterranean skies. In March AD 630, the Sasanians even returned the True Cross to the Byzantine emperor Heraclius, who accompanied it home to the Church of the Holy Sepulchre. During his visit the emperor was so impressed with Modestus' work that he installed him as the new Patriarch of Jerusalem and diverted Palestine's poll tax to restore the holy places. Modestus was the new darling of the Christian Church, and lost no time expanding his mission. Things were looking up.

But this proved to be a false dawn. Who knows to what heights this visionary might have soared? Somehow, somewhere during these years of instability, Modestus ruffled feathers. One dark spring day in AD 631, the new patriarch stopped overnight at the port city of Arsuf,

Roman Apollonia, before sailing up to Damascus where further diverted taxes awaited him. After praying in the local church – whose ruins are today consumed by the dangerously polluted soils of an Israeli munitions factory – and being impressed by the revitalised commerce down by the warehouses, Modestus sat down to dinner. For reasons unclear, a member of his entourage poisoned the patriarch's meal. His death was quick. Modestus had only been in the top job for nine months.

39

Desert City of Saints

Abou GEORGE TOOK the dirt road eastwards towards Mar Saba, one of the oldest inhabited monasteries in the world, rock-cut and hence camouflaged on the side of a steep canyon. Nearby fields surround the cave of Beit Sahour, where a few humble shepherds were minding their own business many moons ago when a supernatural light hovered over their heads and a voice proclaimed Christ's birth.

Sheets of Israel's prefabricated concrete security fence awaited the builders; the odd Israeli army jeep lumbered by burnt-out homes. Being immersed in such rich ancient and modern history – warts and all – was intoxicating. The empty landscape was charged with tension. We drove deeper and deeper into Hamas territory.

Modestus had not been ready to die – he left no will behind or plans for a successor. In the years following the Persian Invasion the monk kept his unswerving eye firmly on the goal of rebuilding the city of God. Nothing else mattered. Yet if I was right, with the Patriarch Zacharias captive, it was Modestus who spirited away the Jewish treasures from the Church of the Holy Sepulchre in AD 614. After the sack of Jerusalem, the city was filled with vengeful Jews until Heraclius yet again expelled them in 630. In this climate I suspect Modestus took the wise decision to keep the Jewish treasures under lock and key, away from prying hands. As his name suggests, the future patriarch was a private man well capable of keeping decisions close to his chest.

By summer 631, Modestus was dead; three years later, Muslim forces invaded Syria. Islam was on the move. According to the late eighth-century account of al-Waqidi, *Kitab al-magazi* (Book of the Wars, 2.758), the prophet Muhammad was advising his troops to

Attack in the name of God. Fight the enemies of God and your enemies in Syria. You will find there men in cells isolated from people. Do not oppose them. You will find others in whose head Satan lives like nests. Cut them off with your swords. Do not kill a woman, a nursing infant, or an old man. Do not strip any palm tree.

In 640, King Herod's old port of Caesarea fell after a seven-year siege. The Graeco-Roman heritage, dead in the West for over a hundred years, was now also officially ended in the eastern Mediterranean. Islam would remain master of Palestine for the next 1,280 years until the collapse of the Ottoman Empire and emergence of the British Mandate in 1920. The secret of the Temple treasure's hiding place died with Modestus and was buried amid the chaos of the Arab Conquest. Christianity was overrun and the Byzantine Empire shoehorned back into the Bosphorus.

So where would Modestus have concealed the Second Temple gold menorah, silver trumpets and bejewelled Table of the Divine Presence? Certainly out of town, beyond Jerusalem, and most obviously in one of the numerous monasteries manned by silent monks in the wilderness of Judaea. However, archaeologists have identified a baffling forty-two monastic retreats ringing Jerusalem. Which one fitted the bill?

The answer is logical. Even in his capacity as patriarch, Modestus was still the superior of the Monastery of St Theodosius. Today, this retreat survives at Deir Dosi, 12 kilometres east of Bethlehem and close to the West Bank village of Ubeidiya. Here was my date with destiny, but I would need to walk on eggshells: for political reasons I didn't want either the Israeli or the Palestinian authorities to get wind of what I was working on. Furthermore, the monastery lies deep in Hamas territory. I had been warned to watch my back.

St Theodosius was born at Marissa in Cappadocia (modern Turkey) in AD 423, before assuming a life of piety in Jerusalem. The record of his life, penned by his disciple Theodorus, Bishop of Petra, confirms that he was an extreme ascetic who renounced all material comforts:

> for dreading the poison of vanity from the esteem of men, he
> retired into a cave at the top of a neighbouring desert mountain, and
> employed his time in fasting, watching, prayers, and tears, which almost

continually flowed from his eyes. His food was coarse pulse and wild herbs: for thirty years he never tasted so much as a morsel of bread.

In time, his piety attracted a large following, forcing him to abandon his cave and open a monastery, whose crypt overlies another cave where the Three Wise Men, the Magi, allegedly rested on their way to visit the infant Christ. Both the fame and size of the establishment rapidly grew until the monastery of Theodosius became, according to Theodorus, 'a city of saints in the midst of a desert, and in it reigned regularity, silence, charity, and peace'. The complex housed three infirmaries for the sick, aged and feeble, and ended up like the United Nations: Theodosius pursued an inclusive open-door policy, building four churches,

> one for each of the three several nations of which his community was chiefly composed, each speaking a different language; the fourth was for the use of such as were in a state of penance, which those that recovered from their lunatic or possessed condition before-mentioned, were put into, and detained till they had expiated their fault. The nations into which his community was divided were the Greeks, which was by far the most numerous, and consisted of all those that came from any provinces of the empire; the Armenians, with whom were joined the Arabians and Persians; and, thirdly, the Bessi, who comprehended all the northern nations below Thrace, or all who used the Runic or Slavonian tongue.

Theodosius died in AD 529, and after Modestus' poisoning in 631 the monasteries of the Judaean desert dwindled like dried-up vines. Nobody has ever studied scientifically the ancient ruins of the Monastery of St Theodosius, so its precise history under Early Islam remains a mystery. Its widespread popularity certainly ceased, yet I remained intrigued by what secrets survived within its walls.

We rounded a corner and were suddenly confronted by the Greek Orthodox monastery of Theodosius, key to so much secret history, perched on the edge of a deep valley. I imagined Modestus wearily arriving here by horse so many centuries ago, burdened by mysterious boxes. The same sense of isolation remains; nothing stirs. The air is thin and dry. Even in winter the ancient landscape is desperately parched; its thin soils support little life. Scars of white bedrock peer out of a hillside bare of sustenance. The only people who can live here today are the monastery's four guardians and the Abediyah Bedouin, whose tin-can and matchstick camp I spied halfway down the valley.

My heart pounded at the prospect of the unexpected as I approached the monastery gates. Its walls were certainly built of ancient Byzantine stone masonry, embedded within the plaster of the latest reincarnation. The tops of a red-brick dome and tower, both sur-mounted with a cross, peered tantalisingly above the 10-metre-high walls. The closer I got, the more I sensed something was not quite right. The outer walls were covered with Arabic graffiti, and all the windows and doorways were sealed with reddish-brown iron gates and grilles. Were these to keep people in or out?

With the entrance clearly barred and no sign of life visible, I walked along the monastery's façade looking for a way in. No luck. The monastery was defended like a medieval castle and silent as the grave. The only link to the outside world seemed to be a slither of orange baling twine hanging between the inner wooden door and the iron grille. I pulled the string sharply and a bronze bell hanging high above my head inside the monastery announced my arrival. A minute passed with no response. Abou George looked at me and sighed. I hadn't come all this way – across the seas and nearly six centuries of history – to be fobbed off. I yanked the bell rope twice again and hollered a 'hello' at the gate. There wasn't even a letterbox to peer through. Finally, footsteps stirred somewhere deep in the bowels of the monastery.

The muffled voice of an elderly woman spat out something in Greek, completely incomprehensible. In slow English I asked her if we might enter the great monastery. No reply. Abou George then tried in Hebrew and Arabic. Nothing doing. The sister had departed. Yet again I heaved on the rope. Tired legs approached and a severe voice firmly told us to 'Go away. Entry not possible.' And that was that. Perplexed, I wondered if the people within were busy, fearful or had something to hide.

Before I could collect my thoughts a couple of Palestinian police cars skidded to a halt, covering us with a cloud of dust. Three young policemen jumped out and engaged Abou George in conversation, largely one-way traffic. Clearly embarrassed, George, a private and

quiet man, was forced to display his passport and explain his movements so far off the beaten track. I was explained as a British tourist
visiting the holy places. The team seemed satisfied. They looked me
up and down and sped off. Abou George shrugged.

If I couldn't get inside the monastery, I was at least committed to
poking about its grounds to satisfy my curiosity. In particular, I needed
to find out if a monastery really did exist here at the time of the
Persian Invasion. I left Abou George looking awkward, locked inside
his car with Israeli number plates in the heart of Hamas territory, and
headed down the valley. The monks had grown prickly cacti all along
the monastery's walls to discourage entry. Eventually I clambered over
the fencing and found myself in an unpromising field.

The monastery turned out to be a simple affair, comprising a
central courtyard surrounded by towers and side-wings housing a
chapel and accommodation. Two stone terrace walls protected the
core building. Greyish-white bedrock interrupted by shallow pockets
of soil surrounded me, suitable for nothing other than the hardy olive
tree. After scanning the landscape in vain for standing structures, I
spent the next hour surveying the soil and got my answers: enough
white mosaic cubes, clay rooftiles and fragments of oil-lamps, pottery
bases and rims to be certain that a monastery stood on this site in the
sixth and early seventh centuries AD. In particular, I picked up and
drew the rims of some bag-shaped amphorae and a bowl with a simple
incurving profile known as Jerusalem Fine Byzantine Ware.

Thrilled with my results, I was just about to make my escape and
liberate Abou George when I spied a pile of soil out of the corner of
my eye and froze in my tracks. A cold flush of anxiety gripped me.
The heap of soil was fresh and beneath it was the entrance to an
underground cave. I was not equipped with a torch, and since most
of the entrance was concealed anyway, there was no way of gaining
access. What was going on?

Further along the hillside were three other pockets of freshly
disturbed soil, clearly less than a week old, above what looked like cave
entrances. Unfortunately, I knew exactly what I was looking at: the
telltale signs of illicit metal detecting. Treasure hunters had beaten me
to the monastery. Why had they focused on this ancient site? How
had they known about its antiquity? Had someone perhaps tipped

them off? Impossible. Nobody outside my very tight circle knew what I was up to in the West Bank.

What was certain, and a shocking piece of news that made my mind race and heart pound, was the revelation that the hills surrounding the Monastery of St Theodosius were honeycombed with underground caves and cavities. Maybe this was another compelling reason why Modestus brought the Temple treasure to his old monastery. The same local geology that had created the cave where the Three Wise Men slept on their way to Bethlehem had also riddled the region with secret subterranean hideouts. One thing was certain, only God now knew what the treasure hunters had already got their hands on.

Troubled, I returned to the car and an equally disturbed Abou George, who jumped out of his skin when I rattled on the window. George was clearly not amused at having been left alone for an hour, here of all places. He felt like a sitting duck and was very keen to head for home. 'Not safe here,' he told me, 'very dangerous security situation. Everywhere not safe.'

However, before he could start the engine I was off again. A yellow tour van had pulled up outside the monastery and it seemed the guide was receiving the same short shrift as me. He turned out to be a jovial Palestinian from Bethlehem called Ilias, who had recently returned from studying in Denmark and Portugal.

Ilias assured me that my welcome at the monastery gate was nothing personal. 'They're not letting anyone in. Many times I come; we don't know why. It's really amazing. Is written in books it must be open every day. Little bit disappointing. The sister refuses to speak.'

He was both deeply frustrated and embarrassed. The West Bank's economy was shattered and he was fearful of losing his only source of income, limited tourism. Ilias explained how the monastery felt trapped and isolated, ringed by Hamas sympathisers. The proof was all around, and he pointed to the black and red graffiti coating the monastery's walls that read 'Youth . . . we are a river of giving. We don't know weakness' (the calling card of Hamas) and 'You remain in our Palestinian hearts, Abu Ammar', Yasser Arafat's *nom de guerre*.

Since returning from Europe, Ilias had been under huge strain. Nothing changes in the Wild West of the East, he told me. 'The politics is still the same. There's no development on the ground, so the people are getting more depressed, as if they've given up. I've never seen this look in their eyes – no meaning to life, no belief, no trust.'

Yet again I realised just how fortunate I was to be able to return to a relatively predictable, stable world. This everyday battle for existence encapsulated everything malignant about the Middle East. I had my answers, and both Abou George and I were relieved to be heading back to the civilised comforts of Jerusalem and, in my case, on to London. At the checkpoint out of Bethlehem we sat on the ground and left the military police to search the car for contraband and bombs. I took the opportunity to check my digital photos and quizzed Abou George about the holes on the hillside surrounding the Monastery of St Theodosius. George works in the building industry and certainly knew of no current or scheduled development work there.

After looking at my photos, out of nowhere George added, 'Maybe they are looking for gold or treasure.'

'Is there treasure there?' I replied, playing innocent.

'Who knows? Maybe,' concluded Abou George cheekily, a twinkle in his eye.

40

City of God, World of Man

B ACK IN JERUSALEM I ended up where I had started, along streets where Jewish sedition had turned the Holy City blood red in AD 69. The Wailing Wall was teeming with tourists free to enjoy the ripest fruits of globalisation. The struggle for life on the West Bank seemed from a different planet.

My quest was complete, and the tides of history washed over me in waves. The present felt unreal; mind and body were in chronic need of decompression. Pottering around the Old City of Jerusalem before flying back to London, I hoped that the urban buzz and oriental smells would bring me down to earth. But nothing happened; I remained marooned between time and space.

After so many years pursuing the elusive trail of the Temple treasure, my final clue left me in a quandary. Should I return to the West Bank with a scientific team of archaeologists and a fluxgate magnetometer to bounce sonic pulses through the soil in search of ancient cultural anomalies? Would the Israeli and Palestinian authorities even grant me a research licence if they knew my true objectives? What if the Temple treasure had already been looted from an underground cave behind the Monastery of St Theodosius?

I flicked on my iPod and sat on a bench behind the Wailing Wall watching Jews worshipping their god and Muslims quietly making their way on to the Haram al-Sharif to pray to Allah. The Herodian masonry separating both is less than two metres wide, but a chasm broader than the Red Sea divides their ideologies. What psychological fear triggers racial hatred, I wondered? I wasn't alone. The Black Eyed Peas playing 'Where Is The Love' on my iPod were similarly confounded, questioning the disappearance of human values, equality and the rise of human animosity. In the shadow of the Jewish Temple

Mount and Muslim Dome of the Rock the cries of the victims of the suicide bombers and of children of the Intifada reverberated around the holy rocks.

The Temple treasure of Jerusalem is all things to all men. To many, it is the gold at the end of the rainbow, the key to riches beyond dreams. If the menorah, silver trumpets and Table of the Divine Presence materialised in the antiquities market they would quite simply be priceless and stir up the mother of all political storms.

Out of curiosity, I had discussed the financial implications of the discovery of the Temple treasure with Dr Jerome Eisenberg, Director of Royal-Athena Galleries in New York and one of the world's most successful dealers in antiquities. He confirmed that these masterpieces are 'the greatest religious treasures known to man, well beyond the value of any object or painting on the planet'. Eisenberg stressed that no precedent exists for marketing ancient art of such religious significance. So there would be no objective means of setting a reserve price or insurance value for the Temple treasure. 'Certainly some city slicker would pay $1 billion for the Mona Lisa,' he pointed out, 'which means that in the case of the value of the Temple treasure, the sky's the limit. You would be talking billions rather than hundreds of millions of dollars.'

But the spoils of Vespasian are not just the greatest treasure on earth. As the symbol of an ancient Jewish House of God and the dream of a messianic future, the Temple treasure is also a source of immense danger. Justinian was right. Every civilisation that possessed it was jinxed: early Israel, Rome, the Vandals and the Byzantine Empire. Behind me the source of today's trouble and hatred, the Temple Mount, continued to seethe with rage. Yet much of the violence surrounding it is based on inaccurate historical assumptions popularised in the last hundred years.

Both Judaism and Islam have a track record of manipulating reality to accentuate rights of territorial possession. Only in 2004 was a famous ivory priestly sceptre, long given pride of place in the Israel Museum as an eighth-century BC original from the Temple of Jerusalem, denounced as a forgery. Inscribed 'Belonging to the Temp[le of YHW]H, holy to the priests', we now know that while the artefact dates back to the thirteenth or twelfth century BC, the inscription is a fake. An inappropriate surface patina and incorrect syntax betray the mind and hand of the forger.

Even more controversial is a fifteen-line Hebrew inscription incised on a sandstone tablet, which surfaced in 2003. The text purports to be a record of renovations ordered by Jehoash, the biblical ruler of ninth-century BC Judaea. Here the king commands the Temple priests to take 'holy money . . . to buy quarry stones and timber and copper and labour to carry out the duty with faith'. Again scientific tests of the patina and studies of the language have condemned the object. Allegedly uncovered in a Muslim cemetery east of the Temple Mount, its convenient provenance is extremely suspect. The Temple treasure is intimately enmeshed in these deadly political claims for indigenous origins.

The question of racial diversity has long perplexed humanity. Ancient intellectuals understood cultural difference in terms of environmental determinism – they blamed it all on the weather. In his late fifth-century BC *Airs, Waters, Places*, the first known treatise on the principles of public health, the Father of Medicine, the Greek Hippocrates, argued that the reason why 'the Asiatics are less warlike and more gentle in character than Europeans is the uniformity of the seasons, which show no violent changes either towards heat or towards cold, but are equable'. In later discussions, he added, 'For uniformity engenders slackness, while variation fosters endurance in both body and soul; rest and slackness are food for cowardice, endurance and exertion for bravery.'

Rome maintained a similar sense of what, much later, would become known as natural selection. Vitruvius, for instance, believed:

> those who are born in colder regions, by their fearless courage are better equipped for the clash of arms, yet by their slowness of mind they rush on without reflection . . . Since, therefore, the disposition of the world is such by Nature, and all the other nations differ by their unbalanced temperament, it is in the true mean within the space of all the world and the regions of the earth, that the Roman people holds its territories. For in Italy the inhabitants are exactly tempered in either direction, both in the structure of the body, and by their strength of mind in the matter of endurance and courage . . . Thus the divine mind has allotted to the Roman state an excellent and temperate region in order to rule the world. (*On Architecture* 6.10–11)

The debate over geography, social superiority and the racial divide endures today in the Arab-Israeli conflict. Jerusalem is universally judged to be the centre of the religious world. Both Jews and Muslims alike claim the greater territorial rights. History and archaeology, however, challenge the accuracy of this blinkered reasoning.

Right-wing Jews lay claim to the Temple Mount as the epicentre of Jewish worship since the dawn of time. Yet not one shred of archaeological evidence exists for a Solomonic Temple on this spot of the grandiose form envisaged in the First Book of Kings. If there was a place of worship, then archaeological evidence suggests it would have resembled and functioned like a typical regional Canaanite temple. Whisper it quietly, but the religious doctrine of monotheism seems only to have been cemented when the Israelites were undergoing a cultural identity crisis in Babylonian exile. Only then did Yahweh abandon his consort, Asherah. It should also be remembered that the wise ruler who liberated the Jews and 'let my people go' was King Cyrus of Persia – an Iranian.

King Solomon is venerated today as the archetypal wise ruler, who ran the kind of Jewish nation many right-wing Jews would like to see restored in Israel. In reality, he was a human being with flaws like any other. I suspect the king would be rather embarrassed by the character reference preserved in the Old Testament. Not only does the Midrash assert that Solomon missed the opening ceremonies of dedication of his own Temple after a long night of passion, but he also married out:

> King Solomon loved many foreign women along with the daughter of Pharaoh: Moabite, Ammonite, Edomite, Sidonian and Hittite women, from the nations concerning which the Lord had said to the Israelites, 'You shall not enter into marriage with them, neither shall they with you; for they will surely incline your heart to follow their gods;' Solomon clung to these in love . . . So Solomon did what was evil in the sight of the Lord. (1 Kings 11.1–6)

Commentators who later compiled the Old Testament had problems sweeping the king's misdemeanours under the carpet. In reality, however, Solomon was simply following contemporary political protocol for the good of the nation. Taking foreign wives and allying your royal house with the strongest Iron Age superpowers was how political alliances were forged and peace maintained in antiquity.

These truisms certainly do not create a factual vacuum permitting the Palestinians to assume final rights over Jerusalem: they also have fallen into the trap of myth-making. Yasser Arafat constantly boasted that the Arabs set down roots in Israel before the Jews as descendants of the Canaanites and Jebusites. This is a complete fabrication. Historically, the majority of modern Palestinians are related to the waves of Arab tribesmen who conquered Palestine in AD 638. Their origin thus lies on the fringes of Iran and Iraq. By tying the name 'Palestinian' to the Peleset and Philistines, groups of Sea Peoples who fled south from the Aegean in the early twelfth century BC following the coastal sea-lanes, Arafat also linked the Palestinian cause to rootlessness rather than the lands of Canaan.

Why do politicians insist on focusing on ethnic differences rather than myriad religious and social similarities? Historians and archaeologists expose universal laws of human behaviour that make a mockery of such artificial constructs. The sequential prosperity, decline and fall of the four civilisations met during my quest for the Temple treasure – Israel, Rome, the Vandals and the Byzantine Empire – confirmed a pattern of long-term action and reaction. Take the Colosseum in Rome. Paid for by the emperor Vespasian with spoils plundered from the Jewish Temple in Jerusalem, eventually even this wonder succumbed to the surging tide of history. In 1452, Pope Nicholas V ordered the removal of 2,522 cartloads of its stones for lime production. That lime ended up bonding the walls of the Basilica of St Peter, today inside the Vatican City. So in one sense, Israel's Jewish birthright does indeed still languish imprisoned in the heart of Rome. History teaches us that we are only ever mere custodians of our ancient heritage.

In my own small way I knew I was also guilty of fuelling the battle for Jerusalem, and thus the Arab-Israeli conflict, by exposing the truth behind the Temple treasure and offering some people new dreams, others deathly nightmares. There and then in the heart of Jerusalem's Old City I decided to leave my revelations to fate. In Plato's *Laws*, written in the mid-fourth century BC, the Greek philosopher pondered the ethics of buried treasure and concluded that:

I should never pray to the gods to come across such a thing; and if I do, I must not disturb it nor tell the diviners . . . The benefit I'd get from removing it could never rival what I'd gain by way of virtue and moral rectitude by leaving it alone; by preferring to have justice in my soul rather than money in my pocket, I'd get — treasure for treasure — the better bargain.

Plato, of course, was writing about an ideal state of mind. Even so, I would like to think that my decision to end the pursuit for the long-lost Temple treasure of Jerusalem was the most rational and responsible reaction. I had reached the end of the line. Perhaps, as I write, the most powerful objects of biblical faith are locked away in some bank vault, with billions of pounds being negotiated on a private sale. I hope not and cross my fingers that the treasure hunters who had been scouring the West Bank left empty-handed.

One thing is certain, the Temple treasure isn't in the Vatican, nor crushed beneath the ruined cities of Rome, Carthage, Istanbul or Jerusalem. The gold menorah, silver trumpets and precious Table of the Divine Presence ended up in a 'city of saints', hidden beneath the Monastery of St Theodosius in the wilderness of Judaea. As I bade my farewell to Jerusalem, I stared one last time at the Temple Mount, and offered up a little prayer that the treasures remain lost for all time, sealed beneath swirling desert sands far from the treacherous clutches of man.

Select Bibliography

ANCIENT SOURCES

All books published by Harvard University Press form part of the Loeb Classical Library series

R. Atwater, *Procopius of Caesarea. Secret History* (New York, 1992)

S. Brock, *The Khuzistan Chronicle* (unpublished)

A. Butler, *The Lives of the Fathers, Martyrs and Other Principal Saints*, Vol. I (London, 1926)

E. Cary, *Dio's Roman History* (Harvard University Press, 1927)

F. H. Colson, *Philo I* (Harvard University Press, 1929)

F. C. Conybeare, 'Antiochus Strategos. The Capture of Jerusalem by the Persians in 614 AD', *English Historical Review* 25 (1910), 502–17

H. Danby, *The Mishnah* (Oxford, 1933)

H. B. Dewing, *Procopius of Caesarea. History of the Wars* (Harvard University Press, 1916)

—— *Procopius of Caesarea. Buildings* (Harvard University Press, 1940)

D. E. Eichholz, *Pliny. Natural History X, Books 36–37* (Harvard University Press, 1962)

L. Ginzberg, *The Legends of the Jews, I: From the Creation to Jacob* (Philadelphia, 1975)

—— *The Legends of the Jews, III: From the Exodus to the Death of Moses* (Philadelphia, 1975)

—— *The Legends of the Jews, IV: From Joshua to Esther* (Philadelphia, 1975)

F. Granger, *Vitruvius. On Architecture* (Harvard University Press, 1934)

M. Hadas, *Aristeas to Philocrates (Letter of Aristeas)* (New York, 1951)

E. Jeffreys, M. Jeffreys and R. Scott, *The Chronicle of John Malalas* (Melbourne, 1986)

H. L. Jones, *The Geography of Strabo* (Harvard University Press, 1923)

W. H. S. Jones, *Hippocrates* (Harvard University Press, 1977)

C. Macdonald, *Cicero X* (Harvard University Press, 1977)

C. Mango and R. Scott, *The Chronicle of Theophanes Confessor* (Oxford, 1997)

R. Marcus, *Philo II. Questions and Answers on Exodus* (Harvard University Press, 1953)

J. Moorhead, *Victor of Vita: History of the Vandal Persecution* (Liverpool University Press, 1992)

M. H. Morgan, *Vitruvius: The Ten Books on Architecture* (Oxford, 1914)

A. Palmer, *The Seventh Century in the West Syrian Chronicles* (Liverpool University Press, 1933)

H. Rackham, *Pliny. Natural History IV, Books 12–16* (Harvard University Press, 1945)

—— *Pliny. Natural History IX, Books 33–35* (Harvard University Press, 1952)

J. C. Rolfe, *Ammianus Marcellinus III* (Harvard University Press, 1939)

H. St J. Thackeray, *The Letter of Aristeas* (Harvard University Press, 1918)

—— *Josephus. The Jewish War* (Harvard University Press, 1927–8)

W. Whiston, *The Works of Josephus* (London, 1890)

<hr />

Roots

G. Alföldy, 'Eine Bauinschrift aus dem Colosseum', *Zeitschrift für Papyrologie und Epigraphik* 109 (1995), 195–226

A. Claridge, *Rome: An Oxford Archaeological Guide* (Oxford, 1998)

K. Hopkins and M. Beard, *The Colosseum* (London, 2005)

S. Kingsley, *Shipwreck Archaeology of the Holy Land* (London, 2004)

A. La Regina (ed.), *Sangue e Arena* (Rome, 2001)

Israel – Land of God

M. N. Adler, 'The Itinerary of Benjamin of Tudela', *Jewish Quarterly Review* 16 (1904), 453–76

J. M. Allegro, *The Treasure of the Copper Scroll* (London, 1960)

M. L. Ambrosini, *The Secret Archives of the Vatican* (London, 1970)

A. Asher, *The Itinerary of Rabbi Benjamin of Tudela* (Berlin, 1840)

G. J. Brooke and P. R. Davies (eds), *Copper Scroll Studies* (Sheffield, 2002)

M. Broshi and H. Esshel, 'Daily Life at Qumran', *Near Eastern Archaeology* 63.3 (2000), 136–9

J. A. Brown, *John Marco Allegro. The Maverick of the Dead Sea Scrolls* (Grand Rapids, 2005)

E. Cline, *Jerusalem Besieged. From Ancient Canaan to Modern Israel* (University of Michigan Press, 2004)

M. Gichon, 'Industry', in M. Fischer, M. Gichon and O. Tal, *'En Boqeq. Excavations in an Oasis on the Dead Sea, Vol. II: An Early Roman Building on the Dead Sea Shore* (Mainz, 2000)

S. Goldhill, *The Temple of Jerusalem* (London, 2004)

P. C. Hammond, 'The Nabataean Bitumen Industry at the Dead Sea', *Biblical Archaeologist* 22.1 (1959), 40–48

J. E. Harper, 'Too Much to Believe? 26 Tons of Gold and 65 Tons of Silver', *Biblical Archaeology Review* November/December (1993), 44–5, 70

S. Harter, F. Bouchet, K. Y. Mumcuoglu and J. E. Zias, 'Toilet Practices among Members of the Dead Sea Scrolls Sect at Qumran (100 BCE–68 CE)', *Revue de Qumran* 21.4 (2004), 579–84

Y. Hirschfeld, *Qumran in Context. Reassessing the Archaeological Evidence* (Massachusetts, 2004)

J.-B. Humbert, 'Interpreting the Qumran Site', *Near Eastern Archaeology* 63 (2000), 140–43

J.-B. Humbert and J. Gunneweg, *Khirbet Qumran et Ain Feshkha II. Etudes d'anthropologie, de physique et de chimie* (Fribourg, 2003)

P. Kyle McCarter, 'The Mystery of the Copper Scroll', in H. Shanks (ed.), *Understanding the Dead Sea Scrolls* (New York, 1992)

R. Lanciani, *Ancient Rome in the Light of Recent Discoveries* (London, 1888)

M. R. Lehmann, 'The Key to Understanding the Copper Scroll. Where the Temple Tax was Buried', *Biblical Archaeology Review* November/December (1993), 38–43

J. Magness, *The Archaeology of Qumran and the Dead Sea Scrolls* (Michigan, 2002)

E. Mazar, *The Complete Guide to the Temple Mount Excavations* (Jerusalem, 2002)

J. T. Milik, *Ten Years of Discovery in the Wilderness of Judaea* (London, 1959)

B. Putnam and J. E. Wood, *The Treasure of Rennes-le-Château. A Mystery Solved* (Stroud, 2003)

N. A. Silberman, 'In Search of Solomon's Lost Treasures', *Biblical Archaeology Review* 6.4 (1980), 30–41

R. de Vaux, *Archaeology and the Dead Sea Scrolls* (London, 1973)

L. H. Vincent, *Underground Jerusalem. Discoveries on the Hill of Ophel (1909–1911)* (London, 1911)

Temple Treasure

P. R. Ackroyd, 'The Temple Vessels – A Continuity Theme', *Studies in the Religion of Ancient Israel* (Leiden, 1972)

D. Barag, 'The Table of the Showbread and the Façade of the Temple on Coins of the Bar-Kokhba Revolt', in H. Geva (ed.), *Ancient Jerusalem Revealed* (Jerusalem, 2000)

M. Bockmuehl, 'The Trumpet Shall Sound. Shofar Symbolism and its Reception in Early Christianity', in W. Horbury (ed.), *Templum Amicitiae. Essays on the Second Temple Presented to Ernst Bannel* (Sheffield, 1991)

A. Demsky, 'When the Priests Trumpeted the Onset of the Sabbath', *Biblical Archaeology Review* November/December (1986), 50–52

J. Fergusson, *The Temples of the Jews* (London, 1878)

H. Geva, 'Jerusalem. The Temple Mount and its Environs', in E. Stern (ed.), *New Encyclopaedia of Archaeological Excavations in the Holy Land* (Jerusalem, 1993)

—— 'Searching for Roman Jerusalem', *Biblical Archaeology Review* 23.6 (1997), 34–45, 72–3

E. R. Goodenough, *Jewish Symbols in the Greco-Roman Period, Vol. 4: The Problem of Method. Symbols from Jewish Cult* (New York, 1954)

—— *Jewish Symbols in the Greco-Roman Period, Vol. 8: Pagan Symbols in Judaism* (New York, 1958)

R. Hachlili, *Ancient Jewish Art and Archaeology in the Land of Israel* (Leiden, 1988)

—— *The Menorah, The Ancient Seven-Armed Candelabrum. Origin, Form and Significance* (Leiden, 2001)

V. A. Klagsbald, 'The Menorah as Symbol: its Meaning and Origin in Early Jewish Art', in A. Cohen-Mushlin (ed.), *Jewish Art* (Jerusalem, 1987)

B. Lalor, 'The Temple Mount of Herod the Great at Jerusalem. Recent Excavations and Literary Sources', in J. R. Bartlett (ed.), *Archaeology and Biblical Interpretation* (London, 1997)

L. I. Levine, 'The History and Significance of the Menorah in Antiquity', in L. I. Levine and Z. Weiss (eds), *From Dura to Sepphoris: Studies in Jewish Art and Society in Late Antiquity* (Rhode Island, 2000)

—— *Jerusalem. Portrait of the City in the Second Temple Period (538 BCE – 70 CE)* (Philadelphia, 2002)

A. Mazar, *Archaeology of the Land of the Bible, 10,000–586 BCE* (Cambridge, 1993)

B. Mazar, *Beth She'arim. Report on the Excavations 1936–1940* (Jerusalem, 1973)

C. L. Meyers, 'Was There a Seven-Branched Lampstand in Solomon's Temple?', *Biblical Archaeology Review* September/October (1979), 47–57

J. Montagu, *Musical Instruments in the Bible* (London, 2002)

J. Patrich, 'The Structure of the Second Temple. A New Reconstruction', in H. Geva (ed.), *Ancient Jerusalem Revealed* (Jerusalem, 2000)

N. Rosovsky, 'A Thousand Years of History in Jerusalem's Jewish Quarter', *Biblical Archaeology Review* 18.3 (1992), 22–40

H. Shanks, 'Excavating in the Shadow of the Temple Mount', *Biblical Archaeology Review* November/December (1986), 20–38

D. Ussishkin, *The Conquest of Lachish by Sennacherib* (Tel Aviv, 1982)

L. Yarden, *The Tree of Light. A Study of the Menorah. The Seven-Branched Lampstand* (London, 1971)

—— *The Spoils of Jerusalem on the Arch of Titus. A Re-investigation* (Stockholm, 1991)

Revolution

N. Avigad, *Discovering Jerusalem* (Oxford, 1980)

A. M. Berlin and J. A. Overman (eds), *The First Jewish Revolt. Archaeology, History and Ideology* (London, 2002)

R. H. Darwall-Smith, *Emperors and Architecture: A Study of Flavian Rome* (Brussels, 1996)

H. Geva, 'Excavations at the Citadel of Jerusalem', in H. Geva (ed.), *Ancient Jerusalem Revealed* (Jerusalem, 2000)

M. Goodman, *The Ruling Class of Judaea. The Origins of the Jewish Revolt Against Rome AD 66–70* (Cambridge, 1987)

B. Levick, *Vespasian* (London, 1999)

T. Rajak, *Josephus. The Historian and his Society* (London, 2002)

Imperial Rome

A. Claridge, *Rome: An Oxford Archaeological Guide* (Oxford, 1998)

K. Coleman, 'Entertaining Rome', in J. Coulston and H. Dodge (eds), *Ancient Rome: The Archaeology of the Eternal City* (Oxford University School of Archaeology Monograph 54)

J. DeLaine, 'Building the Eternal City: the Construction Industry in Imperial Rome', in J. Coulston and H. Dodge (eds), *Ancient Rome: The Archaeology of the Eternal City* (Oxford University School of Archaeology Monograph 54)

D. R. Dudley, *Urbs Roma* (Aberdeen University Press, 1967)

J. Goodnick Westenholz, *The Jewish Presence in Ancient Rome* (Jerusalem, 1994)

P. J. Holliday, *The Origins of Roman Historical Commemoration in the Visual Arts* (Cambridge, 2002)

J. H. Humphrey, *Roman Circuses. Arenas for Chariot Races* (London, 1986)

F. S. Kleiner, 'The Study of Roman Triumphal and Honorary Arches 50 Years After Kaehler', *Journal of Roman Archaeology* 2 (1989), 195–206

—— 'The Arches of Vespasian in Rome', *Mitteilungen des Deutschen Archäologischen Instituts Romische Abteilung* 97 (1990), 127–36

H. J. Leon, *The Jews of Ancient Rome* (Massachusetts, 1995)

B. Olsson, D. Mitternacht and O. Brandt (eds), *The Synagogue of Ancient Ostia and the Jews of Rome. Interdisciplinary Studies* (Stockholm, 2001)

M. Pfanner, *Der Titusbogen* (Mainz, 1983)

L. Richardson, *A New Topographical Dictionary of Ancient Rome* (Baltimore, 1992)

H. S. Versnel, *Triumphus. An Inquiry into the Origin, Development and Meaning of the Roman Triumph* (Leiden, 1970)

Vandal Carthage

A. Cameron, B. Ward-Perkins and M. Whitby, *The Cambridge Ancient History, Vol. XIV. Late Antiquity: Empire and Successors, AD 425–600* (Cambridge, 2000)

F. M. Clover, 'Carthage and the Vandals', in J. H. Humphrey (ed.), *Excavations at Carthage 1978 Conducted by the University of Michigan*, Vol. VII (Ann Arbor, 1982)

—— *The Late Roman West and the Vandals* (Aldershot, 1993)

S. Ellis, 'Dining: Architecture, Furnishings and Behaviour', in R. Laurence and A. Wallace-Hadrill (eds), *Space in the Roman World: Pompeii and Beyond* (Rhode Island, 1997)

A. Ennabli, *Pour Sauver Carthage. Exploration et Conservation de la Cité Punique, Romaine et Byzantine* (Tunis, 1971)

L. Ennabli, *Carthage. Une Métropole Chrétienne du IVe à la Fin du VIIe Siècle* (Paris, 1997)

J. Humphrey, 'Vandal and Byzantine Carthage: Some New Archaeological Evidence', in J. F. Pedley (ed.), *New Light on Ancient Carthage* (Ann Arbor, 1980)

H. R. Hurst, *Excavations at Carthage. The British Mission, Vol. II, 1: The Circular Harbour, North Side. The Site and Finds Other Than Pottery* (Oxford, 1994)

S. Lancel, *Byrsa I. Rapports Préliminaires des Fouilles (1974–1976)* (Rome, 1979)

—— *Carthage. A History* (Oxford, 1995)

A. Lézine, *Carthage. Utique. Etudes d'Architecture et d'Urbanisme* (Paris, 1968)

D. J. Mattingley, 'Oil for Export? A Comparison of Libyan, Spanish and Tunisian Olive Oil Production in the Roman Empire', *Journal of Roman Archaeology* 1 (1988), 33–56

A. H. Merrills, *Vandals, Romans and Berbers. New Perspectives on Late Antique North Africa* (Aldershot, 2004)

C. Sintes and Y. Rebahi, *Algérie Antique* (Marseille, 2003)

H. Van Mater Dennis, *Hippo Regius from the Earliest Times to the Arab Conquest* (Amsterdam, 1970)

Constantinople – New Rome

P. Allen, 'The "Justinianic" Plague', *Byzantion* 49 (1979), 5–20

S. Bassett, *The Urban Image of Late Antique Constantinople* (Cambridge, 2004)

A. Cameron, *Procopius and the Sixth Century* (London, 1985)

M. Harrison, *A Temple for Byzantium. The Discovery and Excavation of Anicia Juliana's Palace Church in Istanbul* (London, 1989)

W. Jobst, B. Erdal and C. Gurtner, *Istanbul. The Great Palace Mosaic* (Istanbul, 1997)

M. Maclagan, *The City of Constantinople* (London, 1968)

C. Mango, 'The Triumphal Way of Constantinople and the Golden Gate', *Dumbarton Oaks Papers* 54 (2000), 173–88

—— (ed.), *The Oxford History of Byzantium* (Oxford, 2002)

M. Mass (ed.), *Readings in Late Antiquity. A Sourcebook* (London, 2000)

—— (ed.), *The Cambridge Companion to the Age of Justinian* (Cambridge, 2005)

D. Stathakopoulos, *Famine and Pestilence in the Late Roman and Early Byzantine Empire. A Systematic Survey of Subsistence Crises and Epidemics* (Aldershot, 2004)

The Holy Land

S. Gibson and J. E. Taylor, *Beneath the Church of the Holy Sepulchre Jerusalem. The Archaeology and Early History of Traditional Golgotha* (London, 1994)

Y. Hirschfeld, *The Judean Desert Monasteries in the Byzantine Period* (New Haven, 1992)

B. Isaac, *The Invention of Racism in Classical Antiquity* (Princeton University Press, 2004)

W. E. Kaegi, *Byzantium and the Early Islamic Conquests* (Cambridge, 1992)

A. Ovadiah, 'Early Churches', in E. Stern (ed.), *The New Encyclopaedia of Archaeological Excavations in the Holy Land*, Vol. 2 (Jerusalem, 1993)

J. Patrich, 'Monasteries', in E. Stern (ed.), *The New Encyclopaedia of Archaeological Excavations in the Holy Land*, Vol. 3 (Jerusalem, 1993)

R. Schick, *The Christian Communities of Palestine from Byzantine to Islamic Rule* (New Jersey, 1995)

Index

menorah *(cont.)*
39; thrown into River Tiber, 39;
ensign of Israel, 95; in ancient
art, 95, 96, 100; Hanukkah, 95,
101; prototype in Exodus, 96–7;
seven-branched, 97–9, 110,
113–14; Tabernacle, 97, 99, 110;
in Solomon's Temple, 97, 110;
base, 98–9; Egyptian inspiration,
99; in Zechariah, 99; on coins of
Mattathias Antigonos, 100;
pagan decoration, 101; in Beth
Shearim, 106; symbolism,
113–14; value, 301
Mesopotamia, 108, 111
Messene, 103
Messiah, 24, 103, 125
Metellus, 183
Metzger, Yehuda, 38
Midrash, 303
mikveh, 20, 82, 86, 142, 177
Milik, Józef, 75, 76, 90–1
Minerva, 12, 14, 247
Mishnah, 30, 31, 32, 118
Mithredath, treasurer, 23
Modestus, Patriarch, 290–5
Modi'in, 28
Mohammed, Prophet, 51, 69, 293
Mons Porphyrites, 208
Moors, 248, 249, 268
Moses, 19, 20, 45, 96, 98, 104, 110,
112, 115, 121
Mount of Olives, 45, 102, 103, 288,
291
Mussolini, Benito, xi, 173, 195
Myron, 9, 217

Nabataea, 83
Nablus, 44
Nahum, Book of, 75

Naples, 4, 6
Napoleon Bonaparte, 26
National Treasure, film, xii
Nazis, 27, 71
Neal, James, 17
Nebuchadnezzar, King: destruction
of First Temple, xii, 22, 23, 46,
100, 110, 115; loots Temple
treasures, 17, 67
necromancers, 17
Nero, Emperor: Jewish factions,
132; financial irregularities, 136,
152, 174; poetry, 148; commits
suicide, 149; Colossus, 199;
memory damned, 200; great fire
of Rome, 204; art collection,
206
Nerva, Marcus Cocceius, Emperor,
174
Netanyahu, Benjamin, 44
New York, 17
Newton, Sir Isaac, 71
Nicholas V, Pope, 304
Nicomacus, 206
Nike, 7, 106
Nile, River, 112
Noah's Ark, xi, 70
North Africa: invasion of Emperor
Leo, 235; Byzantine invasion of
Justinian, 235, 237; Hippo
Regius, 249–50, 268
Numbers, Book of: manufacture of
the Temple trumpets, 121–2
Numidia, 248

obelisks: in Piazza della Minerva,
162; in Piazza della Rotonda,
163; in Constantinople's
hippodrome, 267
Olbia, 215